JACK THE RIPPER
AND ABRAHAM LINCOLN

JACK THE RIPPER
AND
ABRAHAM LINCOLN

One man links the two greatest crimes
of the 19th century

TONY MCMAHON

Troubador Publishing Ltd
Unit E2 Airfield Business Park
Harrison Road, Market Harborough
Leicestershire LE16 7UL
Tel: 0116 279 2299
Email: books@troubador.co.uk
Web: www.troubador.co.uk

ISBN 978 1 80514 364 2

British Library Cataloguing in Publication Data.
A catalogue record for this book is available from the British Library.

Printed and bound by CPI Group (UK) Ltd, Croydon, CR0 4YY
Typeset in 11pt Minion Pro by Troubador Publishing Ltd, Leicester, UK

For Mike

Contents

Introduction   ix

Acknowledgements   xvii

1	The Indian Herb Doctor	1
2	The Sexuality of Abraham Lincoln	51
3	John Wilkes Booth: Actor and Prima Donna	87
4	Tumblety Networks America's Elite	104
5	Washington's Clandestine Gay Network	147
6	The Killing of Lincoln	172
7	Tumblety after Booth and Lincoln	195
8	Becoming Jack the Ripper	222
9	Death and Annie Chapman's Rings	249

Epilogue: The Littlechild Letter and the Sewer Club   295

Index of Names   304

Introduction

Two of the greatest crimes of the 19th century are linked by one man: Dr. Francis Tumblety. An Irish American serial killer who prowled the streets of London in the year 1888, committing horrifying murders, was also implicated in the plot to assassinate President Abraham Lincoln. It scarcely seems possible, but this individual, arrested as a suspect in the Jack the Ripper killings, was held behind bars twenty-five years earlier for his alleged role in Lincoln's death.

It's astonishing to imagine that the real Jack the Ripper committing his foul deeds in 1888 could also have been one of the gang of conspirators that murdered President Lincoln in 1865. Yet that is the truth that emerges from contemporary newspaper reports, court records, and police files. New evidence, presented in this book, firms up the case against Tumblety as a presidential assassin and a Victorian serial killer.

Yet who was this man? It's a story that defies credulity. A mid to late 19th century celebrity doctor, notorious in the United States, who exploited the newly emerging popular press to become an instantly recognisable figure. Far from operating in the shadows, everybody knew the flamboyant Dr Tumblety and his dubious potions and ointments. For every cynic and critic, there was a loyal patient. His fan base, extending through all social classes, generated repeat fortunes.

He was a master of public relations, crafting an outlandish persona to promote his business. Dressed in a plumed helmet, fake cavalry uniform, sporting a walrus moustache, he processed down Main Street in North American cities from New York to Detroit, Toronto to Montreal. Then later crossing the Atlantic to bring his pills and herbal remedies to Liverpool and London, all the time buying acres of classified advertising in the newspapers.

But, like some high-profile celebrities in our own time, there was a darker side to Tumblety. His underlying true self was monstrous with repeated allegations of assaults, manslaughter, and medical fraud. In addition, reported abuse of young men taken on as employees and servants – his so-called "valets" – and a private sex life that flouted the law, although in fairness to Tumblety, those legal prohibitions were homophobic and unjust.

Tumblety glossed over his shocking conduct by making money. Wealth validated his existence. Morals and ethics be damned. He was a boy from the ghetto determined to succeed in a society with no welfare safety net. In this period, it was every man and woman for themselves. Failure meant a return to the poverty of his childhood, which had been miserable and friendless. The Indian Herb Doctor, as he styled himself, was determined to never be pulled back to the penniless existence of his early years.

There were plenty of people like Tumblety, reinventing their backstory and crafting a mysterious or enigmatic persona - forgetting who they had once been and embracing their new fictional self. The novelist Herman Melville parodied this world of liars and hucksters in *The Confidence Man*, written in Tumblety's lifetime. [1] In truth, many of today's social media

---

1   Herman Melville, *The Confidence-Man* (Penguin Classics, 1991)

influencers would have thrived back then, deciding what they wanted to be famous for and then projecting it as truth to the world.

Tumblety has been derided as a buffoon with his fancy costumes and quack doctor cures, but he was in a fight for survival in a very uncaring world. His character was complex. Tumblety was a gay man with a very active sex life conducted at great risk to his person. But he was also violent and reckless with little regard for the health of his patients and he mixed in very questionable company. Most astonishingly, he somehow got embroiled in two of the greatest crimes of the 19th century.

His sexuality is fascinating because he simply didn't hold back. Even as police files on him grew and court cases threatened to ruin him financially, he couldn't resist the lure of the cruising grounds and the company of handsome young men. The resulting hatred and contempt his sexuality generated against him fed a burning anger. Over time, this exploded into a murderous rage.

How many times could he endure public humiliation as the details of his private life were aired in the courts and the newspapers? Despite the repeat fortunes amassed and acts of public philanthropy, his sexuality was cited repeatedly as a means to drag him all the way back down to the gutter.

Yet there was a bonus to his sexuality. An unexpected upside. Because Tumblety was able to tap into clandestine networks of like-minded gentlemen extending into the military top brass, through Washington's political scene, and right up to the White House. Thanks to these networks, he was protected from prosecution and imprisonment on several occasions. Just as the net seemed to be closing in and all hope was lost, somebody in authority would intervene and get Tumblety off the hook.

At the heart of the first great crime that he was involved in – the assassination of President Abraham Lincoln – is the stunning revelation that he was on "intimate" terms with both the president and his killer, John Wilkes Booth. Evidence unearthed from contemporary sources shows that despite his denials, Tumblety not only knew Booth but employed one of his co-conspirators, David Herold, and possibly introduced Booth to yet another plotter, Mary Surratt. He also wrote about being very close to Lincoln's Secretary of State, William Seward, who he called "Billy", and enjoyed candlelit dinners with senior Union army officers during the American Civil War.

There is the constant insinutation of amorous liaisons with both President Lincoln and John Wilkes Booth. To investigate further, we detour into the sex lives of Lincoln and Booth with some surprising findings. For example, the airbrushing out of Lincoln's bed sharing with a succession of young men and his infatuation with Booth. All of which raises the scarcely credible notion that Lincoln, Tumblety, and Booth were in some kind of love triangle. As one is immersed in the story, this doesn't seem so implausible. [2]

The dilemma with the main protagonist is that just as you find yourself rooting for the irrepressible Tumblety, he shows his true colours. Underneath the charisma and chutzpah, Tumblety was a psychopath. Manipulative, narcissistic, unremorseful, exploitative, and completely lacking in any empathy.

Even as Tumblety enjoyed fame in the United States as a celebrity doctor, he was under constant surveillance. The police and the Pinkerton detective agency tailed him for decades, until he was an old man. In large part, they focused on his homosexual cruising, labelling this behaviour "vice" or "obscenity". Several times, he was arrested while chatting up a target for his passions. But the police also had a bulging dossier on the charges he faced over the years for manslaughter, illegal abortion, and the repeat financial fortunes that the authorities suspected were a result of fraudulent business practice. The police clearly relished picking

---

2   Larry Kramer, *American People: Volume 1, Search for my Heart* (Farrar, Straus and Giroux, 2015)

Tumblety up off the streets for homosexual cruising because they were sure to find thousands of dollars in cash, plus diamonds, on his person. He must have enriched several corrupt officers over his lifetime.

Tumblety despised women. When Scotland Yard arrested the Indian Herb Doctor in 1888, they were convinced he was the Ripper after conferring with American police counterparts. Firstly, there was the doctor's claim to have once been married to a woman he discovered was engaged in prostitution behind his back, resulting in a lifelong hatred of both women and sex workers. Secondly, he would fly into a violent rage when anybody questioned why no females were present at his all-male soirées.

Thirdly, and most disturbingly, Tumblety owned a collection of uteruses in glass jars, kept in a cabinet of curiosities, that he displayed proudly to dinner guests over the cigars and port. Given that Jack the Ripper's victims were eviscerated in the most shocking manner, Scotland Yard required no further evidence. Even in a society where the social position of women was perilous, Tumblety's misogyny shocked jaded police officers.

Tumblety was an outsider. An outsider who wanted in. Being born a Roman Catholic Irish American came with its own baggage in the first half of the 19th century. His family had emigrated to the United States, escaping famine and deprivation in Ireland. They met with hostility and contempt in their new home city of Rochester, New York. But Tumblety turned his Celtic roots into an asset. He tapped into well-organised Irish networks, for example almost running for parliament in Canada on an Irish ticket and he was later protected by the Tammany Hall machine in New York, which was dominated by Irish Democrats.

Tumblety was a serial killer. A string of deaths can be linked to Tumblety from the 1850s onwards up to his arrest as Jack the Ripper in 1888. We know of two verifiable manslaughter charges;

the killing of Lincoln; the Ripper murders; but he may also have been involved in a string of grisly killings in Texas and a copycat Ripper homicide in New York, occurring after he returned from London. There were also further incidents of violent assault, which ended up in court.

If he was simply a brute, his story would be dull to relate. But Francis Tumblety lived his life with an eye fixed on his own autobiography, which he published in several editions. Today he would have sold his story to a TV network for a handsome sum.

Such was his obsession with self-promotion that journalists even raised the possibility that Tumblety was involved in the Lincoln assassination and Jack the Ripper murders as part of a high stakes public relations strategy. Was he a compulsive liar who would say or do anything for newspaper coverage whatever the risk? Put another way, was he prepared to risk being hanged over Lincoln's death in 1865 and the murder of five women in 1888 just to publicise his medical business? This seems far fetched and makes no sense. No doctor would want to be associated with what happened to Jack the Ripper's victims in Whitechapel. More likely, his arrest in 1865 and 1888 was founded on a genuine belief by law enforcement in both cases that he was guilty.

Tumblety was a homicidal huckster moving in the highest circles and the murkiest depths. His life takes us from the Civil War through Reconstruction, the Gilded Age, and the so-called Progressive era. We empathise to a degree with the discrimination he faced as a gay man (the author is LGBT himself and half-Irish), but we recoil at his long record of fraud, violent assault, and murder.

The final decade of his life has been completely overlooked but provides essential clues confirming our worst fears about Tumblety. He fled London in 1888 after being accused of being Jack the Ripper. For many, that is the end of the story. But how to explain a copycat Ripper killing in a Manhattan hotel not long afterwards; the reported suspicion of police and journalists that his valet at the time may have been a murderer; and clear evidence that he was still capable of physical attacks on strangers.

All of which presents an intriguing question: how did Tumblety repeatedly evade justice? In 1865, he was clearly associated with at least two of the killers of President Abraham Lincoln, but avoided the scaffold. In 1888, when he jumped bail and fled London, after facing the prospect of going on trial as Jack the Ripper, no attempt was made to extradite him from the United States back to the United Kingdom. Why? How did Tumblety slip through the justice system time and again?

The answer is his networks. He built a support infrastructure around himself that made him largely immune to the threat of imprisonment or capital punishment. As will be seen, just as the police or courts thought they had him in their grasp, up popped an influential person to get him off the hook. A powerful figure from the Irish American community or even a like-minded gentleman of the same sexuality who felt obliged to support another gay man against establishment persecution.

In 1903, Tumblety gasped his last breath at a hospital in St. Louis. To the medical staff, he looked like a tramp down on his luck. But at his death, a sizeable portfolio of investments came to light, subsequently fought over by his family for years. The Indian Herb Doctor had always carried vast amounts of cash and diamonds on his person and his bank balance was very healthy. What surprised those removing the clothes from his corpse was the discovery of two very cheap brass rings out of keeping with his expensive tastes.

Those rings bore a striking similarity to those ripped from the fingers of Annie Chapman – the second victim of Jack the Ripper.

Acknowledgements

Jonathan Ned Katz, author of *The Invention of Heterosexuality* and *Gay American History*, interviewed to help my understanding of how Civil War era Americans viewed sexuality, challenging our modern idea of the rigid dichotomy between homosexual and heterosexual.

Mark Segal, founder of the Gay Liberation Front and former President of the National Gay Newspaper Guild, famously invaded the CBS Evening News in 1973 as Walter Kronkite was presenting. Mark's archive of sixteen cubic feet of personal papers and artifacts was donated to the Smithsonian Institution in 2018. Interviewed with regards to his insights into President Lincoln.

The staff in the Rare Books reading room at the British Library in London who endured my many requests.

Mike Dent, Managing Editor of *Wired* (UK) who patiently subbed my copy at every stage.

One

The Indian Herb Doctor

America was still stunned. The President of the United States, Abraham Lincoln, had been shot dead in April that year. Only weeks before, the unprecedented carnage of the American Civil War had ended with victory for the anti-slavery Union forces led by Lincoln. Then jubilation turned to horror and anguish as the assassin John Wilkes Booth fired at the president as he watched a play at Ford's Theatre in Washington DC.

"It seems even yet a frightful dream," said Senator James Dixon of Connecticut on hearing the news, "rather than a reality in the hour when his wisdom and his patriotism were about to be crowned with the success they deserved." Dixon was among thousands that attended a sad procession bringing the president's body to the Capitol, the centre of government, to be placed in the rotunda, beneath the mighty dome.[3]

Months later, Americans strove to return to some kind of normality. But the war and Lincoln's death had changed everything. For one man, it had been an especially traumatic

---

3   The Death of Abraham Lincoln, United States Senate

1

year. An imposing Irish American with a swirling, walrus moustache whose sartorial preferences bordered on the garish. Well known, though not necessarily admired, in American cities from New York to Detroit, as well as Cincinnati where he now found himself.

Dr Francis Tumblety was a high-profile herb doctor with no verifiable medical qualifications. But that hadn't prevented him making a great deal of money and becoming very famous. Arguably an early example of what we call "celebrity" today, brought to prominence by the emerging popular press. However, in recent months, he had become a talking point for all the wrong reasons. A criminal charge had been brought against Tumblety that if true wouldn't just have destroyed him financially but resulted in the death penalty. Not the kind of publicity he usually sought.

Tumblety had spent several weeks behind bars in Washington's Old Capitol Prison by order of the Secretary of War, Edwin Stanton. Accused of direct involvement in both the assassination of President Lincoln and a bizarre plot to spread yellow fever in Union-controlled cities during the recent war by means of infected blankets. The fact that mosquitoes spread the disease wasn't yet fully understood.

After a few weeks, Tumblety was released and enraged at his treatment, bought newspaper column inches to fulminate against the authorities. But many sceptical readers reckoned: no smoke without fire. Especially as one of Tumblety's employees, David Herold, had been found guilty of involvement in the Lincoln assassination and hanged on 7 July 1865. His neck failing to break and for five minutes, the hapless young man was gradually strangled to death. Tumblety's association with Herold looked decidedly suspicious to contemporary journalists.

Tumblety had been forced to flee Washington DC before his arrest in St Louis. Accusations of gross indecency had seen him hounded out of the American capital. By the end of 1865, he was in Cincinnati trying to rebuild his business selling patent medicines that, allegedly, could cure every ailment from pimples to cancer. What he needed badly was a public relations splash. Something that would remind the public that he was their champion against the medical establishment as well as dulling the memory of his association with the Lincoln assassination. Another one of his high-profile stunts in other words.

The Roman Catholic congregation gathered for Holy Mass at the Cathedral Basilica of Saint-Peter-in-chains could hardly have anticipated the vision that was about to glide down the aisle. Cincinnati's faithful filled the pews of an ostentatious structure that strove to resemble a basilica of the late Roman Empire. Three years earlier, gold-topped Corinthian colonnades had been added along with sumptuous Greek-style mosaics - a perfect backdrop for Dr Tumblety's dramatic entrance.

Tumblety steadied himself for his march towards the altar. He was among his co-religionists, many of whom shared his Irish heritage. Like the Tumblety family, they had fled the terrible famine that had ravaged their mother country seeking opportunity in the New World. This glorious cathedral was a monument to their achievement in the face of contempt and hatred heaped on their heads by the Anglo-Protestant elites. In a place like this, Tumblety believed he would be welcomed.

Though maybe not by everybody. All around him, rows of congregants shuffling in the pews as they awaited the priests, altar boys, wafting of pungent incense, and the holy rite of Mass sung in Latin. These well-heeled parishioners were potential clients for his herbal cures and a source of help when he got into trouble. Many were Irish Americans conveniently positioned in government or law enforcement who might rescue Tumblety when the police and courts closed in on him yet again. Even when he found himself in a sordid pickle with another young, handsome man, the doctor expected to be saved by a well-placed fellow Irishman in the mayor's office or the police department.

There were other congregants who shared Tumblety's sexuality. A clandestine network that dared not speak its name. Like him, they might have found themselves under surveillance by police and private detectives on account of the same-sex attraction that was about to be labelled 'homosexual' by the emerging science of psychology. After church, these gentlemen drifted to the parks and fashionable streets, ostensibly for a Sunday stroll.

Cruising in cities as far flung as Toronto, New York, Washington DC, and Detroit had left Tumblety with an impressive record of vice-related brushes with the law. Sometimes, regrettably, these matters ended up in court. The doctor never emerged entirely unscathed from these proceedings. Not least because the newspapers took a rather sadistic pleasure in regaling their surprisingly knowledgeable readers with the salacious details, albeit in coded language.

It was nearly time. The mass was about to start. Tumblety didn't ponder for a moment the blasphemy of upstaging the priests with his own procession. This profane display would be a statement that he was back in business. Resurrected yet again! Back from the dead having come dangerously close to the hangman's noose that year. If Stanton had got his way his neck would have been stretched alongside poor David Herold. The very thought made him shudder.

Tumblety had been forced to deny ever having known Herold despite the numerous witnesses that had seen them together. The young, doomed Lincoln plotter following Tumblety like a whipped dog behind his master. As for John Wilkes Booth, Tumblety repeatedly denied ever having met Lincoln's assassin. This was an outright lie. A retired police officer would detail decades later how he had encountered Booth and Tumblety as a giggling, inseparable duo in the city of Buffalo. Like Herold, Booth was now also dead. Shot in the neck while fleeing after killing the president.

Three men Tumblety had known so intimately – Abraham Lincoln, John Wilkes Booth, David Herold – were all in their graves. But for Tumblety, there was simply no time for grief or remorse. Pausing for a split second to consider the enormity of what had happened would be taking time out from making money. Unlike America's silver-spoon-in-the-mouth elites, the awkward boy from the Irish ghetto in Rochester, upstate New York, couldn't afford the luxury of mournful contemplation.

It was time for yet another phoenix-like renewal and a part of him revelled in these moments where he cocked a snook at his critics, refusing to bow out and disappear. What he was about to do fitted into a well-established pattern of bold and garish stunts that generated the desired coverage in the newspapers and got the tills ringing again. Achieving notoriety was at the heart of his business strategy and whatever his detractors thought, nothing would stop Tumblety turning shameless self-promotion into wads of cash.

The mass had begun. While the priests processed and the incense burner was swung at the altar, Tumblety swept in with the arrogance of a Medici prince. Slack-jawed, the congregation gazed in horror as an African American page moved on the balls of his feet before the doctor, carrying a huge prayer book on a velvet covered stand, heralding the arrival of the great man himself.

The bible carrier was the latest in a long string of valets, handsome young men picked up by Tumblety on the streets then kept on the payroll until relations soured, as they almost invariably did. The doctor expected his valets to be compliant assistants and lovers. One journalist wrote of the "mesmeric force" that Tumblety exercised over these impressionable youths. An ability to completely control their actions, reducing them to servile obedience.[4]

---

4   "Tumblety", *St Louis Globe-Democrat*, January 5, 1889

Behind this immaculately dressed valet came the main attraction, a picture of unrestrained flamboyance. But if the doctor was expecting his return to prominence to be applauded, then he was in for a nasty shock. Most of the congregation knew Tumblety. Not just because of the whole Lincoln affair, but his sexual escapades were the talk of polite society. There were those who sniggered in amusement, but the majority were scandalised. As for his fellow Irish Americans, some felt they had to support and protect Tumblety as one of their own, but others were unable to overlook the doctor's all too visible homosexuality.

Heads shook as Tumblety sashayed past, wearing his ridiculous parody of a cavalry uniform, dripping with jewellery, while flanked by overly groomed male adolescents. The cathedral hummed with angry murmuring. This time he really had gone too far and his blasphemous vulgarity had to be nipped in the bud. The cathedral busybodies homed in on the doctor. The message they delivered through gritted teeth was clear: either worship less ostentatiously or go elsewhere.[5]

Another more violent version of what happened that day has a man named Holy John, "the stern Sexton", booting the doctor down the cathedral steps.[6] However, even this humiliation was grist to the public relations mill for Tumblety. While the congregation vented their collective spleen, the city was plastered with handbills promoting his miracle cures and the local newspapers were stuffed with classified advertising. Paid-for puff pieces proclaiming Tumblety's arrival in Cincinnati featuring letters from past patients declaring they were now free of cancer, dyspepsia, or gout.

Glowing testimonials from fellow celebrities exalted Tumblety's genius allegedly penned by the likes of English author, Charles Dickens and even the recently assassinated

---

5 "Ah there! Tumblety", *The Springfield News-Leader*, January 11, 1889

6 "Dr Tumblety's Career", *The Cincinnati Enquirer*, December 5, 1888

President Lincoln, among many other worthies and dignitaries. These commendations betrayed a suspiciously similar template: *I suffered from a terrible disease. Mainstream physicians were not only unable to cure me but are arrant fools. Only Doctor Tumblety's herbal cures based on the wisdom of the Native American tribes put things right. I cannot recommend Doctor Tumblety highly enough.*

This barrage of propaganda from Tumblety, who spent considerable sums on classified advertisements, was relentless. Not only did he boast about his cures but abused local physicians by name. He presented himself as a David-like figure up against the Goliath of the medical establishment and there was no depth to which these charlatans would plunge to discredit Doctor Tumblety, he told newspaper readers. Many agreed and duly filled his coffers repeatedly.

But from where had The Indian Herb Doctor, as he styled himself, originated? In truth, Francis Tumblety was a man who rose without trace. Even the date and place of his birth are shrouded in mystery. He was most likely born in Dublin, Ireland in the first half of 1830. Although other accounts have him entering the world in either counties Roscommon, Meath, or Cavan. However, an American newspaper in 1904, after his death, opined that Tumblety was born in 1834 in Rochester, New York state though evidence is scant.[7]

Decades later, when he stood accused of being Jack the Ripper, the city of Saint John, New Brunswick in north-east Canada - Tumblety's base of operation around 1860 - was keen to scotch rumours he was born there. [8] Being associated with a man then accused of multiple murders in Whitechapel wasn't going to help the city's image.

One of Tumblety's "intimates" told a newspaper in 1888

---

7   "Fight for Tumblety's Cash?", *The Sun*, June 26, 1904
8   "Tumblety", *St. Louis Globe-Democrat*, January 5, 1889

that the doctor was "the son of a wealthy Irish gentleman in Dublin and a well-educated physician". Another believed that he had studied medicine at Dublin's prestigious Trinity College. Tumblety produced diplomas by way of proving it was his alma mater. However, asked in the 1990s about these qualifications, the college found it had no records showing a Francis Tumblety had graduated at any time between 1850 and 1900.[9]

In reality, Tumblety's early years were almost certainly a grim and dark place despite his attempts to weave a more exotic backstory. His sad past loomed over him until the end of his life. Back in Rochester's Irish ghetto as a youngster, Tumblety was reportedly a pathetic sight. Described by one neighbour as a dirty, awkward, ignorant, uncared for, good-for-nothing boy devoid of education. A loner with no friends.

As he landed himself in various scrapes over the years, Tumblety adopted a fake identity or altered the spelling of his surname slightly. We know he became Twomblety when operating in certain cities, for example London in 1888. The doctor might have tried to excuse this subterfuge with the excuse that the spelling of Irish surnames was still very fluid in the 19th century, as they were anglicised from the ancient Gaelic. The name Tumblety pops up in the public records as Tumbelty, Tumelty, Tomelty, Tumilty, and so on, derived from the Gaelic Tomaltaigh. Census takers and priests at the baptismal font often inadvertently renamed a family with a stroke of the pen.[10] His own parents were registered in censuses taken in Ireland as "Tumilty". Tumblety even complained in 1875 that hotels in San Francisco never spelled his name correctly in all his many visits.[11]

---

9   Liam Reid, "Ripper may have studied at Trinity", *Sunday Tribune*, October 5, 1997

10   "Last name: Tumblety", *The Internet Surname Database*, https://www.surnamedb.com/Surname/Tumbelty

11   "Personal notes", *San Francisco Chronicle*, December 24, 1875

However, he also adopted names that in no way resembled his own. The aliases Blackburn and Townsend would be deployed during the Lincoln and Ripper episodes respectively. There is even an astonishing assertion that Francis Tumblety was an entirely fake identity adopted by an impostor named Mike Sullivan. It's an intriguing story.

While still using his original name, the young Sullivan went to work under a doctor in Rochester. That doctor, an entirely different person, was called Tumblety. Sullivan murdered him and assumed his identity. Determined to set up his own medical practice and make a fortune from the credulous, he fled to Buffalo, New York state before flitting across the border to Montreal and then Saint John, New Brunswick in Canada.[12]

Yet another version of Tumblety's life story was shared with a California newspaper in the aftermath of Tumblety's arrest in London as a Jack the Ripper suspect. A man described as Tumblety's brother stated that the real Dr. Tumblety had been a British Army surgeon in the Canadian city of Halifax, New Brunswick.

This British Tumblety enjoyed a degree of success across North America. His servant was a young man named Dobson who learned a considerable amount about medicine from his employer. In 1856, Tumblety died and was buried in Halifax. Dobson slipped away having stolen the dead surgeon's diplomas and valuable medical equipment. He then resurfaced two years later in Boston as Dr. Tumblety boasting that women's ailments were his medical forte.[13]

Whatever the truth, Tumblety undoubtedly reinvented himself to escape what the 19th century French novelist Emile

---

12   "Is he the fiend?", *The Buffalo News*, December 1, 1888

13   "Jack the Ripper", *Oakland Tribune*, December 8, 1890

Zola termed "a life sentence in the prison of hunger".[14] Not unlike many other Irish emigrants who adopted new identities as they journeyed to the New World, in the hope of avoiding discrimination based on their surname. Tumblety, though, faced potential hostility for being both an Irish Catholic and a homosexual, so he needed to create an especially dazzling persona that would blind the public to his real self.

The balance of evidence suggests that the doctor was born Francis Tumblety into a large family in Ireland that emigrated out of economic necessity to England and the United States. His parents and siblings arrived in Rochester, New York state when Francis was an adolescent, part of a wave of Irish Catholic immigrants first glimpsing the Statue of Liberty with their resources depleted from the expense of the journey across the Atlantic.

His likely departure from Ireland for America was around 1847, at the height of the infamous Irish potato famine that drove hundreds of thousands of people out of the country escaping starvation. Stories of land and jobs in the New World contrasted sharply with evictions and malnutrition in Ireland. There was plenty of motivation to cross the Atlantic and little reason to return.

Within the immigrant pecking order, the Tumblety family were looked down on. They lived separately from other Irish Catholic families who, in turn, weren't welcome in downtown Rochester. The Irish Catholics, far from their homeland, clustered together in log-cabin dwellings about a mile south from the centre of Rochester, in an area referred to as Dublin.

Tumblety was described as a "good-for-nothing boy with no education".[15] When he was arrested decades later in 1888 as

---

14 Philippa Howden-Chapman, Ichiro Kawachi, "Paths to and from poverty in late 19th century novels", *Journal of Epidemiology & Community Health*, Vol. 60, No. 2, 2006, pp. 102-107

15 "Tumblety Facts in the History of the Supposed Whitechapel Fiend", *St Louis Globe-Democrat*, January 5, 1889

a suspect in the Jack the Ripper case, a certain Edward Haywood who, by then worked in the Bureau of Accounts at the US State Department, remembered a scruffy urchin toddler, about two or three years of age, running around the filthy banks of the Erie Canal in the early 1830s.[16] Confusingly, this places Tumblety's birth in Rochester, but the evidence for Dublin, Ireland is much stronger.

By Tumblety's own admission in a later autobiography, he had little by way of formal schooling. His learning came from serving apprenticeships and plagiarising the ideas of others, though he always added his own special twist. From an early stage, he developed a knack for self-promotion and self-aggrandisement, revealing both considerable drive and flair coupled with a devious and low cunning. He combined tremendous self-belief with a deep vein of insecurity.

Tumblety was sometimes described as illiterate but there's a small mountain of correspondence to male conquests suggesting otherwise. If anything, the doctor possessed that Irish love of the spoken and written word, as well as the ardent belief that the truth should never get in the way of a good story. Tumblety was loquacious and his autobiography, which ran to several editions, displays an acerbic wit. His tongue and his pen charmed clients and lovers into submission.

Life was tough in 1830s and 1840s Rochester. The longer-established citizenry were in no mood to offer a helping hand to newly arrived Irish Catholic economic refugees. They found themselves shunned and marginalised by both New England, Presbyterian 'Yankees' and New York Episcopalians or 'Yorkers'. Indeed, the previous bitter animosity between Yankees and Yorkers evaporated as the two groups viewed with alarm the rapidly growing Irish Catholic presence in their midst.[17]

---

16 "The Missing Tumblety", *Democrat and Chronicle*, December 3, 1888

17 Blake McKelvey, "The Irish in Rochester", *Rochester History*, October 1957, Vol. XIX, No. 4

But the Irish Catholics continued to arrive regardless though they faced violence and discrimination. As early as 1820, the vestry of St Patrick's chapel was vandalised and as a result, a company of Irish Volunteers was set up for self-defence. Far from being cowed by bigotry, the Irish Catholics redoubled their efforts to strive for future success.

St Patrick's chapel was soon rebuilt as the much grander St Patrick's church. And by 1829, the Irish Volunteers were marching on the Fourth of July parade. A year later, there are records of some English and Scottish Rochester residents celebrating St Patrick's Day alongside their Irish Catholic neighbours. This resilience and relentless determination to forge ahead no matter how others regarded you became a hallmark of Tumblety's character. Ingrained in him was the bold and uncrushable spirit of Rochester's Irish Catholic community.

In the 1830s, Rochester's pious Protestants were swept up by the Second Great Awakening. This revivalist movement had been creeping across the United States since the Revolutionary War. Its arrival in Rochester resulted in the city's theatre being reduced to a stable and its only circus turned into a soap and candle factory. Grog shops were closed. The Sabbath was to be strictly observed.[18] And the burgeoning rapprochement with the city's Catholics ground to a halt. For most of the city's Irish, this was a terrifying victory for religious bigotry.

In the decades after the creation of the United States, the trend had been towards secular tolerance with a blind eye turned to lewd behaviour, irreligious outbursts, and even pornography Since the American revolution, a refreshing liberality had emerged, with the New World championing free speech in contrast to the hidebound superstition and oppression to be found in the Old World. America's republic had been founded

---

18   Eddie Hyatt, *2000 Years of Charismatic Christianity* (Charisma House, 2002)

by men of learning and the ability to express oneself in whatever way was very much in the spirit of the Constitution.

But sadly, for a homosexual adolescent growing up in Rochester's Irish ghetto, that climate of relative tolerance was ending. In 1842, the Tariff Act was the first federal legislation prohibiting indecent and obscene material. The intention was to snuff out the post-Revolutionary War boom in pornography. Yet in the same decade, Francis Tumblety set out to make a living from prurient images as a small-time porn baron, deliberately snubbing his nose at the new puritan wave.

The market for illegal images was obvious to the entrepreneurial youngster. A new surge of Irish immigrants was arriving from the mother country to work on the construction of the Erie Canal and as labour for the lumber and flour mills, for which Rochester was famous. Tumblety later handed out bags of flour to the poor as part of his highly publicised philanthropy. The growing trade and commerce on the canals meant potential customers for erotic content to pass the time on long, tedious waterborne journeys.

Tumblety regarded with a commercial eye the canal 'packets' plying their trade on the waterways. Large vessels carrying passengers, freight, and mail along hundreds of miles of canals connecting the Great Lakes and rivers that would eventually be superseded by the railways. The Irish Catholic ghetto boy recognised a captive market and the opportunity to monetise its basest instincts. Bored male passengers would surely part with some cash in return for risqué material to alleviate the tedium?

One of the boats he boarded with his stash of pornography belonged to a Captain W. C. Streeter. Years later he recalled the shifty teenager, who introduced himself as Frank Tumblety, appearing on his canal boat selling smutty pamphlets "of the kind Anthony Comstock suppresses".[19]

---

19   "The Missing Tumblety", *Democrat and Chronicle,* December 3, 1888

Anthony Comstock (1844–1915) was an anti-vice campaigner active in the second half of the 19th century who once boasted he had destroyed fifteen tons of pornographic books and four million images.[20] Continuing the spirit of the Second Great Awakening, he combined his government role as the United States Postal Inspector with his Christian moral activism as secretary of the New York Society for the Suppression of Vice. There was no conflict of interest in his view.

Tumblety was active in New York and other north-eastern cities running his Indian herb doctor business during the height of Comstock's influence and power. Unfortunately, for Tumblety, two of Comstock's targets were homosexuality and patent (trademarked and non-prescription) medicine. His views on homosexuals were unequivocal:

> *Inverts (a derogatory Victorian term for LGBT people) are not fit to live with the rest of mankind. They ought to have branded in their foreheads the word Unclean. Instead of the law making twenty years' imprisonment the penalty for their crime, it ought to be imprisonment for life… They are wilfully bad, and glory, and gloat in their perversion.[21]*

Suggestions in the 1890s that the law should be tolerant of same-sex activity, provided it was in the home, were met with a furious response from Comstock:

> *Why propose to have the law against them now on the statute books repealed? If this happened, there would be no way of getting at them. It would be wrong to make*

---

20 Paul Buchanan, *The American Women's Rights Movement* (Branden Books, 2014)

21 Kahan, Benjamin, "The Walk-In Closet: Situational Homosexuality and Homosexual Panic in Hellman's The Children's Hour", Criticism, *Wayne State University Press*, 2013, Vol. 55, No. 2

life more tolerable for them. Their lives ought to be so intolerable as to drive them to abandon their vices.[22]

Comstock stood in the tradition of the 17th century Puritans and early 19th century Second Great Awakening while Tumblety was the living embodiment of everything he abhorred. We have no copies of what Tumblety was selling on the canal packets but from witnesses who knew the young man at the time, it would have undoubtedly fallen foul of the morality police.

Selling titillating literature on the canals wasn't a long-term prospect for an ambitious young fellow like Tumblety. Medicine offered a more assured career path and, as he would discover, the potential to make enormous amounts of money. His medical apprenticeship was served with a certain Dr. W. C. Lispenard based at No. 14 Exchange Place in downtown Rochester, behind the old post office. Lispenard's real name appears to have been Ezra J Reynolds. Possibly he adopted the name Lispenard to bolster his credibility as a purveyor of "French" cures for the French pox, an old term for syphilis. Venereal ailments were very much his specialism as he boasted in an 1856 classified advertisement:

Young men, who, by indulging in secret habits, have contracted that soul-subduing, mind prostrating, body-destroying vice, should apply to Dr Lispenard without delay.[23]

Nobody, he assured the newspaper readership, left his office "half cured". He could tackle gonorhoea (his spelling), gleet (discharge from the urethra caused by gonorrhoeal infection), and syphilis. He even penned a handy guide on "the diseases of the genital organs" for both sexes written in plain English

22 Ibid: "The Walk-In Closet: Situational Homosexuality and Homosexual Panic in Hellman's The Children's Hour"

23 "A book for the million", *Buffalo Evening Post*, June 21, 1856

outlining preventative measures and what to do if stricken. Priced twenty-five cents in pamphlet form and fifty cents bound in muslin.

Three years earlier he had produced a cheaper priced guide for married couples and those about to wed. "Subjects never before alluded to in any work in our language are here explained".[24] It included full anatomical descriptions of both sexes' genitals; remarks on the "premature decay" that could result from "secret habits"; and the latest medical discoveries. This publication was advertised as far afield as Detroit and given the low availability of sex education at the time; sales were brisk.

Much of Lispenard's sales patter foreshadowed the language and approach Tumblety took in the decades ahead. He boasted of his thousands of patients successfully treated at a low price and urged them to come forward and offer their testimonials. Tumblety dispensed with that formality and to the anger of some patients, published unauthorised testimonials under their real names sharing very embarrassing details.

Lispenard repeatedly trashed the competition. Physicians and apothecaries were rogues and charlatans. Ignorant pretenders who sadly continued to open stores selling ineffective cures "until public indignation shall drive their proprietors from the city with shame and infamy branded upon them".[25] In contrast, his offices were "commodiously arranged" offering patients total privacy.

Tumblety's testimonials also mentioned rival mainstream physicians by name decrying their ineffectiveness. This rebounded frequently on him, as furious doctors colluded with the courts, police, and journalists to bring Tumblety down in city after city. Poking the medical establishment was an effective short-term strategy to make money but in the longer term, it

---

24   "Most Extraordinary Work!", *Detroit Free Press*, May 17, 1853

25   Ibid: "Most Extraordinary Work!"

incurred the wrath of mainstream physicians with devastating consequences.

Lispenard was by no means the only physician making grand claims for his cures. Dr Wilkins in Memphis, Tennessee in the 1850s was also tackling the same "secret habits" that led to "soul sickening, mind harrowing, and body-destroying disease". Like Lispenard, he claimed to be the sole agent for a French contraceptive pill, or rather "preventive powders",[26] Meanwhile, Dr Williams in Louisville, Kentucky was the sole agent for Dr. DeWee's Female Monthly Regulator while also treating young men "who have undermined their health by excessive indulgence".[27]

During the 19th century, medicine was an unregulated market. Federal regulation of drugs was only introduced in the United States in 1906. And it took until the 1950s for a clear distinction to be made between over the counter and prescription medications. Customers in the 19th century could obtain the same drugs with or without a prescription from somebody setting themselves up as a pharmacist or physician, such as Francis Tumblety.[28]

There were early attempts to regulate this free-for-all. In 1820, eleven establishment physicians met in Washington DC and drew up a list of recommended drugs in a compendium called the United States Pharmacopoeia. This was supposed to contrast with all those questionable cures bearing trademarks such as Hamlin's Wizard Oil and Lydia Pinkham's Vegetable Compound that might simply be a mix of water with alcohol

---

26 "Southwestern private medical dispensary", *The Memphis Daily Avalanche,* April 23, 1859

27 "Louisville Private Dispensary", *The Louisville Daily Courier,* March 23, 1860

28 "A History of Drug Advertising", *The Millbank Quarterly,* 2006, Vol 84, No. 4, pps 659-699

or opium.[29] That said, the 1820 list is now regarded as equally ineffective with its emphasis on ingredients like quinine, morphine, and ether. In truth, the concoctions sold by quacks like Lispenard and his student Tumblety were only marginally less effective than the officially sanctioned medications - and if anything, less dangerous in many instances.

During his apprenticeship to Lispenard, Tumblety began styling himself as the Indian Herb Doctor. More than likely, he took the title from another quack in Rochester, R. J. Lyons. Both men promoted themselves as the one and only Indian Herb Doctor for many years. In 1857, Tumblety complained in the pages of the *Toronto Globe* that "an impostor" had been operating under his professional title.[30]

However, there were plenty of other Indian Herb Doctors aside from these two. Dr S. H. Frazier in Pennsylvania did brisk business using this name in the 1840s.[31] Ebenezer Horton was selling an Indian wonder cure extracted from the root of the Wahoo tree across several North American cities at the same time,[32] while Bryant Parker in Monroe County, Georgia presented himself as the German and Indian Herb Doctor.

He pursues the German method of judging disease by the urine, in which he has never failed to give general satisfaction to the thousands who have applied to him.[33]

---

29 J. H. Young, "The Toadstool Millionaires: A Social History of Patent Medicines in America before Federal Regulation", *Princeton University Press*, 1961

30 "From the Toronto Globe, August 1, 1857", *The Gazette*, November 3, 1857

31 "The Indian Herb Doctor", *Pennsylvania Republican*, March 1, 1848

32 "Extract of Wa-ahoo, an Indian medicine", *Detroit Free Press*, April 6, 1841

33 "German and Indian Herb Doctor", *The Weekly Telegraph*, September 8, 1846

Even though the medical establishment was sceptical about so-called "Indian cures", the American public was far more enthusiastic. There was a widespread belief that ancient medicines developed over the centuries by the American Indian tribes could succeed where modern medicine was perceived to have failed.

For example, one patent medicine was branded Dr Kilmer's Indian Cough Cure Consumption Oil. Sadly, for the American public, this had little or nothing to do with tribal wisdom and everything to do with clever marketing. Tumblety and others tapped into the tension between the public's rising expectations about their health and the inability of establishment medicine, at that stage, to deliver. As one of Tumblety's advertisements put it:

Our people are tired of theories. When a man is sick he wants the physician who prescribes remedies that are sure to cure him, and such a person is found in Dr Tumblety, Indian Herb Doctor.[34]

To prove his credentials as a genuine Indian Herb Doctor, Tumblety's Toronto office displayed a large pair of buck horns over the door which he boasted had been presented to him by an Indian chief named Sundown, "a savage of the plains, with whom he was intimately acquainted".[35] This claim by Tumblety has been too hastily derided in some quarters because there was indeed a Chief Sundown "of the six nations" who toured the United States with an exhibition of the religious customs and rites of the Mohawk and Penobscot tribes. Both these tribes are still based in south-east Canada, the Great Lakes, and over towards New Brunswick, Maine, and New York state - exactly the areas where Tumblety was operating.

---

34 "Local News", *Evening Star*, April 19, 1862
35 Ibid, "The Indian Herb Doctor – More about Him"

In January 1851, Sundown could be found entertaining audiences at the Knickerbocker Hall in New York.[36] It hardly stretches credulity that the incipient showman and purveyor of "Indian" herbs went to see a real-life native American put on his show and that Tumblety, the incorrigible networker, would have buttonholed Sundown at some point. The buck horns may have been a gift from the chief or bought at the equivalent of the souvenir shop at the theatre.

Tumblety's claim to have knowledge of Indian medicine led some to believe that he was part native American. He may even have spread this rumour himself. One newspaper felt sufficiently moved to warn its readers that the fraudster in their midst was indisputably one hundred per cent Irish. There wasn't an ounce of Mohawk blood in Tumblety.

In every town and city where Tumblety appeared as the herbalist messiah, it was to a grand fanfare. Creating quite a spectacle, he processed down Main Street on a circus horse resplendent in military garb, his chest festooned with medals. On top of his head was a plumed cavalry helmet and running by his side, a garishly dressed valet, sometimes impersonating a native American child. This exhibitionism disgusted some, but it was a brilliant piece of 19th century marketing.

The servile role of valet chasing behind Tumblety's horse would be assumed for a while by the Lincoln assassination plotter, David Edgar Herold (1842–1865). A few months before John Wilkes Booth (1838–1865) shot the president, his doe-eyed accomplice Herold was trailing behind the Indian Herb Doctor on the streets of Brooklyn giving out handbills for pimple cures. This unlikely scene was commented on in the newspapers after the assassination of Lincoln with journalists wondering how on earth Tumblety and Herold had come to know each other. And why did Herold abase himself in this demeaning role?

---

36   "Grand Indian Exhibition", *New York Tribune*, January 8, 1851

The answer lies in the fact that Tumblety knew Lincoln's killer, John Wilkes Booth. Booth introduced Herold, who had worked as a pharmacy assistant, to Tumblety while simultaneously recruiting him to his murderous plot. Herold was, by all accounts, very immature and obsessed with boys. He fell very easily under Tumblety's spell as other young men had done before and would do in the future.

The connection between Tumblety, Booth, and Herold would be revealed to police by Booth's teenage errand boy after Lincoln's murder leading to the Indian Herb Doctor's arrest in 1865 as an alleged plotter in the president's assassination. However, unlike Booth and Herold, Tumblety would emerge bruised but alive. At the time of his arrest and imprisonment, newspapers in St. Louis reminded their readers of the familiar sight viewed so often on Main Street in many American cities:

> *This Dr. Tumblety is probably the individual who, it will be remembered by the people of this city and Brooklyn, formerly flourished here under the title of the 'Great Indian Herb Doctor' and who made himself conspicuous wherever he appeared by the astounding 'loudness' of his apparel, the immensity of his nicely waxed mustache, and the dignified stride with which he moved along the street.*[37]

He choice of attire was impossible to forget:

> *He was usually "dressed within an inch of his life", and a little beyond the extreme of fashion. He was decidedly the biggest "swell" which the town contained, and when he appeared in the Park for his regular airings he never failed to create a sensation.*[38]

---

37 "The Situation", *New York Daily Herald*, May 7, 1865
38 Ibid: "The Situation"

Tumblety acknowledged in an 1866 autobiography that his public relations inspiration was the great American showman, P.T. Barnum (1810–1891), the manager of several variety troupes and attractions. Barnum perpetrated the Feejee Mermaid hoax, a stuffed mythical creature with the body of a monkey and the tail of a fish and introduced the public to the three-foot-four inches entertainer, General Tom Thumb.

Circuses nearly always arrived in town with a raucous display. But Barnum took things to a new level, tapping into the emerging worlds of PR and marketing, aided by the growth of the popular press. An early example of guerrilla marketing was his deployment of an elephant, attached to a large plough, working his farm. This land happened to be next to a busy railroad linking New York and New Haven, Connecticut with thousands of passengers gawping daily at the curious spectacle.[39] All of which drummed up interest in Barnum's next venture.

Tumblety brought Barnum-like tactics to the world of medicine though he was reticent to admit it:

Although no great admirer of Barnum, I nevertheless regard him as a great authority in the matter of successfully conducting a business, and he himself considers advertising as the great element of his success.[40]

Tumblety made good use of his own impressive physicality in these Barnum-esque processions down Main Street. The doctor was over six feet tall, well-built, smooth-skinned, and often described in the non-murderous sense as a lady-killer. Female admirers reportedly swooned at the sight of this dashing Irish American with his sweeping walrus moustache riding past. A journalist in Buffalo summed Tumblety up

---

39 "Barnum's Elephant", *New York Tribune* article quoted in the North Wales Chronicle, May 12, 1855

40 Francis Tumblety, *A few passages in the life of Dr. Francis Tumblety*, 1866

succinctly: "He is a tall, dark, queer-looking man, with a regular hussar mustache, and certainly has had rare luck in acquiring notoriety".[41]

When he set up shop in a city for the first time, there were multiple appearances with numerous costume changes. As he slipped into something new, the previous costume was handed over to the valet to wear. This ritual might happen hourly. To keep the public enraptured, Tumblety appeared one moment as an English sportsman with tremendous spurs attached to his boots and then transformed the next into a Scottish Highlander replete with kilt and sporran.[42] As he rode past potential customers, unauthorised billboards were being pasted up at prime locations.

In 1859, a railway company was mocked for imitating Tumblety's approach to promotion:

> *The Great Western Railway magnates appear to consider advertising in newspapers such an expensive luxury, that they have actually devised the novel expedient of following in the wake of quacks and rat-killers, by placarding the sidewalks after the fashion of Dr. Tumblety, and Parson the rat exterminator.*[43]

Conspicuous consumption and great acts of philanthropy were Tumblety hallmarks and he made sure the press was well briefed in advance. As late as the 1890s, a few short years before his death, Tumblety sent a cheque for $200 to the New York Herald "for the purchase of bath tickets to be distributed free among New York boys".[44]

---

41   "Dr Tumblety", *The Buffalo Sunday Morning News*, December 16, 1888

42   "Dr Tumblety", *Buffalo Courier*, March 13, 1862

43   "A new way of saving money", *Semi-Weekly Spectator*, June 15, 1859

44   "Table talk", *The Buffalo Commercial*, September 8, 1891

Earlier in his career, Tumblety placed advertisements in the newspapers announcing his imminent appearance on the steps of the Merchants' Exchange in Buffalo to distribute fifty sacks of flour to the poor and dispossessed. At the same time, the city was deluged in newspaper advertisements and handbills. The very next day, Tumblety plus bags of flour duly materialised. This marketing strategy certainly worked with a local newspaper declaring "his charity was more than repaid".[45]

One newspaper proprietor in Buffalo was suspicious about Tumblety's claimed wealth. He telegraphed contacts in Toronto, where Tumblety was known to have previously operated, who might have more information. To his amazement, the Bank of Toronto responded that Tumblety's credit was sound. "His check is good for $60,000 in this bank". [46]

Tumblety made repeat fortunes and spent money lavishly, "buying champagne by the case and cigars by the box".[47] He desperately sought acceptance from the old moneyed elites though on some occasions exhibited contempt for authority using his new-found wealth. For example, after being fined in one courtroom, he threw a stash of dollar bills at the magistrate as if to declare that his deep pockets now made him untouchable.

Tumblety swamped the newspapers with long, classified adverts running across multiple columns, which we would now term 'advertorial'. This was another lesson from Barnum acknowledged in his autobiography:

> Now I know that there is a vast amount of humbuggery
> in the advertising market; but I am also aware, as every
> sensible observer must be, that no matter how beneficial
> or excellent, no article can be fairly presented to the public

45   "The Indian Herb Doctor – More about Him", *The Brooklyn Daily Eagle*, May 10, 1865

46   Ibid: "Fight for Tumblety's Cash?"

47   Ibid: "Fight for Tumblety's Cash?"

without the aid of the press, and to this end advertising is the only medium.[48]

A newspaper reader would find two, three, or four columns listing his cures and testimonials. This PR puff sat alongside legitimate news stories lending an objective credibility to his marketing, especially when the letters of commendation came from well-known figures across the United States, Canada, and Europe. If judges, mayors, and military officers were cured, then the trust of patients, and their money, could be placed with this worker of medical miracles.

The letters from satisfied patients named the doctors deemed to have failed before Tumblety put things right. John Deren of 13 St Paul Street wrote:

This is to certify that I have been troubled with Scrofula or King's Evil in my right leg for the last sixteen years. I tried some of our most eminent Physicians (Drs Godfrey, Crawford, Waller, etc) but received no benefit. I was persuaded to try the Indian Herb Doctor, Francis Tumblety, and in a very short time was perfectly cured.[49]

One multi-column advertisement began with the cry: *News to the Afflicted!!!*[50] This listed "certificates from the citizens of Montreal", basically letters from Tumblety's satisfied patients claiming to have been entirely cured of diseases ranging from jaundice, heart palpitations, and dyspepsia.

The patients' names and details were by and large accurate, but many had not given their permission to be featured in Tumblety's advertising. For example, a well-known pilot

---

48   Ibid: "A few passages in the life of Dr. Francis Tumblety"

49   Ibid, "News to the Afflicted"

50   "News to the Afflicted!!!", *The Gazette*, December 19, 1857

suffering from a tapeworm visited Tumblety and after taking several medications, believed he was cured. Without asking his patient, Tumblety placed a glowing commendation in a newspaper with a forged signature by the pilot. Seeing his intimate medical details in print sent the pilot into a rage and he resolved to beat the herb doctor to a pulp with a club. For some reason, the attack never transpired.[51]

However, Tumblety's dog was stabbed by somebody with a grudge and despite the offer of a reward, no information was forthcoming.[52] While the assailant may have been a rival quack doctor or a disenchanted gay fling, it could very easily have been a patient whose medical record was now public knowledge via one of his many newspaper testimonials.

One of Tumblety's first bases of operation was Hamilton, Ontario, in Canada. Like Rochester, across the border in the United States, it bordered Lake Ontario. In 1854, he was selling patent medicines in the city, taking breaks to ride around the streets on his distinctive horse promoting his business. Tumblety hired "the small brother of a big Irish chambermaid" to assist him. They developed a routine whereby the boy pretended to have a dreadful toothache and very publicly yelped in pain.

The skilful doc would instantaneously cure him before the gaping rustics.[53]

However, on one occasion, Tumblety gave his assistant a dose of what one must assume was a pain killer of some description and it threw the boy into convulsions. This wasn't the intended performance for potential patients. Tumblety

---

51 "Tumblety Facts in the History of the Supposed Whitechapel Fiend", *St Louis Globe-Democrat*, January 5, 1889

52 Ibid: "Tumblety Facts in the History of the Supposed Whitechapel Fiend"

53 "Doc. Tumblety", The Brantford Daily Expositor, November 30, 1888

sneaked away and returned in haste to his hotel. Unfortunately, the Irish chambermaid followed and by all accounts was well versed in the Marquis of Queensbury boxing rules giving him "a black eye, badly disarranged his hair and made such a laughing stock that he had to leave the city".[54]

Nevertheless, Tumblety was printing testimonials for years from pleased customers in Hamilton claiming to have been cured of everything from scrofula to cancer. Two bottles of the doctor's wonder medicine banished lip cancer from a certain Eliza Duffy. While another Hamiltonian had been cured of "ague", an old-fashioned term for malaria, through the external application of "vegetable remedies".[55]

In 1856, Tumblety set up a pharmacy in New York on a block at 13th Street and 6th Avenue. By then, he would have been in his mid-twenties. A very telling incident occurred featuring Tumblety's fondness for both poetry and pornography. It was remembered in an interview thirty-two years later with the veteran journalist Fred Hart after Tumblety had been arrested as a suspect in the Jack the Ripper case.

As a twenty-one-year-old just out of school, Hart was sucked into Tumblety's orbit - an experience he wouldn't forget. Not just Hart but his slightly younger friend referred to as Burchard with whom the doctor formed an instant affinity. One gets the impression from what happened next that Hart was frozen out of the burgeoning relationship between Tumblety and Burchard. The doctor clearly hit on Hart's more handsome and impressionable buddy.

Tumblety was resolved to bring down a rival drug store located close by, run by somebody we only know as Giles. The road to victory against his enemy was obvious to the Indian Herb Doctor. Burchard and Tumblety simply had to pen a

---

54   Ibid: "Doc. Tumblety"
55   "Be Wise Before It Is Too Late!", *The Gazette*, September 18, 1857

pornographic poem denigrating Giles in the vilest sexual terms and distribute it widely in the area. No respectable person would ever want to enter his pharmacy again.

Hart thought this was a terrible idea and backed away. Burchard, however, acquiesced, even though he was the stepson of a Presbyterian minister, whose church was on the same block. Burchard seemed unfazed by the potential reputational damage to his father if this all went horribly wrong. Because he was, as Hart later wrote, "wild, erratic and brilliant, and wrote rhymes with great facility",[56] Tumblety had found his pornographic muse.

Burchard's excuse for undertaking this libellous work was that he needed the money and Tumblety was always generous with young men he liked. However, Burchard's claim to be in dire financial straits doesn't ring true. He was a trust-fund kid with an income from his father's estate and a large legacy on the way in a few months when he attained his majority. Burchard's father, before dying, had been a leading New York shipping magnate. So, poverty doesn't stack up as an excuse for getting involved in this caper. Far more likely, Burchard shared Tumblety's appetite for a thrill.

Burchard churned out an impressive fifty verses on the hapless Giles - undoubtedly with plenty of input from Tumblety, drawing on his days as a purveyor of literary smut on the canal packets. There was no aspect of this man's character left untrashed by their poison pen. Regrettably, none of this obscene poetry has survived. Tumblety had the verses printed and a copy mailed in a sealed envelope to every resident in the Ninth Ward.

If Tumblety imagined this wouldn't be traced back to him then he was rapidly disabused. Giles immediately notified the police, who knew exactly which door to knock on. Tumblety was arrested. Law enforcement dragged the young doctor away for questioning. Sitting across the table from a police officer,

---

56   "Dr Tumblety", *The San Francisco Examiner*, November 23, 1888

Tumblety began to back-pedal furiously, a disagreeable trait throughout his career. Tumblety was happy to court disaster to obtain some great PR but threw anybody under the bus to extricate himself from the resulting perilous situation.

Showing no loyalty to Burchard, the Indian Herb Doctor betrayed him to the police as the author. The trust fund kid got wind of Tumblety's treachery and fled New York, holing up with relatives in Connecticut until the whole affair blew over. Tumblety, in contrast, got a year's imprisonment in what was nicknamed the Tombs. This was a mausoleum-like prison in lower Manhattan, officially termed the New York City Halls of Justice and House of Detention.

At some point in his early career, Tumblety was reportedly married to a woman. His wife was a little older and he had fallen desperately in love with her and she "promised to reciprocate his affection".[57] After a brief courtship, they got married. However, even before the honeymoon had ended, his wife was flirting with other men. Tumblety became very upset and remonstrated while she responded with a flood of kisses, whispering into his ear that the silly doctor was a "dear, jealous fool". Assured he must have imagined it all, Tumblety believed her.

Shortly afterwards, Tumblety was in a horse-drawn cab, on his own, passing through a very undesirable neighbourhood when his jaw dropped to the floor. There was his wife entering a "gloomy-looking house". It was clear that the building was being used as a brothel. Gentlemen approached, collars up and hat brims down, shiftily making their way through the front door. On further investigation, Tumblety discovered to his horror she hadn't just plied her trade there but at several other similar places. At this point, the heartbroken and furious doctor "gave up all womankind".[58]

---

57   "The Missing Tumblety", *Democrat and Chronicle*, December 3, 1888
58   Ibid: "The Missing Tumblety"

This story came to light in 1888 when Tumblety was arrested as a suspect in the Jack the Ripper case and was held up as proof that he had a long-term, visceral hatred of prostitutes rooted in a failed and loveless marriage. He certainly showed no evidence of having sexual relations with any woman ever again despite the female fan club that he generated in every city where he operated. His flowing moustache, military garb, and command of a horse drove some women mad, according to journalists. But Tumblety had no interest in women as wives or lovers.

Whether this tale of being married unwittingly to a female sex worker has a single grain of truth is something we shall probably never know but it certainly coloured opinion when he was arrested in 1888. His account of betrayal by his first love echoes, in our time, the dubious Jilted Bundy Theory. The view that the serial killer Ted Bundy embarked on his murders after the failure of a relationship with a woman, Diane Edwards, also known as Stephanie Brooks. The theory isn't accepted by psychiatrists and is the kind of 'incel' logic that places the blame for attacks on women upon the victim instead of the perpetrator.

Tumblety published an autobiography in 1866, updated over the years, which neglected to mention his failed marriage to an alleged prostitute. The story was recounted to a dinner party guest, Colonel Dunham, and reported in the newspapers after the Jack the Ripper arrest. As will be seen, the veracity of Dunham's account of Tumblety's marriage to a sex worker has been questioned.

In Tumblety's autobiography there is a curious reference about his murderous disposition towards the opposite sex. This self-glorifying work waxes lyrical about the doctor's journalist friends at the newspapers being "lavish in their encomiums and frequently indulged their poetic fancy in complimentary effusions". Or put another way, the reporters to whom he regularly fed stories about himself penned a few witty ditties about the doctor. One poem was published in the *Saint John*

Albion during his curtailed stay in the city of Saint John and begins with a description of Tumblety processing down Main Street:

> *Dr Tumblety rode a white steed*
> *Into St Johns in its time of need*
> *Determined to cure with herbal pills*
> *All the ailing of their ills*
> *Dr Tumblety had a greyhound*
> *A beautiful animal I'll be bound*
> *The dog looked up in the Doctor's face*
> *As he rode along at a slapping pace.*[59]

Then four lines of verse foreshadowing events over two decades later:

> *Tumblety had a killing air*
> *Though curing was his professional trade*
> *Rosy of cheek, and glossy of hair*
> *Dangerous man to widow or maid.*[60]

A poetic lady-killer here. In a couple of decades, he would become the real thing.

Another interesting vignette in Tumblety's autobiography is his description of being on very intimate terms with President Abraham Lincoln and leading American political and military figures. This is often dismissed as the exaggerated claims of a fraudulent braggart. But as will be seen, American journalists were sufficiently convinced that Tumblety and Lincoln were associated in some way to demand the president distance himself from the doctor.

---

59 Francis Tumblety, *A few passages in the life of Dr. Francis Tumblety*, 1866
60 Ibid: *A few passages in the life of Dr. Francis Tumblety*

Tumblety networked frantically in both Canada and the United States as he set up shop in a string of cities from Detroit to Montreal. If it suited his purpose, he was the most nationalistic of Irishmen beating the drum of Republicanism and bemoaning the condition of those left behind in the motherland. At the same time, he tapped into underground gay networks which he sniffed out with remarkable ease.

In the late 1850s, Tumblety played the Irish card to great effect when he was based for a period in the British American provinces that would become the Dominion of Canada in 1867. Tumblety was running his business in Montreal, whose Irish community was divided in its view of the city's foremost Irish politician, Thomas D'Arcy McGee (1825–1868). Incredibly, Tumblety decided to embark on a career in Canadian politics on the Irish ticket by taking on the powerful and influential McGee.

McGee was running to be the representative for Montreal in the Canadian parliament in elections held in December 1857. He was known to Irish communities on both sides of the Canada-United States border as a determined fighter for Irish Catholic interests. Described by the Montreal press in fearful terms as "a sort of raw-head and bloody bones" while his supporters assured the city's discomforted Protestants that they would find no greater "lover of civil and religious liberty".[61]

Born about five years before Tumblety in Carlingford, County Louth in Ireland, McGee had risen to prominence far faster than the doctor. Tumblety emigrated to the United States aged seventeen around 1847 while McGee left Ireland at about the same age but bound for Boston. Unlike Tumblety, who had to struggle from grim obscurity to his current social position, McGee's outspoken teenage support for Irish self-determination and powerful use of language landed him a job as a reasonably paid journalist almost immediately.

---

61   "The Nomination for the City of Montreal", *The Gazette*, December 15, 1857

McGee was lauded back in his native Ireland where he returned attempting to lead a revolution against British rule in 1848. When this failed, he made a quick escape back across the Atlantic to New York. Resuming his career as a journalist, McGee became a champion of Irish American interests both in the United States and neighbouring Canada. Like Tumblety, he moved with ease across the border between the two countries. It was a line both men chose to disregard. For McGee, the Irish communities in the key urban centres from New York and Boston to Rochester and Montreal were a single diaspora with a common interest. He even advocated, at one point, an American invasion of Canada as being in the best interest of Irish American communities in the region.

When hostility towards Irish Catholics increased in the 1840s, with growing anti-immigrant sentiment, McGee called for an Irish American homeland to be created on either side of the Canada-United States border, earning himself the nickname, Moses McGee. A conference was held in Buffalo, New York state in 1856 to discuss McGee's idea but it came to nothing. There was to be no green exodus of Irish Americans to any Promised Land.

A year later and McGee was singing a different political tune. Gone was the idea of an American invasion or an Irish homeland. He now argued that Irish interests in North America would be best served if Canada achieved a semi-devolved status within a British Empire run by a constitutional monarchy. He offered himself as a candidate for Montreal in the December 1857 parliamentary elections on this basis.

Although his views were becoming more conservative, his earlier revolutionary tendencies had irritated the Roman Catholic church and many leading Irish Americans in both the United States and Canada. One commentator even questioned McGee's Irish ethnicity asserting that his "physique" pointed to an African heritage.[62] This was a crude appeal to anti-black racism within the Irish communities.

Irish Canadian bigwigs opposed to McGee cast around for a credible alternative candidate who could defeat him and better represent the Irish interest. That person would receive strong support from the clergy who had still not forgiven a younger McGee for characterising the Catholic priesthood as the greatest enemy of Irish progress. Tumblety pushed himself forward as a good Catholic boy from the old country with a strong moral backbone and a large financial fortune that made him a credit to the community. He already had a high public profile thanks to his ceaseless newspaper promotion and combined with his striking physical presence, Tumblety possessed an almost Trumpian appeal for his Irish American contemporaries who were seemingly unaware of the darker side to his character.

His candidacy was soon being discussed in the Canadian capital, Ottawa where his fame had already spread:

> *It is hinted that Dr. Tumblety will offer himself as a candidate on grittish principles, in case of a vacancy in this constituency, and that he is now feeling the pulse of the people. The Doctor having amassed a fortune in the treatment of all 'the ills that flesh is heir to,' in which treatment he has ever been successful, now philanthropically proposes to devote his brilliant abilities to the cure of the dangerous diseases affecting the body politic and is proudly conscious of the success that awaits him in the effort.[63]*

It's easy to overlook the term "grittish" unless you're well versed in 1850's Canadian politics. This was a reference to the

---

62 "Ireland vs T. D. McGee", *The Gazette*, December 22, 1857

63 Francis Tumblety, Article in the Union newspaper, Ottawa, quoted in *A few passages in the life of Dr. Francis Tumblety*, 1866

Clear Grit Party, a wing of the Reform Party in Ontario that resented the privileges of the Protestant church. Since 1791, lands in Canada referred to as the Clergy Reserves had been set aside for the support and maintenance of the Protestant clergy.[64]

Grittish politicians, many being Irish Catholic, allied themselves to Catholic French Canadians in the Parti Rouge, to oppose this religious favouritism.[65] Their demand for secularisation was really a thinly veiled attack on the English heritage Protestant elite. Tumblety's grittish political instincts were more than likely rooted in his childhood among Catholic Irish immigrants abused by Protestant neighbours.

In his autobiography, Tumblety praised the "celebrated" McGee, "a gentleman whose literary and political reputation is well known in this country".[66] However, the Indian Herb Doctor believed he could beat McGee and get elected to parliament. He was confident of gaining high-profile Irish American endorsements from those who loathed McGee.

But Tumblety suddenly pulled out of the running. In a letter to the Montreal *Commercial Advertiser* on 7 December 1857, the doctor confirmed the rumours he was being asked to represent the "Irish interest" against McGee. But at the present time, he wasn't putting his name forward. Something had happened to make Tumblety change his mind. It wasn't clear to anybody, including journalists, why the doctor had shelved his political ambitions.

McGee was duly elected. In a glittering political career, he went on to become a founding father of the Canadian

---

64 "Clear Grit Party", Quebec History, *Marianopolis College*, March 2005, http://faculty.marianopolis.edu/c.belanger/QuebecHistory/encyclopedia/ClearGritParty-ClearGrits-CanadianHistory.htm

65 "The McGee Irish Roman Catholic Clear Grit and Rouge Alliance", *The Gazette*, May 19, 1859

66 Francis Tumblety, *A few passages in the life of Dr Francis Tumblety*, 1866

Confederation.[67] But then on 7 April 1868, he was assassinated outside a boarding house in Ottowa at 2am, returning from a late-nigh parliamentary debate. It was a murder "coolly done" as he leaned forward to put his key in the front door lock. By 9am, his body lay in an anteroom of the house.

His face and grey beard are all clotted with gore; his overcoat is partly unbuttoned; his right hand, ungloved to open the door, lies on his breast. On his feet are warm carpet slippers and woollen socks. His white hat lies nearby all splashed with his life blood, and his walking-stick and other glove near his head. It is a dreadful sight.[68]

On 11 February 1869, Patrick J. Whelan was hanged after being found guilty of shooting McGee dead with a handgun. Whelan was a member of the Fenian Brotherhood, an Irish Republican movement espousing violence which McGee had denounced in the strongest terms. Whelan's last words as he braced for the long drop were, "God save Ireland and God save my soul". The hanging was botched, with those present forced to watch Whelan's hands and fingers wriggle and his untied legs raise as he was asphyxiated.

It was evident that the prisoner died very hard, there being a nervous twitching of the muscles plainly visible for the space of four and three quarter minutes.[69]

These events may never have played out if Tumblety had run against McGee in December 1857. But something happened

---

67 David A. Wilson, "Thomas D'Arcy McGee: Passion, Reason, and Politics, 1825-1857", *McGill-Queen's University Press*, 2008

68 "Further Particulars of the Murder of the Hon. T. D'Arcy McGee", *The Gazette*, April 8, 1868

69 "Execution of Whelan!", *Ottawa Daily Citizen*, February 12, 1869

that autumn which gave the Indian Herb Doctor pause for thought - a criminal investigation which would have resonated very badly with his fellow Irish American Catholics.

On Monday 21 September 1857, a man named Jean Baptiste Simard walked into Tumblety's office on Great St James Street, next to the Bank of British North America. Tumblety took one look at Simard and announced that he could tell exactly what was wrong with him. Simard, though, punctured this incredible display of medical insight pointing out he was calling on behalf of a young woman who was pregnant. Lowering his voice conspiratorially, he asked whether Tumblety could provide something to induce a miscarriage.[70]

Both men knew full well that abortion was illegal. Canada was part of the British Empire and its laws shadowed those of the colonial power. In 1803, the United Kingdom toughened its stance on early termination, making abortion a capital offence punishable by the death penalty and the Canadian provinces fell into line.[71] The legislation was modified two decades later replacing death by imprisonment. However, despite their liberal reputation today, the Canadian provinces in 1850 continued to have the death penalty on the statute books for many crimes from rape to piracy, even after Britain had removed capital punishment for those offences.[72]

With regards to homosexuality for example, New Brunswick officially mandated death for sodomy, despite London opting for imprisonment. But gay men weren't hanging from nooses all over Canada. Tumblety, was a very active homosexual theoretically risking death with every dark alley encounter. Yet he was alive. As one historian described the legal position for gay

70   "Police Court", *The Gazette*, September 24, 1857

71   Stephanie Paterson, "Fertile Ground: Exploring Reproduction in Canada", *McGill-Queen's University Press*, 2014

72   "Capital Punishment in the Colonies", *Hampshire Telegraph and Naval Chronicle*, July 5, 1856

men, there was a dark cloud hanging over them, but it seldom rained.[73] This wasn't just a reticence by the courts to execute gay people but because, beneath the surface, gay men had formed their own networks of protection to fend off the gallows.

Tumblety clearly felt confident enough to proceed with an illegal abortion. As with homosexuality, the law wasn't enforced to the letter, and anyway the money was too tempting. Simard asked if Tumblety really was a doctor and got an indignant response in the affirmative. Tumblety inquired in turn whether Simard was Protestant or Catholic. Simard said he was a Protestant. Tumblety remarked sternly that he was forbidden to assist a Catholic on religious grounds but as Simard was Protestant, he could return in an hour to pick up "the medicine to kill the child" and it would cost five pounds - £100 sterling in today's value.

But Simard didn't reappear that day. Instead, he came back the next morning telling Tumblety the girl was ashamed to visit his office. Tumblety directed Simard to bring her at once. At noon, Simard returned with a young woman named Philomene Dumas. The Indian Herb Doctor leaped into action examining her tongue and pulse and asking about the pregnancy.

She had been vomiting in the morning and felt a pain in her back. Her periods had been "retarded" for about three weeks. Tumblety turned to Simard: "She is caught but I can cure her!".[74] The doctor handed over a bottle of liquid, which he instructed Dumas to taste, proving it wasn't harmful, and a box of pills with printed directions. Then he demanded his five pounds from Simard and told him to "bring me customers".

The very next day, Tumblety was dragged before Charles-Joseph Coursol, the police magistrate as the whole episode had been a sting operation. Simard, it transpired, was a police

73   Graham Robb,*Strangers: Homosexual Love in the Nineteenth Century* (W.W. Norton & Company, 2005)

74   Ibid, "Police Court"

detective. As for Philomene Dumas, her place of residence was a well-known brothel on Perthius Street where the madam was a certain Mrs Foley. It also emerged that Simard was a regular visitor to this establishment though, according to Dumas, "he never slept there".[75]

Police magistrate, Coursol had orchestrated the sting. He was an imposing figure with one foot in the judicial world and the other in politics. Previously a practising lawyer, Coursol would go on to become the Mayor of Montreal and a member of the Canadian parliament. As a young man, he had shown his gutter-level political mettle by organising "a mob of six hundred bludgeon-armed toughs" in 1841 to support a political candidate in Montreal. In 1849, he was embroiled in a major fracas with Tory party supporters.[76]

The Indian Herb Doctor realised he was up against a formidable foe. Like Tumblety, Coursol craved respectability but never forgot his roots with a pair of knuckle dusters handy in his top drawer. If he wanted a fight, then Tumblety would give it to him. The doctor turned to his Irish network, hiring Bernard Devlin (1824–1880), an Irish-born pugnacious lawyer with a moustache that rivalled that of his client. Devlin would go on to battle D'Arcy McGee in the political arena for many years after this case.[77] He was hired alongside another impressive Montreal legal figure, Lewis Drummond. In paying for this formidable duo, the doctor was pouring his money into destroying Coursol.

Devlin defended Tumblety with gusto. He ripped into the police, arguing this had been a wretched example of entrapment designed solely to destroy his client's reputation. Tumblety's valet at the time, a man named John Guy, testified that the medicine had been for headaches and not to induce an abortion.

75   Ibid, "Police Court"

76   "Coursol, Charles-Joseph", *Dictionary of Canadian Biography*, Vol. XI

77   "Elections in St. Ann's Division in Olden Days", *The Montreal Star*, November 21, 1906

Despite this, Coursol denied Tumblety bail, ruling the case should proceed for trial at the Queen's Bench. Devlin appealed above his head to another judge and got that overturned.

The case was eventually heard before a Grand Jury in October 1857 and the court swung round to the view there was no convincing evidence that the drugs administered by Tumblety could induce an early termination. In fact, the ingredients in his patent medicine appeared to be nothing more than cayenne pepper dissolved in some solution. The Grand Jury rejected the case against the Indian Herb Doctor. His Irish network had done him proud.

However, having emerged triumphant though bruised by the experience, Tumblety unwisely disputed Devlin's legal fees. He was only prepared to pay half of the £100 being demanded. The lawyer then sued his client for the balance. Drummond ended up defending Tumblety against Devlin. The court found for Devlin though didn't award him the full amount he wanted. But he soon got his own back on Tumblety for this ingratitude.

Later the very same month, November 1857, Devlin and Tumblety squared off in court yet again. Still seeking vengeance, Devlin took on a case from a third party against the doctor. He defended a porter who had assaulted one of Tumblety's valets, a young man living and working with Tumblety named Joseph Palmer. Devlin would have known full well the real nature of this relationship. After all, Tumblety's sex life was the subject of ribald gossip in police stations and courtrooms.

Palmer was described in court as "a student of Dr. Tumblety", no doubt to stifled guffaws.[78] The porter, George Hunter, had struck Palmer as he ran down the stairs in their building in pursuit of a dog recently gifted to the doctor as a present. Hunter, who was clearly something of a bully, yelled at

---

78 "Assault and Battery", *The Gazette*, November 24, 1857

Palmer, demanding to know why he was running so fast. The valet told the porter it was none of his business.

> *Whereupon he struck me with his fist on the back of the head, and made two or three attempts at me, and said he would make a football of me.*[79]

Palmer then added the pertinent detail that he had no clothes on at the time.[80]

> *Question by Counsel: What! Were you naked?*
> *Answer: No: I had on my trousers.*[81]

Tumblety was supposed to appear as a witness for the prosecution but decided to stay away. Nevertheless, Devlin lost the case, and the defendant was ordered to pay a fine and costs. But the damage was done to the doctor's standing as the newspaper reports of the trial raised eyebrows across town. The reading public could very well guess why his valet was semi-naked during the course of his employment.

Devlin, like his rival McGee, became a major figure in the political history of Montreal in the 19th century. And in just a few short years, his legal services were retained by a very powerful client across the border in the United States: President Abraham Lincoln.

Soon enough, Tumblety was looking for another handsome, young valet. He scoured the usual hunting grounds - parks, theatres, and busy streets buzzing with office workers, shop assistants, students, and those living by their wits. Cruising areas were well recognised in most cities. In 18th century London,

---

79 Ibid: "Assault and Battery"
80 Ibid: "Assault and Battery"
81 Ibid: "Assault and Battery"

for example, a connecting road between Upper and Middle Moorfields, now the south side of Finsbury Square, was dubbed Sodomite's Walk.[82] An 1878 map of Amsterdam included reference to places that "wrong lovers" frequented.

Horse carriages, trains, swimming pools, markets, and even the poor house were venues for illegal homosexual sex.[83] Two men might be seen kissing there by police and then followed for days or even weeks before they were caught having full-blown sex in a public place. But this danger didn't deter men like Tumblety from losing themselves in a big metropolis where they could forget their families and develop new friendships and support networks but also risk rubbing up against criminals for whom seduction was a prelude to robbery.

Most of Tumblety's relationships were fleeting - young men met on the street who might then be employed as "valets". Confronted by the doctor's wealth, some used their new-found position and access to steal from him. In a society with no welfare safety net or workplace protection, the temptation to pocket some of their employer's money clearly appealed to some of the doctor's valets, especially as they more than likely viewed Tumblety as an exploitative older man. When he dragged them before the police and courts, they responded with allegations of improper behaviour and "gross indecency", landing Tumblety in hot water.

The doctor must have felt as if there were few people he could truly trust. One man who earned his lifelong affection and would be a beneficiary in his will was Mark Blackburn. From the scraps of information that we have on Blackburn, it seems that Tumblety picked him up as a seventeen-year-old working-class lad in Brooklyn or New York then installing him as a valet. As

---

82 "Places for Sex", *Historic England*, https://historicengland.org.uk/research/inclusive-heritage/lgbtq-heritage-project/meeting-and-socialising/places-for-sex/

83 David Higgs, *Queer Sites: Gay Urban Histories Since 1600* (Routledge, 1999)

with all his young charges, Tumblety subjected Blackburn to his customary misogynist rants about the evils of women.

He joined the doctor's habitual processions distributing handbills while Tumblety was the focus of attention in his garish uniform on horseback. While his employer was away on one of his many trips, Blackburn was trusted to run the office, bill customers, and bank the cash. In effect, he became an apprentice much as Tumblety had been to Dr Lispenard, learning the ropes and eventually setting himself up in business.

From the 1860s to the end of his life, Tumblety continued an intimate friendship with Blackburn as he matured from adolescence to full adulthood. Even Blackburn's decision to marry, not just once but twice, failed to dim the doctor's affection towards him. Something about this individual overrode the doctor's customary fury towards those of his boys who fell for a woman. The relationship was almost certainly sexual at the outset but shifted to something more platonic though still emotionally deep over the years.

Blackburn didn't accompany Tumblety to Washington DC when he moved there in 1861 but re-joined the doctor in St. Louis, around the time he was arrested as a suspect in the plot to assassinate President Lincoln. He became embroiled in all the publicity surrounding Tumblety at the time being mistaken in one newspaper report for another valet, David Herold, who would hang for his role in Lincoln's murder.

Further confusion was caused by Tumblety listing one of his offices under Blackburn's name. Blackburn also shared the same surname as Luke Pryor Blackburn – a Confederate-supporting physician who was accused of trying to spread yellow fever among Union troops and cities in the Civil War. As will be shown, Tumblety was briefly implicated in Luke Blackburn's plot in a bizarre turn of events. That Blackburn avoided prosecution and went on to become the 28th Governor of Kentucky in 1879.

This brings us to the first death that can be pinned definitively on Tumblety. In October 1860, the doctor was forced to flee Saint John, New Brunswick after the sudden demise of a patient, an old volunteer firefighter named James Portmore.[84] Coroner William Bayard investigated the death and was soon convinced that Tumblety's fake cures had killed Portmore.

During the coroner's hearing, a disturbing incident occurred where there was an attempt to steal Portmore's heart and liver, presumably from the pathology lab where the post-mortem was conducted.[85] Jurors were reportedly shocked by this audacious attempt to remove key evidence. Nobody doubted for a second that Tumblety's fingerprints were all over this. Reading the runes, the herb doctor didn't hang around to hear the jury return the expected verdict of manslaughter. He fled on horseback down the St Andrew's Road and out of the province and country. By all accounts, he cut quite a dash as he pelted down the road:

Tumblety fled from St. John in the night, mounted upon the white horse which he had made so conspicuous during his stay. He took the post-road to St. Stephen and crossed to Calais. He rode with the haste of Paul Revere in his midnight ride.[86]

Farmers along the escape route were startled from their slumber by this figure galloping past wildly.

---

84 "Dr Tumblety", *Buffalo Courier*, October 5, 1860

85 Ibid: "Tumblety Facts in the History of the Supposed Whitechapel Fiend"

86 Ibid: "Tumblety Facts in the History of the Supposed Whitechapel Fiend"

Looking out they could see a tall man on a white charger,
with a big hound running fleetly by his side.[87]

At some point, Tumblety spied a stagecoach carrying mail moving at speed in the opposite direction. Terrified of being recognised and dragged back to the coroner's court, he urged his horse and dog into some nearby bushes. Despite his best efforts, the mail coach driver couldn't fail to recognise this notorious figure as he thundered past.

Tumblety left behind a young valet in Saint John who found himself hauled before the coroner. His now-departed boss, he said, was making a beeline for the town of Calais in Maine, across the border in the United States. One newspaper in Detroit, noting Tumblety's past presence in that city, had no doubt this "unconscionable quack" was guilty running the headline: *Dr Tumblety Kills a Man and runs away.*[88]

So how did the Indian Herb Doctor recover his reputation after the illegal death of a patient? He resorted to a welter of bluster in the newspapers. A smokescreen of hysterical counterblasts leaving the public unsure who was telling the truth. As with the previous illegal abortion, Tumblety depicted a David and Goliath battle between him and the medical bigwigs. This included the coroner, who was a practising doctor. Tumblety claimed his success as a healer had damaged Coroner Bayard's business and he had effectively exposed this man as a bumbling fool, quite rightly taking many of his patients. The manslaughter charge was trumped up by the envious and out of pocket coroner, simply to get him out of Saint John.[89]

---

87   Ibid: "Tumblety Facts in the History of the Supposed Whitechapel Fiend"

88   "Dr Tumblety kills a man and runs away", *Detroit Free Press*, October 7, 1860

89   Ibid: "Tumblety Facts in the History of the Supposed Whitechapel Fiend"

Tumblety got his side of the story printed in the *Eastport Sentinel*, a newspaper in Maine, thundering in the third person that the prosecution of Dr Tumblety in New Brunswick was the work of "a conspiracy on the part of the physicians of the place".[90] And furthermore, the coroner's jury had failed to prove any link between Portmore's death and Dr Tumblety's course of treatment.

The Mayor of Saint John took a different view. He dubbed Tumblety "an arrant quack" who "realized a very large amount of money from poor persons in the city and vicinity, making them pay down large sums before he would undertake to promise cures, which were not always afterward performed".[91]

The mayor corresponded with a Toronto-based magistrate to get more information about Tumblety. The magistrate said the doctor had appeared before him having extorted a watch from a farmer who was unable to pay his medical fees and he had been fined $100 for "practicing (sic) medicine without a license".[92] The magistrate included an intriguing nugget of information in his missive to the mayor claiming that before arriving in Toronto, Tumblety had been touring with "a strolling company of concert or menagerie folks".[93] The idea that Tumblety was at some stage part of a circus troupe might explain his Barnum-style promotion tactics but there is no further evidence to back up this assertion.

Tumblety returned to Rochester at the end of the 1850s after nearly a decade away. Unlike the Prodigal Son of the biblical parable, he was coming back as "a physician of wealth and eccentric habit".[94] Maybe the Indian Herb Doctor expected

---

90   "The Tumblety Case", *Buffalo Courier*, October 27, 1860

91   "Correspondence of the Courier", *The Charleston Daily Courier*, March 23, 1861

92   Ibid: "Correspondence of the Courier"

93   Ibid: "Correspondence of the Courier"

94   Ibid: "Fight for Tumblety's Cash?"

to be welcomed with open arms. The boy had, after all, done exceedingly well. There is no mention of him meeting his extended family in the city and contact may have been minimal in recent years given his incessant moving around and illicit private life.

The accounts that emerged much later about this homecoming paint a rather downbeat scene, as if Tumblety regretted the trip to Rochester almost immediately. Instead of having the opportunity to flash his cash about town, he was reminded once more of his less than salubrious beginnings.

At one point, Tumblety bumped into Captain Streeter on whose Erie Canal packet he had once sold pornographic material although this wasn't a period of his life that the aspiring pillar of respectability wished to reminisce about.

Streeter watched him striding down Main Street in a light fur overcoat nearly reaching his feet and a large greyhound padding alongside him. The doctor shuddered as he caught sight of the old man. Streeter had known him as a friendless child desperate to make his first few dollars by any means necessary. Despite his newfound wealth, he looked "more exclusive and solitary than ever". As he approached, Streeter greeted him.

Hello, Frank, who d'ye do?[95]

Tumblety resented the familiar tone.

Hello Streeter.

And with that perfunctory greeting, Tumblety went on his way. The crusty captain of the canal packet found his arrogant bearing "aristocratic". When Tumblety was implicated as Jack the Ripper decades later in 1888, Streeter seized on the opportunity

---

95   "The Missing Tumblety", *Democrat and Chronicle*, December 3, 1888

to stick the boot into the former teenage pornographer. He gleefully told American newspaper journalists that Tumblety's "mind had been affected by those books he sold" and he wasn't surprised that his name was mentioned in connection with the Whitechapel murders.[96]

The return to Rochester had been a bad idea. If Tumblety hoped to feel better about how far he had risen, that didn't happen. Instead, old faces like Streeter conjured up a terrible past, from which he had escaped by transforming himself into something very different. The teenage Tumblety with ragged clothes was dead. In his place was the Indian Herb Doctor with his plumed helmet, fake medical degrees, and testimonials from the rich and famous. Tumblety embodied the spirit of the period's unregulated, no-holds-barred, aggressive capitalism where sharp practice and an absence of ethics was the order of the day.

This was an era satirised by the novelist Herman Melville (1819–1891), a contemporary of Tumblety. Aside from his more famous novel *Moby Dick*, he also penned *The Confidence Man: His Masquerade* in 1857, just before the Civil War. The action takes place on a steamboat, the *Fidèle*, sailing down the Mississippi. It's a vessel brimming with charlatans, including a fraudster selling stock in failing companies; another traveller hawking miraculous herbal medicines that can cure cancer; and a man in a grey suit fundraising for a dubious charity.

On the *Fidèle*, everybody and anybody might be a confidence trickster. Drawing on Chaucer's *Canterbury Tales,* Bocaccio's *Decameron*, and a bit of Edgar Allen Poe thrown into this literary mix, Melville is teasing the reader to identify the real rogue on board when in fact everybody is the rogue. There is no honesty to be found on the *Fidèle*.

One of the many great insights in Melville's book is his

---

96 Captain W. C. Streeter was interviewed by the *Democrat & Chronicle* in December 1888

realisation that people like Tumblety were choosing their own personality. Playing a role to achieve their ends. "Life is a picnic *en costume*; one must take a part, assume a character, stand ready in a sensible way to play the fool."[97] The mid-19th century was full of de facto existentialists who decided how they wanted others to define them and then projected that reality.

So, far from being entirely unique, Tumblety reflected the spirit of his age. He embraced the opportunity to get rich quick in an unregulated environment where a boy from the Rochester Irish ghetto could build repeat fortunes and move among the top layers of society simply through sheer effort and guile.

As with Melville's characters, Tumblety began his career as a huckster on a waterborne vessel – in his case, selling pornography on the Erie canal packets. He progressed swiftly to become a wealthy if rather irregular man of medicine with his garish public relations performances on Main Street in various cities including a circus horse, cavalry uniform, valet, greyhounds, and plumed helmet.

For this, Tumblety has been decried as a fraud and a clown. But he was a man escaping a grim past in a young country where you could be anything if you convinced enough people. Many others played the same game. As will be seen, one of Lincoln's most dashing and well-known military officers, who processed in dazzling uniforms down Pennsylvania Avenue, also turned out to be a complete fake. His only mistake was to be found out.

Tumblety had spent a significant amount of time up to 1860 in Canada but despite his later claims to have enjoyed his time in Montreal, Toronto, and Saint John, he was being drawn increasingly towards the United States. New York and Washington DC would dominate his life in the first half of the 1860s.

---

97   Herman Melville, *The Confidence-Man* (Penguin Classics, 1991)

The United States was heading for civil war over the issue of slavery. A new president, Abraham Lincoln, would be inaugurated in 1861 only to see the southern states secede and form a new country: The Confederate States of America. But where others saw misery, chaos and division, Tumblety sensed a business opportunity.

Therefore into this political maelstrom Tumblety charged headfirst, establishing his medical business in the American capital, creating an unseemly blaze of garish publicity, and setting in motion a chain of events that would bring him remarkably close to Lincoln and the president's assassin, John Wilkes Booth.

Even if the Indian Herb Doctor had known what lay ahead, there is little doubt that he would still have taken the plunge.

Two

The Sexuality of Abraham Lincoln

Francis Tumblety was to become implicated in two of the most infamous crimes of the 19th century. The first was the assassination of President Abraham Lincoln in 1865, an event that shocked the nation and the world. The second was Tumblety's arrest as a suspect in the Jack the Ripper murders of 1888. If he was in any way guilty of either crime, it presents the astonishing possibility that Jack the Ripper was involved in the killing of the 16th President of the United States.

Tumblety was in Washington DC for most of the Civil War. In his autobiography, he claims that during that period, he developed an "intimate" relationship with Lincoln, his Secretary of State William Seward, and senior Union military officers leading the fight against the Confederates. From what we know of Tumblety's ability to network up to the highest reaches of society, this shouldn't be breezily dismissed. During his time in Canada, after all, he had been considered as a potential member of parliament. And journalists across North America had already turned the Indian Herb Doctor into a proto-celebrity.

Tumblety wormed his way into the White House using all the networks at his disposal and developing unusually deep friendships with the city's top brass. Many of these relationships, as is inferred in his autobiography and other accounts, suggest a degree of intimacy that, as with his valets picked up on the street, tipped over into the physical. Why should it be assumed that Tumblety could not have enjoyed homosexual relations with elite Americans as well as working-class youths? This raises a question over President Lincoln himself and how he might have known Tumblety and the depth of their relationship. Because despite the heroic efforts of some hetero-historians to airbrush this out, Lincoln's sexuality was a talking point during his life and in the years after his murder.

Raising the question of Lincoln's sexuality elicits howls of anguish from certain historians and has done so for over a hundred years. But contemporary sources and his earliest biographers offer tantalising clues to the president's bedroom preferences. Just by detailing the facts offers a compelling case for Lincoln being either homosexual or bisexual - and this in no way diminishes his stellar achievements and greatness.

The first undeniably LGBT President of the United States was Lincoln's immediate predecessor, James Buchanan. As with other gay men in the mid-19th century, there were the usual tall tales of having kissed a woman's hand at a ball at such-and-such a date; or a female love who tragically died leading to a forswearing of all women afterwards out of grief; or the habitual chestnut that a well-documented steamy relationship between two men was merely a typical, platonic arrangement between chaps of that historical period.

Buchanan was the only bachelor President of the United States living with his best friend, fellow politician William Rufus DeVane King (1786–1853), referred to derisively by a previous occupant of the White House, President Andrew Jackson, as "Miss Nancy" to Buchanan's "Aunt Fancy".[98]

---

98   Jean H. Baker, *James Buchanan: The American Presidents Series* (Times Books, 2004)

The two were seen so often together around Washington DC that they became known as the "Siamese Twins", a contemporary slang reference for gays and lesbians.[99] King was a pro-slavery senator from Alabama and would die forty-five days after being made the only ever bachelor vice president to President Franklin Pierce in 1853. When King left the United States to take up a position as the ambassador in Paris in 1844, Buchanan was beside himself, writing to a Mrs Roosevelt:

I am now solitary and alone having no companion in the house with me. I have gone a wooing to several gentlemen but have not succeeded with any one of them. I feel that it is not good for man to be alone; and should not be astonished to find myself married to some old maid who can nurse me when I am sick, provide good dinners for me when I am well, and not expect from me any very ardent or romantic affection.[100]

Buchanan was practically falling out of the closet - and those around him knew it. Americans in the 19th century weren't anywhere near as naïve as some modern historians tend to assume. This faulty thinking, where only recent generations are deemed to understand issues around sexuality, is based on "chronological ethnocentrism", a belief that the past must have been a terribly regressive place from which we have made steady upwards progress.[101] In reality, we have often regressed with regards to social attitudes forgetting how relatively enlightened folks were in previous centuries.

After four rocky years as president from 1856 to 1860,

99   "Our Queer President", *The Chronicle of Higher Education*, October 15, 1999

100 Jim Loewen, "Our real first gay president", *Salon*, May 14, 2012

101 James W. Loewen, *Lies My Teacher Told Me: Everything your American History Textbook Got Wrong* (Touchstone Books, 1996)

Buchanan left the United States on the verge of civil war regarding the question of slavery - an issue that had festered since the Founding Fathers drafted the Constitution. Buchanan's ineptitude made things a lot worse, and he is widely regarded as one of the worst presidents in US history. Unsurprisingly, Aunt Fancy didn't seek a second term at the 1860 Democratic National Convention. Instead, Democrats went into the subsequent election divided and the Republican candidate, Abraham Lincoln, secured a majority in the electoral college.

Even in these enlightened times, the subject of Lincoln's sexuality is taboo. But since his death, certain biographers touched on his love for other men. Carl Sandburg (1878–1967), author of a multi-volume biography of Lincoln, which won the 1940 Pulitzer Prize for history, wrote of the "invisible companionships that surprised me" and when it came to the young Lincoln's relationship with Joshua Fry Speed (1814–1882), Sandburg observed of the future president:

A streak of lavender ran through him: he had spots soft as May violets.[102]

This line was excised from later editions of Sandburg's magisterial history. The first volumes were released in 1926 and readers with any awareness of contemporary urban and literary culture would have guessed the reference. Some recent historians question the connection between lavender and homosexuality, but the link is well recognised. Senator Joseph McCarthy's purge of homosexuals in the American government in the 1950s was subsequently referred to as the Lavender Scare and gay men were referred to during the purge

---

102 Carl Sandburg, "Abraham Lincoln: The Prairie Years and The War Years" (Harcourt, 1926)

as "lavender lads" by Senator Everett Dirksen (1896–1969).[103]

As for violets, they were worn by one of the lovers of the Greek poet Sappho (630–570 BC) and in 1927, a year after that Lincoln volume came out, a play on Broadway – *The Captive* by Édouard Bourdet – featured two lesbian characters with one sending a bouquet of violets to the other. Violet sales in New York apparently crashed at the time.[104] Along with pansies and the green carnation, lavender and violets are the gayest occupants of your flowerbed.

The question that must be fired back at those who think Sandburg wasn't referring to homosexuality is: well, what do you think he was referring to? Is there an alternative explanation that has equal weight? And it's not as if Sandburg was the first historian to stumble across Lincoln's bedroom arrangements. The investigative journalist and author Ida Tarbell (1857–1944) penned *The Life of Abraham Lincoln* in 1900 and her research lifted the lid, or bed sheet, on Lincoln being between the covers with at least one other man.[105,106]

Tarbell was one of a small number of pioneering female journalists in America's "Progressive" era from the 1890s to the 1920s who had no qualms speaking out on taboo subjects and challenging power. Tarbell and her employers at *McClure's Magazine* were sceptical of the Lincoln hagiographies already in circulation. So, the publication opened a "Lincoln Bureau" where those who remembered the late president could walk in and share their memories.

Like Lincoln, Tarbell's childhood had been experienced in a

---

103 Sarah Prager, "Four Flowering Plants That Have Been Decidedly Queered", *Daily Jstor*, January 29, 2020

104 "Queer Botany: The Sapphic Violet", *University of Washington Botanic Gardens*, December, 21 2021

105 Ida M. Tarbell, *The Life of Abraham Lincoln* (Lincoln History Society, New York, 1909)

106 *The Ida M. Tarbell Collection*, collected papers held at Allegheny College donated by Sarah Tarbell

log cabin, backwoods environment, but whereas the president's first biographers, and many since, cast this as some kind of poverty-ridden gloom, she revealed the vitality and unexpected liberality of pioneer life. The young Lincoln, in her estimation, wasn't a shabby, unkempt tramp but neat, elegant, and sporting an elaborate cravat.[107] Her Lincoln was very human - jovial, witty, risqué, and one might even say a little bit camp.

However, she recoiled at the entrance to the bedroom. Undoubtedly aware of rumours that Lincoln had slept with several men, Tarbell couldn't bring herself to put pen to paper on the matter. Mainly because, as a huge supporter of Lincoln, and at the time influenced by socialist ideas, she fretted that his sexuality would in some way besmirch the great man's memory and give succour to reactionary opinion. Given that this was a period when states in the former Confederacy were still riven with racism and hate-filled politics, she didn't want to let the side down.

Despite her reticence, Lincoln's surviving son – Robert Todd Lincoln (1843–1926) – was unnerved about the direction of travel on his late father's biographies and encouraged writers like William E. Barton, Albert J. Beveridge, and Carl Sandburg to create the looming, saintly figure we think of today.[108] However, Sandburg simply couldn't ignore Lincoln's obvious attraction to men. Unlike Tarbell, he put his suspicion in print - in very coded terms – only to have it excised later.

Among the historical cognoscenti, there is a well-recognised list of men Lincoln bedded: Joshua Fry Speed; William "Billy" Greene; Elmer Ephraim Ellsworth; Abner Y. Ellis; and Captain David V. Derickson. A summary of each of these male bedfellows of Lincoln is certainly called for. Let's meet the male lovers:

---

107 Judith A. Rice, "Ida M. Tarbell: A Progressive Look at Lincoln", *Journal of the Abraham Lincoln Association*, Vol. 19, Issue 1, Winter 1998, pp. 57-72

108 Merrill D. Peterson, *Lincoln in American Memory* (Oxford University Press, 1995)

Joshua Fry Speed (1814–1882): Speed met a young and financially hard-up Lincoln in 1837, the day he walked into the Speed family dry goods store looking to buy bedding. Instead, Speed offered to sub-let his own room above the store, which involved sharing the same bed. It wasn't uncommon for men to share a bed for short stays away from home, but this duo remained under the same covers for nearly four years. Everybody who knew Lincoln in his lifetime remarked on the intensity of the relationship between the two men that in Lincoln's case eclipsed that with his own wife.

William "Billy" Greene (1812–1894): Greene not only shared a bed with Lincoln but famously commented on the future president's "perfect" thighs. It was said by contemporaries that nobody was "more intimately acquainted" with Lincoln than Greene who was showered with favours after his bed partner became president.[109]

Elmer Ephraim Ellsworth (1837–1861): The first Union army officer to die in the American Civil War, killed removing a Confederate flag in Virginia, and whose body lay in state at the White House. Described by an inconsolable Lincoln as "the greatest little man I ever met", Ellsworth was five-feet-six, which wasn't particularly small at the time unless set against Lincoln's gigantic six-feet-four. He was no stranger to the president, having studied law under him as a clerk in Lincoln's legal practice. The two men shared a bed and Lincoln broke down in tears in front of a newspaper reporter when told of his death.

Abner. Y. Ellis (1807–1878): Ellis was a merchant in New Salem who later went into business with Speed. He met Lincoln in New Salem in 1833 becoming "intimately acquainted with him". Ellis is one of several sources confirming that Lincoln

---

109 T. G. Onstot, *Pioneers of Menard and Mason Counties* (T.G. Onstot, Forest City, Illinois, 1902)

had "such a great passion for dirty stories".[110] The two men very definitely shared a bed together.

Captain David V. Derickson (1818-1891): Derickson was Lincoln's head of security between September 1862 and April 1863, staying with him at the Soldiers' Home, a retreat used by Lincoln just outside Washington DC. He would sleep with Lincoln only when the president's wife was away. Their use of the same bed became a subject of gossip among Washington's political elite, especially as Derickson wore Lincoln's nightshirt.

So, how to account for these same-sex encounters? Some 20th and 21st century historians have argued that the sleeping arrangements with Speed were platonic, simply involving two young frontiersmen keeping warm and saving money (sic) before they got wealthier in adulthood.

But how does this explain President Lincoln, as he was by then years later, sleeping with Derickson at the Soldiers' Home during the Civil War with its thirty-four rooms, plenty of heating, and the financial security that came with being the American head of state. No longer a cash strapped young man who had to bunk up with a complete stranger, this is Lincoln at the height of his power taking a military officer to bed. One almost expects one of the hetero-historians to counter that this was to optimise his personal security!

The argument used by these historians against the case for Lincoln being bisexual or homosexual can be easily dismissed. The hetero-historians state that we are living in an over-sexualised period of history whereas antebellum and Civil War America downplayed sex, and genitals were far less important than we might imagine.

This is rubbished by the LGBT history camp who counter that gay invisibility at this time should not be construed as a complete absence of same sex activity, platonic or sexual.

110 Letter from Abraham Lincoln to Postmaster General, April 7 1849

Indeed, same sex relations may have been easier before the term 'homosexual' was popularised precisely because the act hadn't been defined and then demonised by doctors, journalists, and legislators.[111]

Over the last hundred years, Lincoln has been reduced to an asexual, expressionless, motionless seated statue or a bust carved into the rock face at Mount Rushmore. This carefully crafted deification of Lincoln, created incrementally since his death, has reduced the real-life president to a "solemn, gloomy cuss, who speaks only in iambic pentameter, a tear forever at the corner of his eye – the result, no doubt, of being followed around by the Mormon Tabernacle Choir, which keeps humming 'The Battle Hymn of the Republic' behind him…"[112]

But there was another vivacious Lincoln who giggled uncontrollably at inappropriate humour, for example the ravings of a fictional pro-slavery preacher, Reverend Petroleum Vesuvius Nasby, conjured up by the journalist David Ross Locke (1833–1888). Nasby was the "Paster uv the Church uv the Noo Dispensashun" (sic) whose spelling was as shocking as the quality of his arguments. In one sermon, the ultra-bigoted Nasby is worried that African Americans (for whom he uses a predictably derogatory term) are about to outnumber white people in his hometown:

I am bekomin alarmed, fer ef they inkreese at this rate, in suthin over sixty yeres they'll hev a majority in the town, and may, ef they git mene enuff, tyrannize over us, even ez we air tyrannizing over them. The danger is imminent![113]

---

111 Michael Ferguson, "Was Abraham Lincoln Gay?", *Journal of Homosexuality*, Vol. 57, Issue 9, 2010, pp. 1124-1157

112 "Gore Vidal's Lincoln Log", *The Washington Post*

113 Petroleum V. Nasby, *The Nasby Papers* (C.O. Perrine & Co. Publishers, 1864)

Lincoln, far from being a "gloomy cuss", took to quoting Nasby's nonsense at government meetings, expecting chuckles from around the table. What he met instead was the stony glare of Secretary of War, Edwin Stanton, a radical Republican who "used very violent language in commenting on the president's fondness for this literature".[114] Stanton would later become enemy number one in Tumblety's pantheon of Washington DC hate figures.

As Lincoln was elevated into a superhuman being, after his brutal assassination, his humanity was left behind. Lincoln, it was said by those promoting him to godhood, displayed humour but never wit. Because wit involved "some bit of sarcasm, some sting of vindictiveness" while "Lincoln's humor was only kindness, for kindness only was in his heart".[115] This homily isn't borne out by the historical facts because Lincoln not only had a caustic turn of phrase when it suited but also a vast repository of saucy put-downs.

For example, the younger Lincoln, free of presidential cares, was annoyed at a friend who hadn't invited him to a wedding. So, in 1829, the twenty-year-old Lincoln penned an extraordinary poem, under the title *First Chronicles of Reuben*. It detailed a same-sex marriage:

I will tell you a joke about Jewel and Mary,
It is neither a joke nor a story.
For Reuben and Charles have married two girls,
But Billy has married a boy.
The girls he had tried on every side,
But none he could get to agree;
All was in vain, he went home again,
And since that he's married to Natty.

---

114 "A daily lesson in history", *The Boston Globe*, January 17, 1907
115 "Abraham Lincoln The American", *The Journal-Press*, February 16, 1928

So, Billy and Natty agreed very well,
And Mama's well pleased at the match.
The egg it is laid but Natty's afraid,
But Betsy she said you cursed bald head,
My suitor you never can be.
Beside your low crotch proclaims you a botch,
And that never can answer for me.[116]

This poem was included in a biography of Lincoln penned by William Herndon (1818–1891) who had also been a friend of the assassinated president and partner in the same law firm. Some believe it's the first mention of same-sex marriage in American history.[117] It's certainly unpopular with those scholars ever since who have "cast it, along with much other Lincoln material, into a historian's limbo of questioned authenticity".[118]

Having appeared in the first edition of Herndon's Lincoln biography, it was quietly excised from the next edition. Yet another example of what is termed today "gay erasure". That doesn't mean that the "gay" label must be affixed to Lincoln, but we can at least recognise there was more fluidity in gender and sexual identity in history, and Lincoln's life story, than some buttoned-up commentators are prepared to accept.[119]

After the president's assassination in 1865, Herndon spent the rest of the year scouring eastern Illinois and southern Indiana for "solid facts and well attested truths" about his former law partner and friend. It was during this research that

---

116 Mark Segal, "Abraham Lincoln: A life in the closet", *Washington Blade*, October 25, 2011

117 Louis Bayard, "So what if Lincoln was Gay?", *The Paris Review*, April 16, 2019

118 Howard Feinstein, "The Chronicles of Reuben: A Psychological Test of Authenticity", *American Quarterly*, Vol. 18, No. 4, Winter 1966, pp. 657-654

119 Bryan C. Keene, Rheagan Martin, "Coming Out: Queer Erasure and Censorship from the Middle Ages to Modernity", *Getty*, October 11, 2016,

he chanced upon *The Chronicles of Reuben* which went on to describe the two men giving birth to a "jelly baby". Clearly, Lincoln gave this a lot of thought. It's very clear this poem was not a one-off. Lincoln was known in his youth for dipping his pen in bile and rattling off some surprisingly coarse verses. In Indiana, where he spent much of his childhood, his racy ditties were remembered by his neighbours "better than the bible".

Even on the verge of becoming president, Lincoln's lewd sense of humour was well-recognised, though he struggled to repress it as he moved closer to the White House, as a Washington DC political operator witnessed:

In 1859 I was in the Supreme Court in the State House. Lincoln was or had been telling his yarns. A man, kind of lickspittle, a fawner, said: "Lincoln, why do you not write out your stories and put them in a book?" Lincoln drew himself up, fixed his face, as if a thousand dead carcasses and a million privies were shooting all their stench into his nostrils, and said: "Such a book would stink like a thousand privies." Lincoln had two characteristics: one of purity, and the other, as it were, an insane love in telling dirty and smutty stories.[120]

In Lincoln's lifetime, Herndon was all but banned from the White House by the First Lady, Mary Todd Lincoln (1818–1882).[121] Quite why she hated him so much isn't entirely clear, but there was an unusual friction between the two. Almost, one might dare to say, a degree of competitiveness. Herndon's dislike of the First Lady was accompanied by a definite feeling of jealousy towards Speed. Lincoln progressed from bed sharing with Speed to a lifelong intimacy which Herndon was unable to

---

120 Emanuel Hertz, *The Hidden Lincoln* (The Viking Press, 1938, New York)

121 David Herbert Donald, *Lincoln's Herndon: A Biography* (Ca Capo Press, 1989)

break into. As one psychologist put it, "Lincoln's closeness to Speed upset Herndon; he couldn't understand it but wished for something like it for himself".[122]

One unexplored angle to Lincoln's sexuality is whether the sense of being an outsider, that many gay and bisexual men feel even before they have realised their identity, increased his sympathy, or empathy, for America's most oppressed outsiders: the African American slaves. Though in the case of his presidential predecessor Buchanan, being LGBT clearly didn't lead automatically to an anti-slavery disposition. Gay men in the antebellum and Civil War period could be as bigoted as anybody else.

However, those who argued in favour of slavery often conflated the practice of sodomy, and other 'unnatural' vices, as being equivalent to supporting the abolition of slavery. To the pro-slavery brigade, abolitionists were defying God's will and scripture. This is evidenced in a particularly nasty letter written to an abolitionist publication likening interracial marriage to support for sodomy.

William Lloyd Garrison (1805-1879) campaigned for the abolition of slavery. His weekly newspaper, *The Liberator* thundered against the injustice of African Americans being bought and sold. Garrison showed up the stupidity of the opposing argument by printing, in their idiotic entirety, letters from advocates of slavery. One of these outpourings in 1832 came from a reader who styled himself Hotspur, compared racial intermarriage to the sin of homosexuality:

> *There is another small matter between us, Master Garrison. You don't seem to like the law of your state, which prohibits the unholy alliance between white and black. Suppose you were to take a fancy to a brute; would*

---

122 Charles B. Strozier, *Lincoln's Quest for Union: Public and Private Meanings* (University of Illinois Press reprint edition, 1987)

you not make the same objections to the law against sodomy?[123]

Accusing Garrison of being soft on sodomy was a tactic to shut him up. Mercifully, it didn't work. But it tapped into a climate of deep hostility and danger for LGBT people in the first half of the 19th century. Exactly the period when a young Lincoln was sharing a bed for several years with Joshua Speed that went far beyond a short stay or keeping snug under the covers in the winter months.

The number of people prosecuted for homosexual acts in the early 19th century was low, but the sentences are nevertheless shocking. In May 1824, a certain Nicholas Rickhout was sent to the New York state prison for life for the crime of sodomy.[124] In March 1830, the US Congress considered a new bill for the punishment of crimes in the District of Columbia. Alongside rape, burglary, and horse stealing, the offence of "sodomy or buggery" was to carry a mandatory prison term with hard labour.[125]

In the same year, the state legislature in Tennessee elaborated on the recommended prison terms for different crimes. Sodomy would carry a minimum of five years up to a maximum of fifteen. That ranked it way above all forms of theft and manslaughter. Only murder, arson, rape, and bigamy carried higher maximum terms of twenty-one years.[126]

With the threat of imprisonment or being subjected to barbaric medical treatment, it's little wonder that men with same-sex desires kept their activity a dread secret. They were

123 "To Wm. Lloyd Garrison", *The Liberator,* March 31, 1832

124 (No headline), *Poughkeepsie Journal,* May 5, 1824

125 "Crimes in the District of Columbia", *Alexandria Gazette,* March 18, 1830

126 "New Penal Code", *National Banner and Nashville Whig,* November 26, 1830

unable to define their identity in this kind of intolerant climate but recognised they had specific desires - feelings that didn't require the definition 'homosexual' to be invented first in order to realise them.

Even when late 19th century psychologists began to establish the rigid dichotomy of homosexual and heterosexual, not everybody assumed that one was normal and the other abnormal. Up until the 1920s, some surprisingly liberal voices defined heterosexuality as a "morbid" fixation on the opposite sex.[127] However, soon enough, homosexuality came to be branded abnormal and anti-social versus normal and agreeable heterosexuality. And before long, homosexuality was classified as a mental illness leading to the de facto torture of young men in psychiatric institutions.

In April 1837, a twenty-eight-year-old, tall, studious man, whose gait wasn't unlike that of a giraffe, according to one source, entered a dry goods store in Springfield, Illinois to buy some bedding only to find the price was beyond his means. The twenty-three-year-old male behind the counter took pity on the melancholic new face in town and suggested he could use his bed upstairs. The two men shared the same bed for the next four years.

His exact words as he invited Lincoln to get under the covers: "I have a large room with a double bed upstairs, which you are very welcome to share with me".[128] Lincoln experienced no second thoughts, bounding upstairs, depositing his bags, and re-emerging "beaming with pleasure".[129] This was the beginning of an intensely emotional, lifelong association. Whether it was homosexual has of course been the subject of intense debate and rancour. The amorous duo shared their political views, poetry, went horse riding, attended parties, always returning to the same

127 Interview with the historian Jonathan Ned Katz, January 2023

128 Doris Kearns Goodwin, *Lincoln* (Penguin, 2005)

129 Ibid: *Lincoln*

bed. Speed was, as Lincoln himself put it, his "most intimate friend".[130]

Historians have vexed as to whether this was asexual, homosocial, homoerotic, or just plain homosexual. Speed summed up the relationship himself, "No two men were ever so intimate". In 2005, Lincoln biographer Gore Vidal expressed what every LGBT person thinks when reading the account of the relationship between Lincoln and Speed:

The young Lincoln had a love affair with a handsome youth and store owner, Joshua Speed, in Springfield, Illinois. They shared a bed for four years, not necessarily, in those frontier days, the sign of a smoking gun – only messy male housekeeping. Nevertheless, four years is a long time to be fairly uncomfortable.[131]

And there was a smoking gun - the correspondence between the two men. Especially during the period where Speed was returning to Kentucky to get married while Lincoln was preparing for his wedding in Springfield. Neither of the two men were anywhere near enthusiastic about their respective prospects.

By the time they had spent three years sharing the same bed, Lincoln was thirty-one and Speed was twenty-six. Their families would have been wondering if these boys were ever going to marry. It was one thing to share a bed during a journey or for a short duration, but these two seemed to have no intention of terminating this agreeable arrangement. Eyebrows must have been raised.

There is something almost comical about the way in which Herndon describes Lincoln's bed sharing. He stayed at Speed's

---

130 Ibid: *Lincoln*

131 Gore Vidal, "Was Lincoln Bisexual?", *Vanity Fair,* January 2005

house for periods in a spare bedroom that strangely was never offered to Lincoln. Herndon witnessed Lincoln under the covers with Speed but also sharing a bed with two other men, on separate occasions: Billy Greene and A. Y. Ellis. Yet we are told to believe it was all harmless, platonic fun.

Herndon has been mocked and accused of "heterosexual bias" or naïve innocence. But more likely, Lincoln's long-time friend decided to turn a blind eye to what was screamingly obvious. Sadly, he also removed details about the spare room in Speed's house from later editions of the Lincoln biography which he must have realised would only arouse suspicions.[132]

Herndon details how the duo moved towards marriage with reluctance and trepidation. Their correspondence, which continued throughout this process, makes it clear this wasn't joyous for either of them. Lincoln, parted from Speed, had a complete nervous breakdown - a mental collapse that Herndon thought could lead to suicide. When they met up for a short holiday together with no women present, Lincoln's mood improved dramatically.

Would the sleeping arrangements between Abraham Lincoln and Joshua Speed have excited any interest in the 19th century? To believe some 20th and 21st century historians, one might assume the answer was no. The usual grounds for this view being that men slept together regularly on a purely platonic basis; sharing beds was cost effective; and a great way to keep warm. However, for the long period of time that Lincoln shared a bed with Speed, and later invited his head of security under the covers at the White House, we have contemporary evidence that this conduct would have excited interest.

The main source is a leading medical figure of the era seen as an expert on the homosexual mind and later quoted by newspapers in 1888 in relation to Tumblety being Jack the Ripper. This

---

132 Interview with Mark Segal, January 17, 2023

groundbreaking thinker on matters relating to sexuality was the Lincoln-appointed Surgeon General of the United States Army during the Civil War and founder of the Army Medical Museum: William Alexander Hammond (1828–1900).

Hammond was a pioneer in the field of neurology who founded a sanatorium to treat diseases of the nervous system, studying the causes of mental illness and addiction. His strong desire to improve battlefield medical treatment for Union soldiers during the Civil War was inspired by the example of Florence Nightingale and what she had achieved in the Crimean conflict several years earlier.[133]

In 1862 at the age of thirty-three, he was appointed as the US Army's Surgeon General by President Lincoln. His improvement of hygiene in military hospitals is estimated to have saved thousands of lives at a critical period during the Civil War.[134] But Hammond also became interested in the science of psychoanalysis as it came to public prominence two decades later. He was undoubtedly a pioneer of the new science and had plenty to say about sexual conduct he regarded as deviant.

Hammond turned his mind in 1883 to the various reasons why some men aren't turned on by women. The book, *Sexual Impotence in the Male*, was remarkably candid in discussing such issues as "absence of the power of erection" and "desire extinguished by perversion of the sexual appetite".[135] Hammond observed that "those addicted to pederasty are as a rule devoid of desire towards the opposite sex".[136]

As with excessive masturbation, which he believed was

133 "Dr. William Hammond, Surgeon General", *National Museum of Civil War Medicine*, July 18, 2022

134 Ray Cavanaugh, "William Alexander Hammond", *The Lancet*, May 8, 2018

135 William A. Hammond, *Sexual Impotence in the Male* (Bermingham & Co, 1883, New York)

136 Ibid: *Sexual Impotence in the Male*

another reason for a lack of desire towards women, men who were into same-sex relationships are often "debauchees" seeking a new thrill. Married men and fathers of families aren't immune from this, he noted. But they snap out of this perverted behaviour and return to women at some point. However, some of those into "pederasty" do not. Hammond quoted another academic source on the fate of those who sink into pederasty:

> *One of these men, who had fallen from a high position, to one of the lowest depravity, gathered about him the dirty children of the streets, knelt before them and kissed their feet with passionate submission before asking them to yield themselves to his infamous propositions. Another experienced singularly voluptuous sensations by having a vile wretch administer violent kicks on his gluteal region.*[137]

Men like this had clearly gone insane, Hammond argued. A modern reader immediately notices the conflation of paedophilia and homosexuality under the term 'pederasty'. Characterising homosexuals as potential child abusers was commonplace in learned articles and media reporting in the US and UK up until the 1990s and still bubbles under the surface.

Hammond adds to this another ancient trope that the most depraved are prepared to debase themselves before the poorest in society. This concern echoes the ancient Roman *Lex Scantinia*, whereby a man of senatorial rank could still violate a male slave or prostitute, but woe betide a senator allowing himself to be sodomised by somebody low-born.[138] To let your social class down in front of the slaves was the greatest crime of all.

Hammond describes a young man of twenty years of age who

---

137 Ibid: *Sexual Impotence in the Male*

138 Craig A. Williams, *Roman Homosexuality: Ideologies of Masculinity in Classical Antiquity* (Oxford University Press, 1999)

is clearly homosexual, solely into adult male sexual relationships. But his hostility towards women resembles the feelings of Tumblety on the same subject. This young man had "the most decided repulsion, not only towards women in general, but towards all that could exhibit the least evidence of a feminine origin".[139]

> *He felt himself, however, on the contrary, irresistibly drawn towards men and pictures, statues, and images, representing man in a naked state. He possessed anatomical plates depicting the genital organs of man, the adjuncts to virility, and he was constantly looking out for a chance to see the penis of every man who stopped to urinate in his vicinity.*[140]

Yet another young man had never got over watching a soldier masturbating in a toilet years before. "Strong, handsome, and young men always provoked in me a strong emotion", the patient declared. A Greco-Roman statue like the Apollo Belvedere, with its perfect male musculature, drove this youth crazy with passion. He yearned to invite good looking men back to his house and write them letters on perfumed paper.

> *As to women, however beautiful they may be, they never excite in me the least desire. I have tried to love one, believing thus to turn my ideas into their natural channel, but notwithstanding her beauty and her assistance I have remained entirely unmoved, and erection, so easy with me at the sight of a man, has never even had a beginning. No woman has ever provoked in me the slightest sexual feeling.*[141]

139 Ibid: *Sexual Impotence in the Male*
140 Ibid: *Sexual Impotence in the Male*
141 Ibid: *Sexual Impotence in the Male*

This gay man liked to see women dressed finely but only because he it allowed him to imagine how he would dress if he were a woman. At the age of seventeen, during the carnival season, he had indulged that wish momentarily and dressed as a woman "trailing my skirts on the floor". His lady friends were always astonished at how good a judge he was of "the good or bad taste of their toilets, and at hearing me talk of things as if I were myself a woman".

In the late 19th century, some gay men volunteered or were coerced into an early form of conversion therapy. Hammond describes how this included 'hydrotherapy' which basically meant showers or immersion with ice cold water. Essentially a form of torture. In addition, they were administered bromide of potassium to suppress homosexual desire.

One case study after another, with plenty of salacious detail from Hammond, is enough to convince any sceptic that homosexuality not only existed in 19th century America but was well recognised, even if also condemned and prohibited. The stories have the same basic structure. Men crave sex with other men. Then feel racked with guilt. The doctor duly diagnoses a depraved mental condition. Therapy begins. Some improve while others do not.

Hammond's work was deemed to be cutting edge, influenced by the emerging field of psychoanalysis in the last quarter of the century. But his methods bordered on the brutal in some instances. One patient sexually aroused by other men had the nape of his neck repeatedly cauterised over a ten-day period and the same procedure carried out on his lower dorsal and lumbar regions. This along with bromide of sodium taken three times a day. At the end of which, Hammond proclaimed triumphantly that the patient "could look at a nude statue of a man without feeling any sexual excitement".[142]

---

142 Ibid: *Sexual Impotence in the Male*

At a future date, Hammond would be cited by Billy Pinkerton, the famous private detective, who would spend decades tailing Tumblety across the United States and Europe. In 1888, Pinkerton quoted Hammond in a newspaper interview as proof that Francis Tumblety possessed the right profile to be Jack the Ripper:

> *Dr. Hammond – Surgeon General Hammond – some time ago, when asked as to whether or not he thought that the Whitechapel murderer was an insane man, said that when the murderer of those women was discovered he would undoubtedly be found to be a woman hater and a man guilty of the same practices which I have described Dr. Twombley, or Tumblety, as being guilty of, and that such men were crazy and as likely as not to murder women.*[143]

So, what about Lincoln and Speed sharing a bed for such an extended period? Hammond doesn't refer directly to Lincoln and Speed, even though he may have known about their relationship, when he wrote the book. But he gives the example of a young man working at a tobacco business. For years at school, he had taken the passive role in sexual relations with older boys. Now, he formed "an association for pederastic purposes with a young man who was to take the active while he himself took the passive part".[144]

They drew up an agreement between themselves swearing eternal fidelity and agreed to use the terms husband and wife. But then came the issue of sharing a bed. Far from believing that everybody would find this perfectly normal, the secretive couple had to engage in some subterfuge.

---

143 "The Whitechapel Murder", *The Bottineau Courant*, November 29, 1888
144 Ibid: *Sexual Impotence in the Male*

They took a room together and at night slept in one bed. There were two beds in the room and both were occupied for a few minutes so as not to excite suspicion, and then the one who was in this disgusting arrangement to act the part of the 'husband' came to his 'wife's' bed and remained there during the night.[145]

The passive male in the case study above detailed by Hammond took to wearing female attire. The 'wife' would then wait for the 'husband' to return home from his liquor business. This continued for three years, a shorter period than the four years in which Speed and Lincoln shared the same bed. Throughout the duration of their relationship, the 'wife' knew "that if detected disgrace and severe punishment would be the result".[146]

He endeavoured, however, to reconcile his mind to his conduct, by endeavouring to persuade himself that he could not help doing what he did; that the tendency was born in him, and, that though his body was that of a man, his soul was a woman's.[147]

So here we have Hammond making it very clear in his book that male-on-male sexual desire was a well observed phenomenon in 19th century America, in its many manifestations. Also that two men sharing one bed for an extended period of time, in an intimate relationship, was something that required a degree of subterfuge or a very good excuse. The idea that nobody regarded such a situation as sexual is blown out of the water by Hammond.

---

145 Ibid: *Sexual Impotence in the Male*
146 Ibid: *Sexual Impotence in the Male*
147 'Ibid: *Sexual Impotence in the Male*

Once in office as president, the head of state had an adoring LGBT admirer. From his window, the gay American poet and contemporary of Lincoln, Walt Whitman (1819–1892), watched President Lincoln trot by every day to the White House. This was his first term in office and within months, the country had fractured into two halves. The United States of America led by Lincoln and the Confederate States of America led by Jefferson Davis with a rival White House in Richmond, Virginia.

Lincoln was under unbearable personal and political pressure. For the first time since the country had gained its independence from Britain, it had split between northern states opposed to slavery and the southern states in favour. The president arrived in the city each morning flanked by about twenty-five to thirty-five cavalry officers in random formation. This regular occurrence caused barely a ripple of interest on the capital's streets. But where was Lincoln coming from each day?

Between 1862 and 1864, Lincoln spent most nights outside Washington DC at a place called the Soldiers' Home, originally established as an asylum for injured military officers.[148] This was a rural retreat from the city with cooler air as opposed to the stifling, swampy heat of downtown Washington. Buchanan had developed the Soldiers' Home as a presidential retreat and Lincoln agreed it was a charming spot. In addition, the Soldiers' Home, as the name suggests, was crawling with soldiers. When Mary Todd was away, the president invited two captains, David Derickson of Company K and Henry Crotzer of Company D, to dinner on a regular basis.

Nothing remarkable in that. Except that Lincoln decided, again when his wife was absent, to get Derickson into bed. There was nothing at all normal or customary about this arrangement. Soldiers might have bunked up together but the President of the United States getting between the sheets with an army captain

---

148 Matthew Pinsker, *Lincoln's Sanctuary* (Oxford University Press, 2003)

set tongues wagging. Especially when Lincoln remarked to another officer with a "twinkle in his eye" that the "Captain and I are getting quite thick".[149]

This gossip spread like wildfire. Virginia Woodbury Fox was the wife of Assistant Secretary of the Navy Gustavus V. Fox and a close Lincoln confidant. On 16 November, 1862, she wrote down a short account of what was going on between Lincoln and Derickson which can still be found in The Library of Congress. Who would have thought it? An officer in the One Hundred and Fiftieth Regiment, Pennsylvania Volunteers, Second Regiment, Bucktail Brigade under the covers with Lincoln:

> *Tish says, "there is a Bucktail soldier here devoted to the President, drives with him, and when Mrs. L. is not home, sleeps with him." What stuff!*[150]

Incredibly, some have tried to construe the phrase "what stuff!" to mean "gosh, what's all the fuss about?". I'm more inclined to visualise a society gossip palpitating at the thrill of the information she has to divulge. "What stuff!" being the Civil War equivalent of that oft-used exclamation of the Millennial generation in our own time: OMG.

Derickson was nine years younger than Lincoln with "intense eyes, a strong nose, and thick black hair".[151] The Pulitzer Prize winning historian Margaret Lèech (1893–1974), who wrote a damning biography of vice campaigner Anthony Comstock, also penned a comprehensive overview of Civil War scandals. She touched on the Derickson affair:

---

149 H. S. Huidekoper, "On Guard at White House", *National Magazine*, February 1909 quoted in Lincoln's Sanctuary, Pinsker, Matthew, Oxford University Press, 2003

150 C. A. Tripp, *The Intimate World of Abraham Lincoln* (Free Press/Simon & Schuster, 2005)

151 Ibid: *The Intimate World of Abraham Lincoln*

(Lincoln) grew to like the Bucktails, especially Company K., with whose captain he became so friendly that he invited him to share his bed on autumn nights when Mrs. Lincoln was away from home.[152]

Lincoln's bed sharing with Derickson is further confirmed in a book written by his commanding officer in 1895, Lt. Col. Thomas Chamberlin. Lincoln's new lover was directly under his command. Nothing his subordinate did escaped Chamberlin's attention:

Captain Derickson, in particular, advanced so far in the President's confidence and esteem that in Mrs Lincoln's absence he frequently spent the night at his cottage, sleeping in the same bed with him, and – it is said – making use of his Excellency's night shirt! Thus began an intimacy which continued unbroken until the following spring.[153]

The exclamation mark is from Chamberlin and not me. This bed sharing happened only when the First Lady was away. Derickson quit the presidential bed when she returned. But not to make way for the president's wife, because Mary Todd had her own sleeping quarters at the Soldiers' Home. Derickson, in other words, enjoyed a unique nocturnal closeness to the president. The reason given for the absence of sexual contact between the presidential couple was the physical damage that had been done to Mary Todd from the birth of the Lincolns' son, Tad.

Eventually, Derickson was given a new posting away from Lincoln, which is cited by defenders of the president's

152 Margaret Leech, *Reveille in Washington: 1860-1885* (NYRB Classics Main Edition, 2011)

153 Thomas Chamberlin, *History of the One Hundred and Fiftieth Regiment, Pennsylvania Volunteers, Second Regiment, Bucktail Brigade* (Alpha Editions, 2019)

heterosexuality as solid proof that the relationship could have been in no way homoerotic or homosexual in nature. More realistically, Lincoln realised that it would have been impolitic and impossible to intervene. Watching the hetero-historians wriggle on the hook of the Derickson liaison is a source of endless amusement.

There is clear evidence that Lincoln, Tumblety, and very like John Wilkes Booth had syphilis, a major killer in this century. Herndon had no doubt that Lincoln had contracted the disease, according to him from a female prostitute in 1835 or 1836. He was murdered before developing the final stage of the disease but Mary Todd, who caught it off her husband, was less fortunate. Booth's promiscuity make syphilis a racing certainty unless he was unbelievably lucky.

Jesse W. Weik (1857–1930) co-authored the Lincoln biography and was told by Herndon about the president's encounter with a sex worker as a young man:

I said to you that Lincoln had, when a mere boy, the syphilis and now let me explain the matter in full which I have never done before. About the year 1835-6, Mr Lincoln went to Beardstown and during a devilish passion had connection with a girl and caught the disease.[154]

Lincoln was supposedly cured of his syphilis by a certain Dr. Daniel Drake of Cincinnati, but Herdon believed he remained infected and passed the disease on to his wife. Through her, it may have contributed to the early deaths of three of the Lincoln sons. "Poor boys", Herndon wrote, "they are dead now and gone. I should like to know one thing, and that is: What caused the death of these children? I have an opinion, which I shall never

---

154 Quoted in Douglas L. Wilson, *Honor's Voice: The Transformation of Abraham Lincoln* (Vintage Books, 1999)

77

state to anyone".[155] Herndon was being a little disingenuous as he most certainly did share information on the president and his venereal disease.

Drake was a prominent doctor in Cincinnati who, unlike Tumblety, had officially accredited medical qualifications but, in a similar manner to the Indian Herb Doctor, bought up many columns of newspaper space offering medical advice that was every bit as faulty as the alleged quack. In 1849, he was advising citizens of Cincinnati on how to cope with a cholera outbreak in the city.

Of the exciting causes…getting wet in a shower, remaining long on damp places, sitting in a current of air, sitting in the open at night, and sleeping with but little bed covering should be carefully avoided… Loading the stomach with any kind of food, especially at night, may bring on the disease, and omitting to eat at the usual time may do the same thing.[156]

Lincoln took mercury for his condition and was still swallowing the "little blue pills" for a few months after his first presidential inauguration in 1861. Mary Todd tried the same medication in 1869, presumably as her health began to be severely impacted, but had a severe reaction.[157] While Abraham Lincoln died before the onset of tertiary syphilis, Mary Todd lived to experience the full insane horror.[158]

As Herndon noted, only one of Lincoln's children by Mary Todd would survive to adulthood: Robert Todd Lincoln.

155 William H. Herndon, Jesse W. Weik, *Herndon's Lincoln: The True Story of a Great Life* (Digital Scanning Inc., 1999)

156 "Epidemic Cholera", *The Cincinnati Enquirer*, May 12, 1849

157 William C. Roberts, "The Pox", *Baylor University Medical Center Proceedings*, January 2004, Vol. 17, No. 1, pp. 89-94

158 Norbert Hirschhorn, Robert G. Feldman, "Mary Lincoln's Final Illness: A Medical and Historical Reappraisal", *Journal of the History of Medicine and Allied Sciences*, Vol. 54, Issue 4, October 1999, pp. 511-542

Robert's wife, Mary Harlan (1846–1937) developed a terrible hatred for the widowed Mary Todd, so much that she made sure her husband was buried away from his mother moving his remains to the Arlington National Cemetery.[159] One reason could have been Mary Todd's increasingly erratic behaviour after the president's assassination, which resulted from a grim combination of grief and syphilis-driven madness.

After her husband's killers were hanged, or in the case of John Wilkes Booth shot resisting arrest, Mary Todd travelled to Europe, then relocated to Chicago. Things got progressively bizarre with the former First Lady as she wandered the streets with cash and negotiable bonds pinned to her undergarments. Shopping expeditions involved buying truckloads of drapes with nowhere to put them and in one month, buying eighty-four pairs of kid gloves for absolutely no reason.

Robert Todd became increasingly exasperated. On one occasion he was staying with his mother in a hotel when she entered the elevator half-dressed, convinced it was the bathroom. The stunned occupants then watched Robert Todd try to negotiate her back to their hotel suite while she screamed, "Murder!". Shortly after this incident, her son reluctantly instigated proceedings to have Mary Todd committed to an asylum.

Syphilis destroyed armies and decimated the populations of entire cities. About 20% of the population of London was estimated to be stricken in the 18th and 19th centuries with a significant percentage of those admitted to the city's asylums having gone mad as a result of the disease.

Lincoln contracted syphilis around the time that Booth was born and Tumblety would have been a toddler. So, assuming that the other two hadn't already gone down with the pox, Lincoln could have infected either Tumblety, Booth,

159 "Church's Lincoln Bells resonate with history", syndicated from *The Washington Post* in the Longview Daily News, July 6, 2002

or both men if they were in some kind of covert homosexual triangle. As we will see, this isn't an entirely unrealistic prospect and the Indian Herb Doctor certainly wanted readers of his autobiography to believe that his relationship with the president went beyond mere friendship. Which raises the intriguing and provocative thought that if Booth believed he had been infected with syphilis by Lincoln, could this explain his irrational fury towards the American head of state leading to the assassination in 1865?

Infection was a death sentence. Before the discovery of penicillin, a sufferer was powerless to resist as their body and mind advanced through the well-recognised stages of the disease. In stage one, weeping sores around the genitals and bodily rashes. Second stage brought wart-like lesions. But it was the final stage that terrified the afflicted with ulcers that caused the nose to crater, blindness, insanity, and death.

In his autobiography, Tumblety claims to have been a physician to Lincoln, visiting him at the White House. It's worth remembering that Tumblety began his career as an apprentice to the venereal disease specialist Lispenard, peddling his cures for the French pox. Is it possible that Tumblety could have been discreetly treating the president for his syphilis?

All of this is impossible, the hetero-historian will declare, as Lincoln was a married man. But as has been increasingly well documented in recent years, Victorian gay men might have a "lavender marriage" with a sympathetic or lesbian/bisexual woman prepared to give them a respectable cover while they continued a homosexual existence. The slightly derogatory term "beard" is used on the gay scene still referring to a woman who agrees to such a scenario.

Or a gay man might lead a dishonest, secret existence on the side - cheating on his wife. These Victorian gays would have found physical satisfaction in the Turkish bath, public toilet, gentleman's club, or theatre saloon. Court records detail the entrapment of many such males who entered a lavatory cubicle with an undercover police officer and left in handcuffs

The challenge for understanding sex and sexuality in the 19th century is, as one writer brilliantly put it, "wresting the Victorians from the prison of dour, prudish stereotypes to which their children and grandchildren consigned them".[160] Gay men may not have known they were homosexual but they knew what they wanted. They also realised what society expected.

Lincoln got married. Tumblety didn't bother. The doctor had no interest in even trying to have a relationship with a woman, even for the sake of appearance. His violent misogyny precluded that. There was the story of the unsuccessful marriage but this looks to us today like a clumsy and unconvincing attempt to legitimise his appalling attitude to the opposite sex. Lincoln was married with children, a necessary prerequisite for success in American politics (with the exception of Buchanan), but dived between the sheets with a succession of male partners. As for Booth, he jumped on anything with a pulse.

Did Lincoln love his wife? Not according to Herndon, who knew Lincoln well but had his own axe to grind against the First Lady. Herndon described Lincoln's marriage to Mary Todd as "a domestic hell on earth", a "burning, scorching hell" and "as terrible as death and as gloomy as the grave".[161] This situation even resulted in domestic abuse.

In 1857, a man named Barrett passed by the Lincoln family home. He witnessed "a long, tall man running and saw a little low squatty woman with a butcher's knife in her hand

---

160 Deborah Cohen, "Before Straight and Gay", *The Atlantic*, March 2017
161 Herndon quoted in *The Intimate World of Abraham Lincoln*

in hot pursuit".[162] The future president was being chased by a murderous Mary Todd. Suddenly, Lincoln noticed a nearby church spilling out and the congregation heading in their direction. This fracas had to be brought to a rapid halt for the sake of his political reputation.

> *He stopt (sic) short and quick; and wheeled around –*
> *caught Mrs. Lincoln by the back of the neck and at the seat*
> *of her drawers – carried or pushed her squealing along*
> *the walk back to the house – Lincoln's home, got her to*
> *the door of the kitchen – opened it – pushed her in, at the*
> *same time – to use Whitehursts expression gave her a hell*
> *of a slap on her seat – saying to her "There now, stay in the*
> *house and don't be a d—d fool before the people."[163]*

Somewhere between 1858 and 1860, Mary Todd was visited by an auctioneer, Charles Lewis, who was her nephew. He had done some business with a senior judge close to Lincoln. As a courtesy, he dropped in on his aunt. She immediately fumed at the young man with "cruel and brutish language" to the effect that he wouldn't get a dime out of her, despite protests that he had no need for her money.

Lincoln, not yet president, came home to find his wife still simmering. According to Herndon, Lincoln was more concerned with the young man's feelings than his wife. He dashed down to the auction house to comfort the "rather accomplished fellow". Lincoln "offered to assist him in all ways" and asked if he would consider coming back home with him. The young man clearly thought this was a terrible idea and declined. He was clearly not the first young man Lincoln brought back:

---

162 Ibid: William H. Herndon, *Herndon on Lincoln* (The Knox College Lincoln Studies Center and the University of Illinois Press Urbana, Chicago and Springfield, 2016)

163 Ibid: *Herndon on Lincoln*

Lincoln as a general rule dare not invite any one to his house; because he did not know what moment she would kick Lincoln and his friend out of the house.[164]

In Herndon's view, this was yet more evidence that Mary Todd was a ghastly ogre:

This woman was to me a terror – haughty – poor when she married Lincoln – imperious, proud, aristocratic, insolent, witty and bitter: she was a gross material woman as she appeared to me.[165]

But then Herndon contradicts himself declaring that in her "domestic troubles I have always sympathized with her". He suggests there is a genuine basis to Mary Todd's sense of grievance. One can imagine what that could be. But Herndon goes cryptic at this point:

The world does not know what she bore and the history of her bearing. I will write it out sometimes. The domestic hell of Lincoln's life is not all on one side... Wait patiently for all the facts. Mrs. Lincoln acted out in her domestic relation the laws of human revenge...[166]

In the arguments on Lincoln's sexuality, one story has loomed large in defence of his heterosexuality. The tale of his love for Ann Mayes Rutledge (1813–1835). Kentucky-born Ann was allegedly the first love but ever since Lincoln's death, historians, friends, and Lincoln family members have argued whether this is a complete fiction or not.

---

164 Ibid: *Herndon on Lincoln*
165 Ibid: *Herndon on Lincoln*
166 Ibid: *Herndon on Lincoln*

In a nutshell, Ann's family had founded the town of New Salem where Lincoln moved to for about six years as a young man. She was engaged to be married to John McNamar (1801–1879) who was struck with fever while away on a trip. When no news arrived about him, Ann assumed he was dead and got engaged to Lincoln. However, McNamar arrived back before the wedding took place and it was called off. But McNamar didn't marry Ann and she subsequently died of typhoid, plunging Lincoln into a severe depression.

Herndon recounted this story, which apparently landed very badly with Mary Todd and Lincoln's first-born son Robert Todd who didn't believe it. Ann Rutledge is often cited as clear evidence that Lincoln was a hundred per cent heterosexual, but the story was first robustly challenged back in 1928 by the Lincoln biographer and associate of Carl Sandburg, Paul M. Angle (1900–1975). He claimed that letters and memorandums ascribed to Lincoln about Ann Rutledge weren't authentic. The style, for a start, was "mawkish and bombastic, when Lincoln was neither".[167]

In a letter to Weik, his writing collaborator, Herndon conceded that the Lincoln-Rutledge love story, this reassuring tale of red-blooded heterosexuality, wasn't landing as hoped. There were details that stretched credulity such as Ann deciding to risk being betrothed to two men at once when McNamar might still be alive. But Herndon persisted with the story as part of his mission after the assassination to deify Lincoln. The sceptics must "look over our evidence" and "have a dream of its truth". Herndon was surprisingly frank about his desire in his closing years to paint only the best picture of his old friend, the dead president:

Lincoln will be in the great, no distant, future the Ideal man of America, if not one of the great Ideals of all the

---

167 "Paul M. Angle, 74, Historian and Authority on Lincoln, dies", *The New York Times*, May 13, 1975

English speaking people and every incident of his life will be sought for – however apparently trifling – read with pleasure and treasured up in the memory of men.[168]

The Rutledge story and other anecdotes that reinforced the president's heterosexuality solidified into rock solid facts even though they were nothing of the sort. Lincoln scholars from the 1930s onwards were almost united in their view that Herndon had manufactured this love affair. He himself wrote of an "idea of a life of Lincoln, and especially so when these little incidents are facts truthfully told".

The critics cannot destroy the truth, he thundered. A truth that he determined and set about ensuring would acquire some kind of scriptural power. If he had ever doubted Lincoln's heterosexuality, he now buried those thoughts under layers of folksy, heart-warming fiction.

Sadly, for Herndon, the stories of Lincoln's various same-sex relationships have refused to remain hidden, despite the best efforts of some biographers. Lincoln was clearly a sensuous man with a wicked sense of humour capable of penning the most outrageous and forward thinking poetry that even touched on the notion of same-sex marriage. He was passionate and developed the strongest of bonds with men with whom he enjoyed a chemistry completely lacking in his marriage to the First Lady.

Taking all that into consideration, Tumblety's claim to be on "intimate" terms with Lincoln doesn't look so far-fetched. All we need to determine is how the doctor came to be so close to Lincoln and the true nature of their relationship.

In addition, how did the doctor find himself arrested over the assassination of a president he claimed to adore so much? What convinced the government to issue a warrant for Tumblety

---

168 Ibid: *Herndon on Lincoln*

and lock him up in 1865, accused of being an accessory to the assassination of the American head of state?

We find ourselves observing the incredible lives of three men connected in some way to each other: President Abraham Lincoln, his killer John Wilkes Booth, and Francis Tumblety. Dare we consider the seemingly outlandish possibility that they were locked in a homosexual love triangle - brought together through the clandestine gay underworld of Washington DC?

Three

John Wilkes Booth:
Actor and Prima Donna

The third point in the triangle of president, assassin, and Francis Tumblety is the assassin: John Wilkes Booth. The events that will be described leading up to the murder of President Lincoln make it abundantly clear that Booth and Tumblety got to know each other very well in advance of the fateful day. The evidence that will be put forward is incontrovertible. Tumblety, despite all his denials to the contrary, knew the killer of Abraham Lincoln.

Tumblety also employed one of the gang that Booth assembled to carry out the murder of Lincoln as well as taking out Vice President Andrew Johnson, and the Secretary of State, William Seward. That was the boyish and rather dim David Herold who would hang for his involvement. Furthermore, Tumblety is alleged to have introduced Booth to yet another conspirator, Marry Surratt, who would become the first woman to be executed by the US federal government for her role in the plot.

After the president had been slain, Tumblety was arrested by order of Lincoln's Secretary of War, Edwin Stanton. The doctor's incarceration should not be dismissed as being just part of a general round up of the usual suspects. He was already a celebrity figure, and his arrest excited a lot of media commentary. Journalists were in no doubt that Tumblety was in some way linked to Booth but how or why did the two men form such a close association? To discover the truth, we must examine Booth's back story.

John Wilkes Booth was born near Bel Air in Hartford County, Maryland. He was the second youngest of twelve children, some of whom became actors or artists. Junius Brutus Booth Jr. (1821–1883) was lauded for his depiction of Cassius in Shakespeare's *Julius Caesar*. In 1864, Junius reprised the role alongside Edwin Booth as Brutus and John Wilkes as Mark Antony. After his younger brother shot Lincoln, he would be imprisoned in Washington DC until the authorities were assured that he hadn't supported the plot.

Edwin Booth (1833–1893) was viewed as a greater actor than John Wilkes, though he had to quit the stage for a while in the aftermath of the Lincoln assassination. Writing to his sister, Asia, after the terrible deed, he urged her to forget the lunatic that John Wilkes had become towards the end of his short life: "Think no more of him as your brother, he is dead to us now, as he soon must be to all the world, but imagine the boy you loved to be in that better part of his spirit, in another world".

Asia (1835–1888) was a poet and writer, apparently given this name because her father believed the Garden of Eden was located in that continent. After Lincoln's death she emigrated to England. What she left us was a sorrowful biography in which she described her brother's "fitful gaiety" alongside a "taint of melancholy". He was a volatile, uncontrollable persona with a tendency to brood in the manner of Edgar Allen Poe.

The handsome young actor charmed his audiences, in spite of his overacting, faulty elocution, and general lack of discipline.[169]

When Booth was a young man, his family began to replace African American slaves with poor white labourers on their estate. But John Wilkes objected to the entire Booth family sitting down to dinner with the male, white, hired workers, as was the custom in the area. His sister interpreted this as snootiness in the memoir she published about her wayward and murderous brother. What she noted though was that her tempestuous sibling resigned himself to eating with the estate's workers provided the women left the room. He, however, would stay despite his earlier misgivings:

Wilkes made a compromise with his pride, as he termed it, and desired us, his mother and sisters, not to be present at the meals with the men, while he sat at the side of his table, giving the head to the oldest workman.[170]

These male-only meals suited Booth but didn't go down well with all the hired hands. One young lad asked if the ladies thought they were too high and mighty to share dinner with them. They clearly didn't find the single-sex arrangement as agreeable as their host. But Booth, as his sister relates, wanted these encounters to remain strictly chaps only.

"Oh, don't bother us about women," Wilkes interrupted quickly, "drink your cider, and, Stonebreaker, give us Ben

169 Lawrence Block, *Gangsters, Swindlers, Killers, and Thieves* (Oxford University Press, 2004)

170 Asia Booth Clarke, *John Wilkes Booth. A Sister's Memoir* (University Press of Mississippi, 1996 edition, original 1888)

Bolt in your heaviest style."[171]

Songs were sung and Booth, with his new working-class chums, strayed off for a nap under the trees before they resumed their labours. His sister described the idyllic scene:

Sons of the soil in the scantiest of clothing, with the sweat of honest labour on their sunbeat faces, with voracious appetites that seemed hungering in the midst of rapid gratification, after the plug of tobacco laid carefully beside their chunk of bread, were not the most delightsome guests to entertain.

Maybe her brother felt differently.

The Booth family were opposed to slavery, except for John Wilkes. As a teenager, he was involved in the American Party, nicknamed the 'Know Nothings', which almost became the nation's second political force. They opposed immigration from Ireland and Germany with a particular animosity for Roman Catholics.[172] This makes the later close friendship between Tumblety and Booth rather unexpected, but not impossible.

In 1859, his determination to defend the institution of slavery led him to enrol in a milita group, the Richmond Grays. This irregular band of volunteer soldiers tracked down the radical abolitionist John Brown who had incited a slave rebellion at Harpers Ferry that year. Booth took a particular delight in being present with other Richmond Grays, in their uniforms, at Brown's hanging.

Booth liked to combine a muscular athleticism with his acting. So, for example, when playing Shakespeare's *Macbeth*, approaching the witches with merely a few short steps was never

---

171 Ibid: *John Wilkes Booth. A Sister's Memoir*

172 Brea Jones, "Posts Make Unfounded Claims About Political Affiliation of John Wilkes Booth", *Annenberg Public Policy Center*, April 22, 2022

going to be good enough. Booth insisted on the set designers creating a ledge of rocks about twelve feet high from which he leaped down on to the stage. A stunt he would re-enact from Lincoln's box after shooting him, only on that occasion breaking his leg in the process.[173]

His *Richard III* was a noticeably lively affair with fight scenes that terrified the audience. This physicality earned him as much as $25,000 a week and over $700,000 a year at today's value. His earnings reached such a level that he spent more time thinking about oil speculation than acting towards the end of his life. Washington DC was in love with Booth, showering him with praise and money. Yet he remained obsessed with killing the president under whose administration he had enjoyed stunning success.

By 1865, John Wilkes Booth had Hollywood-style celebrity status. He was possibly one of the first actors to have his clothes torn at by fans.[174] When leaving a theatre in Boston, for example, the manager yelled at his devoted followers on the sidewalk: "Back up, let him out, let him walk to the hotel".[175] This was a kind of adulation never seen before. Like Tumblety, Booth was profiting from the emergence of a mass media that could turn ordinary mortals into celebrities. In previous centuries, actors had been social dross. But Booth's over-the-top acting and the emerging cult of celebrity elevated him to the very top of society.

John Wilkes was said to be the closest in style to his British-born father, Junius Brutus Booth Senior (1796–1852). He certainly inherited his volatile nature and commanding presence on stage. Booth senior began his acting career in

---

173 "Booth as an actor", *The Courier-Journal*, December 7, 1881

174 Renee Montagne, "Who was John Wilkes Booth Before He Became Lincoln's Assassin?", *NPR*, April 15, 2015

175 Terry Alford, *Fortune's Fool: The Life of John Wilkes Booth* (Oxford University Press, 2015)

Covent Garden, London, with the usual Shakespearian roles. In 1821, he ran off to the United States with his mistress, Mary Ann Holmes, leaving his wife behind in England.

Happiness eluded the head of the Booth dynasty. Despite American audiences lapping up his Hamlet, Shylock, and Iago, he sank into alcoholism and violently unpredictable behaviour on and off stage. Before performances, theatre managers locked Booth Senior in his room to prevent him getting drunk. But there was always a way round this. One anecdote had the thirsty actor bribing a bellboy to feed him brandy through the keyhole using a straw.

Like many of that era, he was a believer in spiritualism, conducting his own bizarre experiments. This included trying to reanimate a dead horse by making his wife lie on top of the deceased animal while he recited some incantations from a book with a gun held in the other hand. This experiment failed. But it's indicative of his unstable mental state.[176]

Support for séances linked the White House and John Wilkes, who seems to have shared his father's interest in the paranormal. The celebrated medium, Charles J. Colchester, gave private performances for the Lincolns, who had lost nearly all their children before adulthood, while around the same time being a drinking partner of John Wilkes Booth. Colchester even acted in a play at Ford's Theatre very shortly before Booth shot Lincoln.[177] After the assassination, Colchester was prosecuted for practising "magic" without a license.[178]

While Edwin Booth was keener to put some distance between himself and his father, John Wilkes channelled that insane effervescence on the theatrical stage. Which is why "people of

---

176 Terry Alford, *In the Houses of their Dead: The Lincolns, the Booths, and the Spirits* (Liveright Publishing Corporation, 2022)

177 Ibid: *In the Houses of their Dead: The Lincolns, the Booths, and the Spirits*

178 "Jugglery and Spiritualism. The United States vs. Charles J. Colchester", *The Buffalo Commercial*, August 21, 1865

taste"[179] held him in less regard as a serious thespian. He was written off by many as a ham actor fit only to play dastardly villains. While Edwin was a natural Hamlet; John Wilkes was better suited to the evil and twisted Richard III. "Edwin Booth will be the delight of the women, and John Wilkes Booth the favourite of the men."[180]

One theatre critic wrote this, comparing John Wilkes to his brother Edwin:

Edwin has more poetry, John Wilkes more passion; Edwin has more melody of movement and utterance John Wilkes more energy and animation; Edwin is more correct, John Wilkes more spontaneous.[181]

As the Civil War raged, so did John Wilkes Booth, increasingly convinced that it was his destiny to bring Shakespeare's play *Julius Caesar* to life on America's political stage. He would be honourable Brutus to Lincoln's imperious Caesar. It would fall to him to put on the performance of a lifetime and avenge the defeated Confederacy.

Edward Morrison Alfriend was a friend and biographer of Confederate President Jefferson Davis. By 1865, he believed that the increasingly deranged Booth was no longer able to distinguish between drama on stage and real life:

I believe that if the truth could be known, John Wilkes Booth in his insanity lost his identity in the delirious fancy that he was enacting the role of Brutus and that Lincoln was his Julius Caesar.[182]

---

179 "The Youngest Booth", *The Nevada Democrat*, August 9, 1862
180 Ibid: "The Youngest Booth"
181 Ibid: "The Youngest Booth"
182 "Pure Fake", *The Courier-Journal*, March 8, 1903

Booth was described by a psychologist as "an actor who never could bring himself to give up fantasies when faced with reality".[183] The Booth biographer, Michael W. Kauffman, characterises Booth as both a psychopath and vainglorious narcissist; a man who compartmentalised his life with one set of friends being entirely unaware of another set.[184]

Many of Booth's qualities matched those of Tumblety, with whom he formed a bond in the lead up to Lincoln's killing:

Physically Booth was a handsome man. He was well liked by his acquaintances, and he exerted a magnetic power over most men with whom he came in contact.[185]

Booth and Lincoln crossed paths in theatreland on many occasions but in the year before the president's assassination, the successful actor stalked his presidential prey with a manic fervour. There was something irrationally obsessive and highly personal about his attitude towards Lincoln, evidenced in a curious incident where the two men faced each other at close range. Booth was on stage. Lincoln was watching him.

This happened at Ford's Theatre, where Lincoln would die while watching the farce *Our American Cousin*. The building was a converted church opened in March 1861, burned down in 1862, and rebuilt. With the customary hyperbole of the time, it was reopened in September 1863 as "the most magnificent theatrical structure in America".[186] Lincoln became a regular and at his first visit after the fire, came to see John Wilkes

---

183 Yoti Lane, *The Psychology of the Actor* (John Day Company, 1960, New York)

184 Michael W. Kauffman, *American Brutus* (Random House, 2005)

185 Francis Wilson, "John Wilkes Booth: Fact and Fiction of Lincoln's Assassination", *The Mississippi Historical Review*, Vol. 16, No. 4, 1930, pp. 572-574

186 "Ford's New Theatre", *The Baltimore Sun*, September 2, 1863

Booth who was also making his debut at the newly refurbished venue.

The day was 9 November 1863. The performance was *The Marble Heart*, a play by Charles Selby, also referred to as *The Sculptor's Dream*. It's a typical overwrought melodrama which suited Booth perfectly. He played Raphael Duchatlet the main protagonist, a French sculptor unable to win over his true love. In a dream sequence that takes him back to ancient Greece, he woos a statue with a marble heart that betrays him for another who can offer great riches. Waking, he is still in the same predicament and dies tragically.

Booth launched himself into the role with gusto in what *The Washington Chronicle* described as a "beautifully emotional play".[187] But there was something unusual in the actor's delivery that evening. Because Booth took the most bitter and furious lines of the doomed hero and aimed them directly at Lincoln who was seated in a box below the one in which Booth would kill him. The so-called "death box". This weirdness didn't go unnoticed. Lincoln's friend, Mrs Clay, who was sat nearby as Booth spat his words at the president, recalled:

> *Twice, Booth in uttering disagreeable threats in the play came very near and put his finger close to Mr Lincoln's face. When he came a third time I was impressed by it, and said "Mr Lincoln, he look as if he meant that for you." "Well," he said, "he does look pretty sharp at me doesn't he?"*[188]

If Booth's intention was to discomfort Lincoln, it had completely the opposite effect. The president was quite taken by the impetuous twenty-four-year-old breathing all over him.

---

187 "The Marble Heart", *The Washington Chronicle*, April 29, 1863

188 Kevin Morrow, "The Lincolns and the Booths", *The New York Times*, December 30, 2013

As the curtain went down, Lincoln sent a note backstage asking Booth to join him immediately at the White House.[189] This wouldn't be the last time that Lincoln attempted to get Booth over to the executive mansion and, reportedly, was rejected on every occasion.

The idea of Lincoln having something of a man crush on Booth is downplayed by some historians, but it was corroborated by two reliable sources at the time. The first is the noted American journalist and author, George Alfred Townsend (1841–1914) who wrote under the nom de plume, Gath. He would achieve national fame for his coverage of Lincoln's assassination and the aftermath as the Washington correspondent for the *New York World*.

Townsend reported that as Booth made his final bow, Lincoln "applauded the actor rapturously and with all the genial heartiness for which he was distinguished". Backstage, Booth reacted with racist petulance. "When told of the president's delight, said to his informant that he would rather have the applause of a Nigger".[190] Townsend added that Booth made a point of avoiding Lincoln as the theatre audience and actors departed.

This account was verified by Frank Mordaunt (1841–1906), a well-regarded "actor of rugged emotional roles"[191] and member of the National Theatre Stock Company. He stated that "Lincoln was an admirer of the man who assassinated him".

I know that, for he said to me one day that there was a young actor over in Ford's Theater whom he desired to meet, but that the actor had on one pretext or another

189 Matthew Pinsker, *Lincoln's Sanctuary: Abraham Lincoln and the Soldiers' Home* (Oxford University Press, 2005)

190 *Inside Lincoln's White House: The Complete Civil War Diary of John Hay* (Southern Illinois University Press, 1999)

191 "The World of Amusements", *The Evening Star*, September 17, 1898

avoided any invitations to visit the White House. That actor was John Wilkes Booth.

On one rather poignant occasion, Lincoln's youngest son – Thomas "Tad" Lincoln (1853–1871) – saw Booth perform and remarked that the actor "thrilled him", which prompted Booth to give Tad a rose. Tad's father then sneaked yet another note backstage to Booth to come over and join him at the White House, but it was rejected like all the others.

Despite Booth telling actors and journalists that his deeply held convictions wouldn't permit him to be Lincoln's guest at the White House, he nevertheless showed up at the president's second inauguration at the Capitol on 4 March 1865, after Lincoln had won re-election. He was even caught in a photograph sitting a few rows behind Lincoln as he addressed the crowds.[192] Down below in the throng were three men who would later hang for their roles in the murder of Lincoln: David Herold, George Atzerodt, and Lewis Powell (also known as Lewis Payne).

The animosity Booth showed towards Lincoln, even to his face, can seem illogical and hysterical as it certainly did to those in his family and circle of friends who were forced to listen to him letting off steam repeatedly. Grasping what it was about Lincoln that so irked Booth is difficult to fathom. Recent analysis suggests he doesn't meet the required criteria to classify as a psychopath, an allegation sometimes fired at Booth. Indeed, one psychologist a decade ago remarked that Booth could have been talked out of his feelings over a beer.[193]

This is a rather salacious assertion that a middle-aged Joshua Speed presented Booth to Lincoln as a "present" after his first inauguration to be serviced as the president pleased. This is

---

192 Rebecca Beatrice Brooks, "Abraham Lincoln was a John Wilkes Booth fan", *Civil War Saga*

193 Kent A. Kiehl, *The Psychopath Whisperer* (Oneworld Publications, 2015)

based on a stash of correspondence between Speed and Lincoln allegedly discovered by the late Larry Kramer, a historian and LGBT activist. The letters were never made public, nor subjected to academic scrutiny.[194] However, the Lincoln biographer Gore Vidal told Kramer, in the 1990s, that he had come to similar conclusions regarding the president's sexuality and same-sex liaisons. Could it be at the root of Booth's hysterical animosity towards the president?

Booth was hugely promiscuous according to most sources. Lincoln had same-sex relationships where beds were shared and there was enormous emotional intensity. The biographers of both men have touched on their mutual infatuation. Star-crossed lovers with Lincoln seeking Booth's affection while the tormented actor convinced himself he had to be rid of the president. As the writer Havelock Ellis once put it: "When love is suppressed, hate takes its place".

Initially, Booth didn't intend to kill Lincoln. At least that is what he told his little gang of conspirators. His scheme was to kidnap Lincoln to provoke a prisoner exchange with the Confederacy - but it was suddenly escalated to murder. Even his fellow plotters, barring the exceedingly violent Powell, were uncomfortable with this change of plan, which explains in large measure why they bungled their respective roles failing to kill others in the administration. They simply couldn't understand Booth's fiery antagonism towards the president. Neither could his colleagues in the theatre. What had Lincoln done to earn such homicidal hostility from this most tempestuous of actors?

Which brings us to the relationship between Booth and Tumblety. After President Lincoln was assassinated, a teenage errand boy working for Booth went on the run from Washington DC, eventually being arrested by police in Brooklyn. Under interrogation by police back in the American capital, he claimed

---

194 Carol Lloyd, "Was Lincoln gay?", *Salon*, April 30, 1999

that Tumblety and Booth "were on very intimate terms".[195] This testimony led to Tumblety's arrest as a suspected accomplice of Booth in the murder of Lincoln.

But the veracity of the boy's statement has been unfairly dismissed with the argument being that he was a cunning thief assuming a false identity to avoid arrest for an unrelated crime. That would seem to torpedo the notion of an alleged intimacy between Tumblety and Booth. But there is another piece of evidence, now revealed, that proves a close connection inexplicably overlooked because it appeared in a Buffalo newspaper fifty years after the end of the Civil War.

Fast forward to 1914 and Europe was sliding into a horrific four-year conflict that would lead to unprecedented slaughter. The United States wouldn't join the First World War until 1917 but maybe the gathering clouds of war had many Americans reflecting on the terrible carnage of the American Civil War. There were still enough veterans around for interviews and reminiscences.

The newspaper article in question included interviews with five local people in Buffalo asked to recall what life in the city was like during the Civil War era. A retired police officer, Captain Thomas Cavanaugh, revealed that he had seen Booth in the city in the early 1860s as he was appearing in a theatre play. But it was the company that he was keeping that is of most interest because Booth was observed by Cavanaugh hanging out with the celebrity doctor, Francis Tumblety. They were very clearly not just casual acquaintances but, in his view, great friends.

The journalist conducting the interview with Cavanaugh was Deshler Welch (1854-1920), a respected hack. He began his reporting career aged twelve and had worked in newspapers at a high level for decades, mainly in his hometown of Buffalo. Over the years, he had picked up many "startling war tales" that were

---

195 "Booth's Errand Boy arrested in Brooklyn", *Detroit Free Press*, May 7, 1865

too contentious to print in the years immediately after the Civil War.

This included shameful violent attacks on African Americans in what was supposed to be a Union city. Also the alarming tale of a sole surviving Union soldier, Charles Stewart, from a regiment that had fought in the Battle of Bull Run. This poor unfortunate had spent twenty-three months in the Libby Prison, a Confederate jail in Richmond, and seen military comrades shot by the guards or killed through starvation.[196]

Welch asked the elderly Cavanaugh for his Civil War recollections and the old police captain began chatting about John Wilkes Booth and his appearance in the city alongside his brother Edwin, another celebrated actor, to play the Shakespearian role of Richard III. Booth's depiction of the evil English king had garnered him much praise. He captured the very essence of this child-murdering monarch of the Middle Ages.

However, he also played Hamlet during his Buffalo visit – a performance that tanked with the critics. One theatre critic, Tom Kean, thought Booth's interpretation of the role was a "failure" and the "mere mediocrity of an amateur". Having delivered such a cruel blow, Kean finished with some mollifying comments about Booth's potential and how he resembled his father, proclaiming the young actor as "just the man for our citizens to admire".[197]

Cavanaugh was in awe of John Wilkes Booth, even though he was convinced that "during that week in Buffalo, young Booth hatched his infernal conspiracy to assassinate Abraham Lincoln". The retired captain described his feelings at the time towards the temperamental actor:

---

196 "J. Wilkes Booth may have hatched plot in Buffalo", *Buffalo Courier*, May 31, 1914

197 Ibid: "J. Wilkes Booth may have hatched plot in Buffalo"

I saw a great deal of him; I was intensely interested in theatrical matters; I wanted to be a real actor myself and I was already in the 'utility'. Naturally, I heard a great deal about his private life, in which I was not slow in manifesting a great deal of boyish curiosity. Of course, there is always a lot of small talk going around both behind and in front of the scenes. I must say I was somewhat fascinated by the young man.[198]

Cavanaugh described his "sparkling black eyes and a fine head covered with curly black hair". But behind the good looks, Cavanaugh picked up gossip about Booth's "lack of ordinary diplomacy" in expressing himself, particularly his hostility towards President Lincoln and the Union cause.

This inchoate anger culminated in a bizarre attack on a local jewellery shop in downtown Buffalo. The firm of Hotchkiss & Co. at 286 Main Street, owned and run by Hiram Hotchkiss, was displaying what were described as "Confederate trophies" in the window – most likely items captured from the enemy forces in battle. Hotchkiss was no doubt keen to display his loyalty to Lincoln and attract custom with this array of Confederate trinkets. But Booth seethed with rage.

He was repeatedly drawn to the display "like a bird hypnotized by a snake" until he could take the sight of it no longer. The impetuous actor adjourned to Tiphaine's liquor store nearby; bought a bottle of wine; downed the entire contents and then hurled the empty bottle into the Hotchkiss store window. This sent glass flying in all directions, attracting a large crowd to view this act of political vandalism. Booth, fortified by alcohol, walked away coolly.

Cavanaugh noted that while Booth used his stay in Buffalo to steel himself to kill Lincoln, he made "a very singular

198 Ibid: "J. Wilkes Booth may have hatched plot in Buffalo"

acquaintance". "In fact, quite an intimacy sprang up between him and a Dr. Tumblety – or Tumulty". This testimony from a reliable witness serving in the police, with no axe to grind, is the smoking gun that proves Booth and Tumblety knew each other prior to Lincoln's assassination - and it wasn't just a casual acquaintanceship.

He (Tumblety) sought Booth and they were seen together treating each other with familiarity.[199]

Tumblety was in Buffalo repeating his old trick of dispensing bags of flour to the city's needy while plastering the better-off neighbourhoods with his marketing material. There must be a strong suspicion that the two men arranged to be there at the same time. Cavanaugh noted that the doctor was "particularly susceptible to the allurements of the theatrical profession". The only thing that meant in the Gilded Age of America was the bawdy and bohemian lifestyle of actors and others in the trade.

Tumblety had almost certainly zeroed in on Booth in Washington DC prior to being in Buffalo. He was no stranger to the city's theatres as these were indoor cruising grounds for gay men in this era. As will be seen, the doctor was so well known in the capital's theatreland that a libellous burlesque was even staged about him over which he took legal action. It beggars belief that Booth would have been unaware of the notorious Indian Herb Doctor, who was forever generating both paid-for and free press coverage. The two would have made their introductions over a whisky in one of the saloons attached to some or other theatre in Washington DC.

The overwhelming proof that Tumblety and Booth were connected is that the doctor employed a member of his gang:

---

199 Ibid: "J. Wilkes Booth may have hatched plot in Buffalo"

David Herold. This was confirmed by newspapers after the president was murdered in 1865. But Cavanaugh made a further bombshell claim that removes any remaining doubt over whether Tumblety and Booth were closely associated:

> *Now the doctor had among his close friends the family of Surrats (sic) in Washington. Mrs Surrat kept a boarding house. I believe that was the first act in the Surrat tragedy, for I think it was through his confidences with the doctor that Booth came to know them.*[200]

Mary Elizabeth Jenkins Surratt (1820–1865) ran a boarding house in Washington DC and was convicted for her alleged role in the Lincoln plot. She hanged alongside David Herold. Her son, John, was effectively Booth's right-hand man, recruiting plotters and organising meetings. But after Booth killed Lincoln, John Surratt wisely skipped across the border into Canada and finally to Europe, where he ended up in the armies of the Papal States.

If Cavanaugh is correct, then Tumblety knew not just two, but three of the Lincoln plotters: John Wilkes Booth, David Herold, and Mary Surratt. The old police officer was convinced that, while in Buffalo, Booth was finalising in his own mind the way he would kill Lincoln. He was still discussing kidnapping with fellow plotters, but assassination was top of his mind. And there was Tumblety hooking Booth up with one of the main plotters: Mary Surratt.

So, what exactly was the doctor up to?

---

200 Ibid: "J. Wilkes Booth may have hatched plot in Buffalo"

Four

Tumblety Networks America's Elite

In November 1860, Abraham Lincoln won that year's presidential election. By the time of his inauguration on 4 March 1861, seven US states had seceded to form the pro-slavery Confederate States of America with their own president, Jefferson Davis. One month later, the American Civil War commenced with Confederate troops firing on Fort Sumter in South Carolina, held by Union troops. The sheer scale of the conflict ahead couldn't have dawned on Lincoln as he prepared to assume the weight of office from the outgoing 15th president, James Buchanan.

On 11 February 1861, Lincoln left Springfield, Illinois travelling by train to Washington DC. The journey took ten days as the newly elected president processed through several cities to present himself to the people before meeting Buchanan for the official handover of power. A journalist on the train with Lincoln noticed that the president-elect was indulging in less of his habitual storytelling, jokey parables, and anecdotes. A new seriousness was descending on him.

He entered New York state stopping off at the state capital

Albany where he greeted crowds from his carriage as it glided down the main thoroughfare. Lincoln passed by the Stanwix Hall Hotel, an elegant and exclusive establishment. From his suite of rooms, John Wilkes Booth glared down at Lincoln. He was performing in a play, *The Apostate*, at the Gayety Theatre on Green Street. Though on this momentous day he was recuperating having injured himself with a prop dagger inflicting a deep wound under his right arm.[201]

Even at this early stage of the descent into civil war, Booth was firing verbal salvos against the president-elect in the bar and lobby of the Stanwix. His loud grumblings didn't go unnoticed. So much so that the Gayety's treasurer warned Booth that if he continued to insult Lincoln in public, attendance at his play would be discouraged.[202]

The scene on Lincoln's arrival in New York was one of barely organised chaos with an "absence of all military display and the utter disregard of formal preparation".[203] The mayor of the city was nowhere to be seen while two hurriedly assembled lines of police tried to hold back the crowd. Lincoln and the soon-to-be First Lady boarded a barouche, a horse-drawn carriage with a collapsible hood over the rear seat. They then rode down Broadway waving to cheering New Yorkers.

Some newspaper reporters observed a very distinguished military officer in full cavalry uniform and a flowing moustache riding a "very warlike steed" directly behind Lincoln's carriage. "He attracted as much attention as did Lincoln himself".[204] It was generally assumed that he was either a close friend of

201 "Accident to a Tragedian", *The Baltimore Sun*, February 14, 1861

202 Peter Hess, "1861: Lincoln and John Wilkes Booth in Albany", *New York Almanack*, December 23, 2019. Essay first appeared in the Adirondack Almanack on June 17 2015

203 The New York Illustrated News quoted in "Mr Lincoln and New York" *The Lehrman Institute*

204 "Correspondence of the Courier", *The Charleston Daily Courier*, March 23, 1861

Lincoln or possibly Norman B. Judd, a member of the House of Representatives from Illinois where Lincoln had begun his political career.

But others knew the true identity of this figure and were mortified. That very month of February 1861, the New York newspapers had been covering Tumblety's acrimonious court case against the Chemical Bank and an estranged teenage male valet, Charles Whelpley, accused of defrauding the doctor.

As ever with Tumblety's attempts to get justice against an errant valet, his private life had been dragged up in all its vice-ridden glory. So, it seemed very odd to journalists that such a disreputable character as Tumblety should now turn up on Lincoln's New York procession riding so close to the president. Why would Lincoln be giving prominence to such a man? One reporter in New York wrote sarcastically that maybe the doctor should clear up a few issues with Lincoln in the coming days:

> *I am afraid Dr Tumblety is in a close place. He has been living at one of our crack hotels and doing the grandee in magnificent style. He must call on Old Abe to rectify, distil and cleans (sic) his character, for some very ugly letters have been received and read in court, slightly touching his personal history and antecedents.*[205]

The reporter went on to insist that Lincoln take time out from the growing hostilities with the southern states to "give an emphatic denial to the assertion that the military-looking gentleman who rode behind him on the occasion of his reception was not an intimate or trusted friend".[206]

This incident is perplexing. One can consider various explanations for how Tumblety came to be riding right behind

---

205 Ibid: "Correspondence of the Courier"
206 Ibid: "Correspondence of the Courier"

Lincoln on this important occasion. He might have taken advantage of the disorganisation to insert himself into the procession, gaining valuable publicity. Or there is the doctor's own claim years later in his autobiography that he knew Lincoln after a chance meeting where he had treated his son for a sprained ankle. Though when his happened isn't specified. Whatever the truth, journalists were aghast.

Gazing on adoringly as Lincoln and Tumblety rode past was the poet Walt Whitman whose homoerotic poetry disgusted prudish opinion at the time and since. He had long yearned for a heroic president "with the tan all over his face, breast, and arms" while being "fully formed, healthy-bodied, middle-aged, beard-faced American blacksmith or boatsman".[207] In Lincoln, he got what he wanted. Whitman's notebooks were stuffed with vivid descriptions of Lincoln as a "Hoosier Michaelangelo" with the "dark brown face, with the deep-cut lines, the eyes, always… with a deep latent sadness in the expression".[208]

That day, he got a perfect view of his idol:

From the top of an omnibus (driven up on side, close by, and blocked by the curbstone and the crowds) I had, I say, a capital view of it all and especially of Mr. Lincoln: his looks and gait; his perfect composure and coolness; his unusual and uncouth height; his dress of complete black, stovepipe hat pushed back on his head; dark-brown complexion; seamed and wrinkled yet canny-looking face; black, bush head of hair; disproportionately long neck; and his hands held behind, as he stood observing the people.[209]

---

207 Jack Veasey, "Walt Whitman: Poet, chronicler of war", *Pride Source*, October 13, 2011

208 Ibid: "Walt Whitman: Poet, chronicler of war"

209 Walter Lowenfels, "Walt Whitman's Civil War" (Hachette, 1989)

Over the years, Whitman, as a government clerk, rubbed shoulders with Lincoln without getting to know the great man. Though, there are accounts of Lincoln reading Whitman's steamy work, *Leaves of Grass* aloud to colleagues in his Springfield office.[210] While on another occasion, he spotted Whitman passing by and is reported to have murmured, "Well, he looks like a man".[211] One can only imagine what Whitman made of the unmissable Indian Herb Doctor riding proudly on horseback behind Lincoln's carriage. Sadly, he never penned those views.

While Tumblety yearned to worm his way into the affections of President Lincoln and sell his patent medicines to America's elite, he was busy at that point being dragged down to the gutter by his own private life. His poor choice of valets, based more on lust than their professional abilities, was a constant source of grief. In 1861, it brought the doctor some very high-profile publicity he could well have done without.

For most of that year, Tumblety was based in New York. Despite his earlier woes in Canada, Tumblety continued to rake in enough money to instal himself in the almost brand new Fifth Avenue Hotel built by the Manhattan real estate speculator, Amos Richards Eno and widely referred to as "Eno's Folly". This had become part of the Tumblety modus operandi, locating himself in a hotel where the city's bigwigs socialised, allowing the doctor to ingratiate himself with the rich and wealthy at the bar, in the lobby, or at the restaurant.

In this kind of environment, he could tap into networks that would help his business and offer protection when required and Tumblety was all too often in need of a well-placed helping hand to get him out of yet another sticky legal situation. The reading room was a busy area at the weekends with top-hatted gentlemen of distinction gathering to peruse the newspapers

---

210 Walt Whitman, *Leaves of Grass* (Penguin Classics, 2017)

211 Ibid: "Walt Whitman: Poet, chronicler of war"

and discuss the rapid descent into civil war that now threatened to tear apart the United States.

Crucially for Tumblety, the hotel was a magnet for bankers, Tammany Hall Democrats (with their pro-Irish leanings), and prominent politicians.[212] Like all luxurious hotels, it also attracted the city's well-heeled homosexuals.

Tumblety's offices were on Broadway, the main thoroughfare snaking through the city. Business was brisk and the doctor deposited his growing profits with the Chemical Bank, also based on Broadway. The bank had been operating since 1824 and sold its first office to the legendary showman, grudgingly admired by Tumblety, P.T. Barnum, though Barnum's extensive reworking of the building weakened its structure, resulting in its collapse into the street in 1848.

There had been a severe financial crisis in the United States in 1857 that Chemical Bank had endured, unlike some of its competitors.[213] This bank, therefore, appeared to be a stable institution with which Tumblety could entrust his significant investments. In any normal circumstances, he would have been viewed as a valued customer - exactly the kind of client the bank desired.

However, nothing with the doctor was ever going to be straight forward. In 1861, Tumblety was residing at the Fifth Avenue Hotel with a young assistant, Charles Whelpley, aged about seventeen or eighteen. Whether they shared a suite or had adjoining rooms is a lost detail. Tumblety instructed Whelpley to cash a cheque with the Chemical Bank for $100, which the doctor duly signed. But three days later, Whelpley seems to have drawn up another cheque for $400 and forged Tumblety's signature.[214]

---

212 "The Fifth Avenue Hotel", *The Bowery Boys*, September 14, 2022

213 "The History of Chemical Bank", *Chase Alumni Association*

214 "Forgery on the Chemical Bank", *The New York Times*, February 22, 1861

Officer Holland of the Lower Police Court arrested Whelpley in February 1861 on a charge of having robbed his employer. The handwriting on both cheques was very similar but the signature on one appeared to be "an imitation of the genuine".[215] What really should have been an open and shut case for Tumblety became something far uglier for him. Instead of Whelpley being on trial for forgery and theft, the doctor ended up in the court of public opinion over his private life and previous criminal record.

Chemical Bank dug its heels in, refusing to compensate their customer. In effect, the bank's lawyers decided to demolish his character to protect their business reputation having let a duff cheque be cashed. Everything was dredged up, including Tumblety's previous clashes with the medical establishment in Canada; allegations of manslaughter and an illegal abortion; and matters that were left unprinted but undoubtedly included allegations of sexual assault by Tumblety against Whelpley.

It was in this court case that Tumblety's very identity was questioned. Lawyers for the bank claiming his real name was Sullivan and that he had assumed the Tumblety name from a doctor many years back to whom "he was a menial servant".[216] This was strenuously denied. As for his various misadventures in Toronto, Montreal, and Saint John, Tumblety dismissed these as conspiracies by the medical and legal establishments against him.

The jury found against Tumblety, some wondering if the doctor had been drunk when he signed the cheque. But the court report in the newspapers added the cryptic observation that other jurors "looked at the matter in a different light".[217] The inference being that at the root of his case was an illegal sexual relationship between Tumblety and his valet.

---

215 Ibid: "Forgery on the Chemical Bank"

216 "Correspondence of the Courier", *The Charleston Daily Courier*, March 23, 1861

217 "Dr Tumblety", *The Kingston Whig-Standard*, May 2, 1861

The reports in the newspapers were spiced with the usual oblique remarks and hints to readers that dear old Tumblety was up to his usual tricks again. Contrary to the widespread perception of Victorians, many newspaper readers were very aware of same-sex activity though when it came to reporting homosexual relationships, journalists "created a coded language that could transmit widespread and commonly understood knowledge while, at the same time, avoiding an explicit treatment of homosexual behaviour".[218] In other words, the references were well understood, but it was left to the reader's imagination to picture the scene.

Sometimes, a newspaper article might make the situation more explicit but withhold the most raunchy details. For example, in September 1864 a New York actor, Frank Lavier, was arrested by a former detective on a charge of "sodomy". He appeared before Justice Giberson and a journalist from the *Evening Star* was present to record the details. Readers were told that Lavier was twenty-one years of age, good looking, intelligent, and from the city. He didn't even deny the charge. But, the reporter concluded, "the evidence is too disgusting for publication, but resulted in the accused being held to bail for court in $500". (Just under $10,000 today.)[219]

Despite Tumblety's private life getting a good airing in court and the newspapers, there was no resulting prosecution for sodomy or assault. If the police and magistrates had wanted to pursue the doctor, they could have constructed a credible case with the help of Whelpley, other disgruntled valets, and the authorities in several cities. Instead, the case was allowed to fade away.

Tumblety, in classic form, reacted to this unfortunate episode with a public relations stunt along the lines of what he

---

218 H.G. Cocks, *Nameless Offences: Homosexual Desire in the Nineteenth Century* (I.B. Tauris Publishers, London, 2009)

219 'A Beastly Fellow', *Evening Star,* September 17 1864

would do a few short years later at holy mass in Cincinnati. He grabbed his circus horse, donned his garish costume, and rode brazenly behind Lincoln's carriage. As if to say, I'm still here and rising once more from the ashes of scandal.

In the latter part of 1861, possibly around November, Tumblety set up in the American capital, Washington DC at No. 11, Washington Buildings, Pennsylvania Avenue on the corner of 7th Street. The number of people in the city was rocketing skywards, without any corresponding improvement to its infrastructure and services. Tumblety positioned himself in a prime location to offer his patent medicines to a growing market. He joined a wave of speculators descending on the city as the American Civil War intensified, described by one newspaper as that "crowd of adventurers who infested Washington". [220]

At the start of the war, the American capital had a population of about 75,080 but that number grew to 200,000 by its close. In response, the federal government was forced to evolve from a relatively small bureaucracy to a behemoth administering military policing, anti-vagrancy laws and struggling to keep a grip on public health. [221] More people meant more sickness.

The water supply was filthy and infected. People were crammed together with coughs and sneezes spreading killer diseases. The authorities were overwhelmed by repeat outbreaks of typhoid and smallpox that hit civilians and soldiers. The Union's military chief, General George Brinton McClellan (1826–1885) succumbed to typhoid while President Lincoln contracted smallpox. The smallpox vaccine had been available for half a century, but many remained un-jabbed despite the advice of physicians. Showing no regard for wealth or power, the pandemics spread among Washingtonians, regardless of social class:

---

220 "Tumblety", *St Louis Globe-Democrat*, January 5, 1889

221 "Washington, D.C. during the Civil War", *American Battlefield Trust*

Within a few days past there have been an unusual number of deaths of well-known citizens, of whom the case of Mr. John B. Sullivan, of the Treasury Department, is strikingly conspicuous. A man of powerful physique and of middle age, it can scarcely be realized that he had succumbed to the insatiate archer, death.[222]

Washington DC was built on classical lines, exemplifying Enlightenment values. It melded ancient Egypt, classical Greece, and imperial Rome, but at street-level it resembled the worst aspects of a medieval city in the Old World. A humid, marshy, southern provincial town where "major thoroughfares turned into hazardous mud traps in rainy weather; geese and pigs roamed freely over much of the downtown area; the city canal was an open sewer, into which dead animals were sometimes thrown".[223]

Little wonder that a dismissive Charles Dickens referred to Washington as a "City of Magnificent Intentions" with "spacious avenues that begin in nothing and lead nowhere". Nobody, he opined, would seriously choose to live in Washington unless obliged. As for the politics, he had nothing but contempt.

Despicable trickery at elections; under-handed tamperings with public officers; cowardly attacks upon opponents, with scurrilous newspapers for shields, and hired pens for daggers...[224]

This was, in short, a rapidly expanding, chaotic metropolis, riven with disease and corruption. In the heart of the city,

---

222 "Deaths of prominent citizens", *The Baltimore Sun*, January 6, 1862

223 "Wartime Drama: The Theater in Washington", Bloomfield Maxwell, CUA Law Scholarship Repository, *The Catholic University of America*, Columbus School of Law, 1969

224 Charles Dickens, *American Notes* (Penguin Classics, 2000)

political monuments globally recognised today like the dome of the United States Congress and the Washington Monument were still under construction. Tools were downed repeatedly because of the military conflict or the money running out. While to the south of the city, Confederate armies menaced with their capital less than one hundred miles away in Richmond, Virginia.

This was what Tumblety made a beeline for towards the end of 1861. Setting up his office on the city's main thoroughfare, Pennsylvania Avenue, and residing on the same street at Willard's Hotel, a centre of political intrigue situated directly opposite the White House. In a remarkably short space of time, Tumblety made his presence felt:

> *He was the general feature of curiosity in the city, drawing attention from the distinguished men of the nation and exciting general remark on account of his peculiarities of dress. It is said he would appear in two or three different outfits upon the street in as many hours, being always known by his tall form and dignified step, his curly hair and mammoth moustache.*[225]

The PR campaign followed the usual pattern. The outlandish horseback processions down Pennsylvania Avenue and entire columns taken over in the local newspapers, stuffed with glowing testimonials. The claims were as suspect as ever. For example, Thomas Griffin was "almost dead with pain" in his chest, back, shoulders and head. But he was soon as good as new thanks to "Tumblety's skill and his remedies".[226] While 7th Street-based S. C. Parrish was stricken with seven weeping sores on his leg and the looming prospect of amputation but was completely cured by the Indian Herb Doctor. Meanwhile

225 "The Indian Herb Doctor", *The Brooklyn Daily Eagle*, May 10, 1865
226 "Additional Testimonials", *Evening Star*, May 5, 1862

down at the Navy Yard, James H. Beall saw his dyspepsia vanish after a course of Tumblety's medicine.

Miracle cures aside, Tumblety was also networking right up to the highest levels of Washington society. His ultimate mission was to get in front of President Lincoln. Preferably to have him as a client and, possibly, his lover. This would be the crowning glory of his achievements to date. His first step towards that enticing goal was to insinuate himself with the leaders of the Union army. Any route into that world was admissible. He certainly played the Irish card to great effect and his autobiography intimates that seduction was also deployed.

On arriving in Washington, Tumblety made contact with a certain General Wordsworth who, according to Tumblety's autobiography (1866 edition), was the Provost-Marshal and Military Governor of the city. This appears to be a misspelling of General James Samuel Wadsworth (1807–1864) though in fairness to Tumblety, his name is misspelt as Wordsworth in a newspaper regarding his failed attempt to become the civilian Governor of New York in 1862.

Wadsworth was based at Arlington House, on the Virginia side of the river Potomac, which had formerly been the residence of General Robert E. Lee. After Lee joined the Confederate States Army in April 1861, Union troops loyal to newly elected President Lincoln seized the property. Despite his position as a Union general and Lincoln loyalist, Wadsworth was a conciliatory figure who found the whole business of war painful. Anti-slavery voices on the Union side complimented the general on his humane treatment of runaway slaves they encountered while on military campaign.[227] While Confederate families living near Arlington House appreciated his kindness and outreach to win their affection.[228]

Despite his lack of bellicosity, he was capable of incredible

227 "Contrabands", *Brooklyn Evening Star*, May 28, 1862

228 "A Loyal Virginian on Gen. Wadsworth", *The Buffalo Weekly Express*, November 4, 1862

martial bravado when the situation demanded. For example, Wadsworth distinguished himself in the 1863 Chancellorsville campaign that saw Union forces push deep into Virgina, resulting in the mortal wounding of Confederate General "Stonewall" Jackson. The general was forced at one point to lead a charge across a river with his troops in boats while he "swam the river on horse".[229]

Tumblety claimed that Wadsworth knew his family in Rochester. It's very tempting to dismiss this assertion – but the evidence is surprisingly compelling. The general hailed from Geneseo in upstate New York, not far from Rochester. In the 1840s, he was a wealthy landowner and a very active local politician running for office in the state. While many election candidates played the anti-Irish "nativist" card, Wadsworth declared his sympathy for the plight of Ireland as it faced an unprecedented famine. He even supported attempts to send massive federal relief to Ireland.[230]

Tumblety emigrated to the United States in the late 1840s and as somebody who became steeped in Irish American politics, he would have been aware of Wadsworth's pro-Irish stance and it's clear that before arriving in Washington DC, he had contacted the general already. Yet another indication of Tumblety's uncanny ability to get himself in front of elite social figures. In no time, Tumblety was attending regular dinners at Arlington House as he described in his autobiography:

There were many pleasant reunions, at which I became acquainted with several United States officers of high rank, who have since recognised the old social time with their continued friendship.[231]

229 "Letters from the Army", *The Wellsboro Gazette* Combined with Mansfield Advertiser', May 20, 1863

230 George M. Weston, "Next Governor of New York", *National Republican*, October 8, 1862

231 Francis Tumblety, *A few passages in the life of Dr. Francis Tumblety*, 1866

These gatherings continued into the night, but Wadsworth made sure Tumblety was safely escorted back to his hotel. One can sense the thrill the doctor experienced as he returned through the darkness flanked by well-built men in uniform:

> *I very often remained there until it was quite late, and at such times the General invariably sent some of his staff officers with me, for my protection, to Willard's Hotel.*[232]

Willards Hotel, at 1401 Pennsylvania Avenue situated right opposite the White House, was abuzz with political machinating throughout the Civil War. In February 1861, months before Tumblety arrived in the city, ex-President John Tyler had convened an unsuccessful peace conference to try and broker a deal between what would become the Union and Confederacy.

Lincoln attended but "had to sneak into the hotel, out of fear he would be assassinated"[233] and didn't leave until his inauguration ten days later. The president, facing the break-up of his country, was smuggled in by a detective named Allan Pinkerton (1819–1884) who would go on to form the Pinkerton National Detective Agency. One of his sons, William "Billy" Pinkerton (1846–1923), made it his business to track Tumblety for decades.

In the 1860s, the American author Nathaniel Hawthorne observed that "the Willard Hotel more justly could be called the center of Washington than either the Capitol or the White House or the State Department".[234] In 2021, the hotel found itself on the front pages when it emerged that Trump supporters

---

232 Ibid: *A few passages in the life of Dr. Francis Tumblety*

233 Gilliam Brockell, "The hotel where Trump allies plotted to overturn the election has a wild and sometimes violent history", *The Washington Post*, October 26, 2021

234 Quoted in "Willard Hotel, Washington DC", *National Park Service*

were based there in the lead up to the Capitol Hill Riots on 6 January 2021.[235]

Willard's, as it was referred to back in the 1860s, was an ideal base for an inveterate networker like Tumblety. It makes his claim to have forged high-level political and military contact very plausible. Because this was a period when it was still relatively easy to gain access to the powerful than it would be today with the high level security surrounding politicians. Tumblety was ideally placed to casually bump into society's leaders and tap influential networks.

The hotel was viewed as being so closely associated with Lincoln that Confederate newspapers reported a failed plot in April 1862 to burn it down. "Fifteen bundles of inflammable material were found distributed in various parts of the building, with slow matches attached".[236] But the politicians kept using the venue, nevertheless. One 1862 newspaper report describes an "avalanche of governors"[237] staying there.

Tumblety's permanent residency at Willard's suggests his business was booming. In his autobiography, he claims to have made $30,000 after expenses in the two-year period 1861 to 1863. In today's value that is just over $1m. And he attributed this fortune to his "treatment extended to the families of the very first people of Washington".[238] As will be seen from the impressive legacy he left at this death; this figure is believable.

With his roving eye for handsome young men, it was inevitable that Tumblety would form a close connection with one of the military officers escorting him regularly to the hotel from one of Wadsworth's dinners:

---

235 Mychael Schnell, "Jan.6 panel to seek information from Willard hotel", *The Hill*, January 2, 2022

236 "Plot discovered to burn Willard's hotel", *The Semi-Weekly State Journal*, April 27, 1861

237 "Personal", *National Republican*, May 1, 1862

238 Ibid: *A few passages in the life of Dr. Francis Tumblety*

With one of these, Captain Bacus, who I think is a near relative of the General, I had the honor of an intimate acquaintance and personal friendship.

Tumblety goes on to say that Bacus "had been previously well acquainted with my brother in Rochester".[239] This may be a brother mentioned in later press reports living in California whose hatred of women rivalled that of Tumblety.

The Indian Herb Doctor also developed a fond friendship with a Kentucky-born army poet and song writer, Captain George Washington Cutter (died 1865). A man upon whom "the wreath of poet laureate of America should have been justly placed".[240] Details about Cutter vary in different sources. His birthplace may not have been Kentucky, as Tumblety thought, but Massachusetts or even Toronto. His middle name at birth might have been Wales and not Washington. His age was disputed. Though one thing is certain – the poet's over-wrought verses replete with muscular imagery appealed to the doctor:

Harness me down with your iron bands,
Be sure of your curb and rein,
For I scorn the strength of your puny hands
As a tempest scorns a chain.[241]

How did he come to be in Washington DC hanging out with Tumblety? Cutter was married twice but both wives didn't accompany him to the American capital. Wife number one was a woman in Indiana from whom he became estranged after leaving her behind. The marriage was subsequently annulled. Then Cutter joined a newspaper in Cincinnati in an editorial

---

239 Ibid: *A few passages in the life of Dr. Francis Tumblety*
240 Ibid: *A few passages in the life of Dr. Francis Tumblety*
241 "The Song of Steam", quoted on the *All Poetry* blog

post and remarried. But Washington DC exercised a magnetic pull, and he ditched wife number two and came back again. What did the city have to offer and why did the wives have to stay away?

In his autobiography Tumblety describes Cutter as having a self-destructive personality then throws up vague statements about him being a genial spirit whose "vices and misfortunes" were "the offspring of congeniality". What exactly is this coded language referring to? Whatever it was, it led straight to the bottle as Tumblety relates:

He fell a victim to drink, and in the embrace of the demon of intoxication, he fell from the lofty pinnacle that was within his reach to the depth of inebriate degradation.[242]

One night, according to a Chicago newspaper, the poet was sitting on a roadside kerb in Washington worse the wear from drink. Through the window of a nearby stately residence came the sound of a soprano singing a patriotic song for which he had penned the lyrics: *E Pluribus Unum*. Tearfully, he lay down in the road and fell asleep.[243] After that incident, Cutter's health declined precipitously. Tumblety nursed him, striving to treat a worsening bronchial condition. His cures, however, were ineffective. In 1865, the captain died.

The most significant social networking breakthrough for Tumblety was to get himself in front of Lincoln. He may have met the president prior to setting up in Washington if we are to assume, as journalists did at the time, that he knew Lincoln already when he processed through New York in early 1861 ahead of his inauguration. Tumblety himself mentions being introduced to Lincoln by an unnamed "distinguished" military

---

242 Ibid: *A few passages in the life of Dr. Francis Tumblety*
243 "George W Cutter", *All Poetry* blog

officer from Boston, Massachusetts but there are no more details about this mysterious individual.

According to one account, Tumblety chanced upon Lincoln by a "watering place" as early as the summer of 1860, when the doctor was still based in New York. The future president's son, Robert, had sprained his ankle and the Indian Herb Doctor set it right. From that moment, the bond between Tumblety and Lincoln was formed. Hence his appearance behind the carriage in New York and everything that would transpire in Washington DC.

By 1861, Tumblety wrote in his autobiography that he was a "constant attendant at the president's *levée*" at the White House.[244] This ceremony originated with the crowned heads of Europe. At the court of the French King Louis XIV in the 17th century, courtiers vied to be chosen to attend to the king as he rose from his bed and got dressed. Hence the word for this ceremony derived from the French verb 'to rise': *lever*.

This ritual was imported to the American colonies by the British with the colonial governor holding court while ditching the rigmarole of being dressed and washed by grovelling flunkeys. After the American revolution the *levée* survived in a less imperial form simply giving public access to the president. This accorded with republican principles that the head of state should be an accessible figure, not remote like a monarch.

The Lincolns threw their first *levée* before the inauguration in Springfield, Illinois. On 6 February 1861, they invited "citizens and strangers" to attend at their house. Lincoln received the guests as they arrived and made their introductions. Mary Todd Lincoln, the First Lady, was attired in "a beautiful, full trail, white moire antique silk, with a small French lace collar" and her neck "ornamented with a string of pearls".[245] Once installed

244 Ibid: *A few passages in the life of Dr. Francis Tumblety*

245 M. E. Burkhardt, "Lincoln's First Levee", *Journal of the Illinois State Historical Society*, Vol.11, No.3, October 1918, pps 386-390

at the White House, the Lincolns continued with the *levées* every Tuesday evening and Saturday afternoon. They were held in the Blue Room with only those known to the Lincolns allowed to linger while everybody else filed past and then departed. As Lincoln's presidential aide, William O. Stoddard, explained:

> *None of the crowd of comers remain in the Blue Room except friends of the family, persons especially invited, and those whose official position gives them the right.*[246]

For Lincoln himself, the whole thing seems to have been an ordeal extending for up to five hours or more. The poet Walt Whitman saw his hero in action "dressed in black, with white kid gloves and a clawhammer coat, receiving, as in duty bound, shaking hands, looking very disconsolate and as if he would give anything to be somewhere else".[247] Tumblety boasted that he made many "valued and cherished acquaintances" at the repeat *levées* he attended suggesting that he was permitted to linger.

One of those he befriended was General Louis Blenker (1812-1863). The attraction of the two men to each other becomes obvious the more one discovers about Blenker. When it came to sartorial extravagance, Tumblety faced strong competition. Blenker was all gold tassels, heaps of braid, and ceremonial swords with his military cap worn at an almost coquettish angle.

Prussian-born Blenker commanded a German American brigade under the overall command of General McClellan's Army of the Potomac. He was typical of many foreign-born Americans, who responded fervently to the call from Lincoln to defend the Union. Often bringing Old-World military experience with them, they dashed to the recruiting offices and

---

246 William O. Stoddard, *Inside the White House in War Times: Memoirs and Reports of Lincoln's Secretary* (Bison, 2000)

247 Walt Whitman, "I see the President almost every day", *The Washington Post*, reprinted February 11, 1979, original article dated August 12, 1863

formed new regiments.[248] Here was an opportunity to show their patriotism and loyalty to the flag.

While referred to as German, the troops under Blenker were in fact an assemblage of soldiers from several European countries and South America. Many of them classified more as adventurers than soldiers. And their uniforms were as varied as the rainbow, according to one contemporary description. Blenker's military camp in Washington DC was so neatly organised with rows of trees planted between the lines of tents that it became an attraction for the city's strolling elite.

One of Blenker's distinguishing features was a penchant for Prussian pomp. McClellan described his visits to the German general's camp as "the most entertaining of my duties".[249] There seems to have been a high degree of theatricality involved. One of McClellan's aides likened the curious martial parade to a "circus" or "opera". As his commanding officer, McClellan, approached, Blenker assembled his "picturesque unit". A bemused McClellan later described the scene:

> *Wrapped in his scarlet lined cloak, his group of officers arranged around him, he would receive us with the most formal and polished courtesy. Being a very handsome and soldierly looking man himself, and there being many equally so among his surroundings, the tableau was always very effective, and presented a striking contrast to the matter-of-fact way in which things were managed in the other divisions.[250]*

248 Frank W. Alduino, David J. Coles, "Ye come from a far-off clime: and speak in many a tongue", *Italian Americana*, Vol. 22, No.1, Winter 2004, pp. 47-63

249 "The Civil War Fifty Years Ago Today", *Omaha World-Herald*, September 28, 1911

250 Ibid: "The Civil War Fifty Years Ago Today"

Then Blenker would bark: "Ordinanz numero eins!" This was a signal for lashings of champagne to be served, bands to strike up, and songs to be sung with gusto. It's not hard to imagine two men with such a passion for dressing up - Tumblety and Blenker - circling each other at a presidential *levée*, each observing the other man's sartorial splendour. They became very good friends.

Indeed, they got so close that Blenker took to sharing details of confidential discussions between Union generals, the US Secretary of War Edwin Stanton, and the president. This was a clear breach of security. Yet Blenker persisted, telling Tumblety exactly what he thought of Lincoln's Secretary of War, Edwin Stanton - the man who would eventually issue the order to arrest Tumblety.

On one occasion, Stanton threatened to remove Blenker from his military post if he ever again made favourable comments about McClellan. Tumblety in his autobiography describes the scene with rather catty references to Stanton:

> *I remember an anecdote told me upon one of these occasions by the General, which will be found characteristic of Secretary Stanton, who really, as far as my experience goes, does not possess a friend in the intelligent or unselfish of any political party. General Blenker had an interview one day with the President at which Stanton was present, and in the course of conversation, he, the General, had occasion to speak of McClellan in somewhat favorable terms, when Stanton, whose countenance darkened with the expression of a fiend, turned upon him and remarked, with a bitter sneer, that if he heard any more such commendations of a man he hated, he would procure his (Blenker's) discharge.[251]*

---

251 Ibid: *A few passages in the life of Dr. Francis Tumblety*

This exchange very likely happened. Lincoln and Stanton were set on removing McClellan from his command of the Army of the Potomac. So, Stanton's irritation at Blenker's comments was understandable. In addition, when Tumblety recounted this incident in 1866, the doctor had only recently been released from the Old Capitol Prison in Washington after being held as a suspected Lincoln plotter on the director orders of Stanton. One can imagine Tumblety and Blenker, resplendent in their respective gaudy military uniforms, over the cigars and port, pouring the vials of their wrath on a man they both hated.

Blenker wasn't the only beautifully dressed military leader to cross Tumblety's path. Serving under Blenker was a "gorgeously bedecked" Hungarian nobleman, Colonel Frederick George D'Utassy. The story of his rise and fall in Washington DC has striking parallels with that of Tumblety and illustrates how men like them could indeed rise through society with remarkable ease at that time.

D'Utassy wasn't at all what he seemed. The imperious, aristocratic title and dashing backstory were entirely fictional and like Tumblety, he created a glittering persona that Washington society desperately wanted to believe. D'Utassy presents us with a tale of military valour combined with epic fraud that reflects badly on the Washington of the time.

Before his mask was torn away, Colonel D'Utassy managed to extract $60,000 ($1.5m today) in financial support for his New York based Garibaldi Regiment from the Union Defence Committee and private contributions from "gentlemen of the highest social position". He was friends with the "first families of the city" and received "costly gifts as tokens of goodwill". When his regiment marched out to the battlefield, the Washington DC crowds cheered him on.

But by July 1863, two years later, the truth was out. His real name was Strasser, a fraudster and perjurer whose life began as a circus horse trainer and clothes dealer on the Hungarian plains. The description of Strasser, aka D'Utassy, at his trial mirrored aspects of Tumblety's life story:

He came to this city some three or four years ago, bringing with him strong letters of recommendation from influential people in Canada, which, with his pleasing personal address and perfect self-control, enabled him to obtain the confidence of our best citizens.[252]

Like the Indian Herb Doctor, he first tried medicine as a route to riches, apprenticed to a certain Dr. Watts. Already styling himself as Dr. D'Utassy or Chevalier D'Utassy, he attended university medical lectures. But whereas Tumblety persisted down the medical route, D'Utassy found that the military was a quicker route to riches. Forming his regiment at the outbreak of civil war, and inserting it under McClellan's Army of the Potomac, he skimmed off a percentage of monies donated straight into his own pocket.

He even took a cut from the pay of his own soldiers and was only caught out when he began trading horses stolen from the army or illegally requisitioned from farmers in Virginia, establishing "a sort of bazar" at the regiment camp. But there was far worse:

The camp was a brothel and a drinking place, beer and liquors being sold openly, and women of bad character imported from Washington, and occupying officers' quarters with his knowledge and consent.[253]

It was with considerable fury that the elite of the American capital realised they had been taken in by a petty criminal.

---

252 "The Career of a Hungarian Adventurer", from *The New York Tribune* quoted in Chester Chronicle, July 11, 1863

253 Ibid: "The Career of a Hungarian Adventurer"

Like Tumblety, he generated a strong visual display to dupe the credulous. Appearing on Pennsylvania Avenue "and in the hotels at Washington in all the glory of gilt lace and embroidered coats with an outrider in Mameluke costume followed at his heels".[254]

Almost a carbon copy then of Tumblety with his outlandish clothes, horse, greyhounds, and trusty valet. D'Utassy and the Indian Herb Doctor gave the public what they wanted. Exotic celebrity that alleviated the tedium of everyday life. The elites of North America couldn't get enough of these rascals, who were given the oxygen of publicity by story-hungry journalists. But once the mask was ripped off, it provoked a wave of angry indignation from those who had previously bought into their yarns.

After an inquiry and resulting court martial, D'Utassy was sentenced to a year of hard labour in the notorious Sing Sing prison. While on trial he was detained at the Old Capitol Prison in Washington.[255] Two years later, Tumblety would be behind bars at the same forbidding location.

In his autobiography, Tumblety claims that he offered his medical services to the Union army and specifically, General McClellan, after he had assumed the leadership of the Army of the Potomac in July 1861. But just in case the general had any second thoughts, Tumblety swanned around military facilities ingratiating himself by degrees with the officers. A later witness account from a military source related that Tumblety made his presence felt in the War Department and the Navy Yard, turning up in his fake cavalry uniform:

He had no business in either place, but he went there to impress the officers whom he would meet. He professed to

---

254 Ibid: "The Career of a Hungarian Adventurer"

255 "The case of Colonel D'Utassy", *Cleveland Daily Leader*, June 1, 1863

have an extensive experience in European hospitals and
armies and claimed to have diplomas from the foremost
medical colleges of the Old World and the New.[256]

Edward Haywood of the Bureau of Accounts at the US State
Department who remembered Tumblety as a child in Rochester
told a newspaper in an 1888 interview, after Tumblety had been
arrested as a Jack the Ripper suspect, that he recalled the doctor
wearing military fatigues in Washington DC in the 1860s,
claiming to be on McClellan's staff.[257]

There was also a curious reported incident where a certain
Lieutenant Larry Sullivan, who also hailed from Tumblety's
childhood city of Rochester, rounded on the doctor in the street
denouncing his fictitious qualifications and experience. Angrily,
he "told the imposter plainly just how great a liar he was".[258]

But Tumblety wasn't to be deterred by such a disagreeable
skirmish. He let it be known that "after much persuasion" the
Indian Herb Doctor of global renown had agreed to an invitation
from General McClellan himself to become a brigade surgeon
even though this would mean "a great sacrifice pecuniarily".[259]
Of course, it didn't. Tumblety continued to build his private
client base among the rich and famous during his brief stint as
an army doctor.

General McClellan was an experienced commander who
had served in the Mexican American War in the 1840s. Along
with twenty other bright and ambitious 1846 graduates of the
United States Military Academy, McClellan was promoted to
a full rank general in the American Civil War. His swift and
confident military action at the start of the conflict kept Kentucky

---

256 "The Missing Tumblety", *Democrat and Chronicle*, December 3, 1888
257 Ibid: "The Missing Tumblety"
258 Ibid: "The Missing Tumblety"
259 Ibid: "The Missing Tumblety"

out of Confederate hands and delivered him the command of the Army of the Potomac and later general-in-chief of all the Union armies in November 1861.[260] Tumblety maintained later that he had always been a huge admirer of McClellan:

When General McClellan was appointed commander of the Army of the Potomac, I partially made up my mind to tender my professional services as surgeon in one of the regiments, and I had the assurance from head-quarters that they would be cheerfully received.[261]

The very idea of a purveyor of patent medicines like Francis Tumblety obtaining a position as an army surgeon may seem laughable but desperate circumstances allowed this to happen. With a shortage of regular, trained physicians, there was enormous pressure on the army to bring in the services of homeopaths and what today would be regarded as quack doctors.

In December 1861, McClellan contracted typhoid. In the first week of illness, he was treated by two homeopathic doctors. This raised eyebrows and tempers among orthodox physicians, especially as McClellan's family were part of the medical establishment.[262] His father, George McClellan (1796–1847), had founded the Jefferson Medical College and was renowned throughout the United States for the number of operations he performed during his lifetime. The general's brother was a doctor. As was his cousin Major John Hill Brinton (1832–1907).

Indeed, Brinton was a distinguished surgeon and the first curator of the Army Medical Museum. In August 1861, Lincoln

---

260 "George B. McClellan", *American Battlefield Trust*

261 Ibid: *A few passages in the life of Dr. Francis Tumblety*

262 Ethan S. Rafuse, "Typhoid and Tumult: Lincoln's Response to General McClellan's Bout with Typhoid Fever during the Winter of 1861-62", *Journal of the Abraham Lincoln Association*, Vol.18, Issue 2, Summer 1997, pp. 1-16

appointed him a brigadier surgeon and in 1862 he worked under the new Union Army Surgeon General William A. Hammond, another Lincoln appointee. Brinton accumulated an extensive collection of "specimens" from the Civil War battlefields including 985 surgical specimens and 103 bits of weaponry "most the most part extracted from the body".

In 1864, Brinton would be sacked from his museum position. This followed the court martialling of Hammond but also may have been the result of his proposal to bring in "volunteer" surgeons equal in rank to regular army surgeons.[263]

Evidence from newspaper reports, and the detective Billy Pinkerton, suggests that Tumblety may have already got into the Union army as a battlefield medic by 1861, the first year of Civil War hostilities. One report has him turning up to visit the 13th New York Infantry Regiment at Fort Corcoran in July that year. This would have made a lot of sense as the 13th Regiment was also known as the "Rochester Regiment" having been founded in Tumblety's home city in April 1861 as the Civil War kicked off.[264] Many of the soldiers were Irish Catholics. So, the Indian Herb Doctor could have made friends very easily.

As for Fort Corcoran, this fortification of earth and wood in north Virginia intended to defend Washington DC from the south, was named after Sligo, Ireland born Colonel Michael Corcoran (1827–1863). Again, an Irish Catholic connection for Tumblety to exploit.

Corcoran was commander of the Irish Brigade 69th New York Volunteer Regiment. He had deeply held Irish Republican sympathies. So much so that in 1859, Corcoran was court-martialled for withdrawing his regiment from a military parade in New York honouring the visit of the Prince of Wales from

263 "U.S. Army Maj. John Bill Brinton", *National Museum of Health and Medicine*

264 "13th New York Infantry Regiment's Civil War Historical Sketch", *New York State Military Museum and Veterans Research Center*

England, the future King Edward VII. His opposition to British rule in Ireland wouldn't permit any involvement in such an event celebrating the British Empire.[265]

Tumblety, who had considered running for political office in Canada on an Irish ticket, can hardly have been unaware of the Rochester and Irish connections of the regiment and the fort's founder. As subsequent events in Tumblety's life showed, he played the Irish card (and covertly the gay card) repeatedly for advancement and to extricate himself from difficult legal situations including vice-related charges. So, to get into the Union army, he would have emphasised his Irish background and Corcoran, as a friend of Lincoln, was possibly yet another route into the president's presence.

Tumblety made a memorable entrance into Fort Corcoran mounted on an Arabian horse. When asked how he had come to own such an animal, Tumblety claimed his steed was a present from the United States Secretary of State, William H. Seward. And later, he returned the compliment by gifting a greyhound to Seward, whom he referred to affectionately as "Billy".

Seward was another flamboyant dresser who bristled that the presidency had gone to what he termed "a little Illinois lawyer", namely Abraham Lincoln, instead of himself. According to Lincoln biographer Gore Vidal, Seward had hoped in 1861 to manipulate Lincoln "through a powerless presidency" and dump him in 1864. But titanic events thwarted that plan.[266]

Seward had been Governor of New York in the 1830s and then state senator from 1849 up until the election of Lincoln as US President a decade later. As a compulsive networker, Tumblety must have reached out to the senator while running his business in Manhattan. And Seward, like all politicians in the

265 Pauline Murphy, "The amazing life of Michael Corcoran: From Sligo to Abe Lincoln's US Civil War Irish Brigade", *Irish Central*, September 21, 2020

266 "Gore Vidal's Lincoln Log", *The Washington Post*

north-east United States, was alive to the importance of the Irish Catholic vote, cultivating their support while keeping one eye trained on his nativist supporters "who regarded Protestantism as synonymous with Americanism and wished to limit immigration and set up extreme obstacles to naturalization".

The nativists detested "the influx of famine-ridden hordes of illiterate, militantly Catholic Irish".[267] But Seward, like other politicians in New York, could see the growing importance of the Roman Catholic Irish vote. Tumblety was a prosperous American Irish businessman with great connections and a high public profile. Exactly the kind of person a local politician would cultivate. The intriguing question, raised by the exchange of gifts, is whether Tumblety and Seward were more than just friends.

Seward was born in the village of Florida in Orange County, New York. As a boy growing up in a wealthy family, one of his playing companions had been a slave child named Zeno owned by a neighbour. His descriptions of being beaten and chained turned Seward into a lifelong abolitionist.[268] As a lawyer in 1846, he defended an African American, twenty-three-year-old William Freeman, accused of murdering a white family of four. A mob bayed outside the courtroom keen to lynch the accused. The jury found against Freeman, and he was hanged, but Seward's speech was publicised widely for its eloquence and sense of injustice.[269]

On the flip side, Seward was a massive snob. After Lincoln became president and he was appointed Secretary of State, he never ceased to look down on his boss and the two men lobbed catty comments at each other. On one occasion, Seward found Lincoln polishing his boots in the Oval Office and remarked

---

267 Joseph J. McCadden, "Governor Seward's friendship with Bishop Hughes", *New York History*, Vol. 47, No. 2, April 1966, pp. 160-184

268 "William H. Seward", *American Battlefield Trust*

269 Walter Stahr, *Seward: Lincoln's Indispensable Man* (Simon & Schuster, 2013)

with haughty disdain that men of their high office "do not blacken our own boots". To which Lincoln fired back, "Then whose boots do you blacken, Mr. Secretary?"[270]

Seward's sexuality has been hotly debated. There still exists the incredibly suggestive correspondence between him and fellow politician Albert Haller Tracy. Even the most ardent defender of the heterosexuality of Civil War American heroes would struggle with these lines from Tracy to Seward on 7 February 1831:

> *My dear Seward – It shames my manhood that I am so attached to you. It is a foolishness from which no good can come. I abjured such feelings years ago, but despite my judgement they have stolen on me again, bringing, I doubt not, as they always have done, fruits meet for repentance.*[271]

It goes on in similar pained tones to declare that his affection for Seward is crowding out his heartfelt feelings for another man, George Boughton. So much so that Tracy couldn't bear to be apart from Seward and suffered "a womanish longing to see you". But then he declares that this is inappropriate for "two grave senators, and I'll leave unsaid three fourths of what I have been dreaming on since I left Albany".[272]

On 4 May in the same year a still distraught Tracy wrote, "You know I love you but how much I dare not trust myself to enquire, far less to express".[273] There is a point where the florid language of the time tips over into an expression of

---

270 Ibid: "William H. Seward"

271 "Letter from Albert Haller Tracy to William Henry Seward, February 7, 1831", *Seward Family Digital Archive*

272 Ibid: "Letter from Albert Haller Tracy"

273 Ibid: "Letter from Albert Haller Tracy to William Henry Seward", May 4, 1831"

same-sex love. From a man to a woman, the intent behind the words wouldn't be questioned. But from a man to a man, it's immediately problematic.

Predictably, in our time, the idea of a homosexual attraction between Seward and Tracy has been discounted on the grounds they were both married. Clearly some hetero-historians, who may have led rather sheltered lives, are unaware that being married to a woman, and even having kids, is no barrier to homosexual activity. Not just casual flings, but even long-running parallel same-sex relationships.

Tumblety's account of being given a horse by Seward and his close relationship with Lincoln's Secretary of State wasn't dismissed out of hand in his lifetime. In 1881, Tumblety was arrested in New Orleans, accused of picking the pocket of a government clerk. The newspaper in his home city of Rochester picked up on the story and harked back to the doctor's claim about the horse:

> *The late Secretary of State had about this time received a gift of horses from abroad and the 'Doctor's' story may have been true.*[274]

But how did Tumblety come to enjoy such a close friendship with the US Secretary of State leading them to exchange gifts and familiarities? They could have met at the president's regular *levées* in the White House or at the theatre or at Willard's Hotel – or at all three of these networking spaces. Somehow, it would appear, the doctor got to know Seward very well.

Tumblety's below the radar activity in Washington didn't go unnoticed among those tasked with ensuring the internal security of the Union. Surveillance techniques and intelligence

---

274 "Another Rochester Character Acquires Unenviable Distinction – W.H. Seward's Friend in a Prison Cell", *Rochester Daily Union and Advertiser*, April 5, 1881

gathering evolved rapidly during the Civil War period and the doctor was an early person of interest. The groundbreaking approach to spying on the population being developed by the Lincoln administration involved both military personnel and a new private detective agency, the Pinkertons.[275]

After an early assassination attempt in 1861 was foiled, the so-called Baltimore Plot, President Lincoln summoned the Scottish-born detective Allan Pinkerton to set up an Army Secret Service that would root out Confederate spies and treason on the Union side. This was a case of the private sector, in the form of the Pinkerton agency, working alongside the public sector, in the form of military intelligence.

Pinkerton arranged for his teenage son William, known as "Billy", to be discharged from army service and to join the new operation. Billy remained at his father's side as he kept a watchful eye on the Army of the Potomac until 1863.[276] From 1861, Billy Pinkerton, by his own admission, began tracking Tumblety after his arrival in Washington. This may have been linked to the doctor's startling appearance at Lincoln's inaugural procession in New York or his socialising with the military top brass, which may have been concerning. Furthermore, there were allegations that while serving as an unqualified doctor in McClellan's army, Tumblety circulated pornographic material to the troops.

For many years, Pinkerton stalked the intriguing figure he saw wearing "a military cap, a black velvet coat, and lavender-colored pants" also noting his "Morocco top boots". He observed that Tumblety could easily have been taken for a "swell army officer".[277] The young detective seemed in awe of the doctor's

---

275 John M. Tidd, "From Revolution to Reform: A Brief History of U.S. Intelligence", *The SAIS Review of International Affairs*, Vol. 28, No.1, Winter-Spring 2008, pp. 5-24

276 "William A. Pinkerton", *Fox River Valley Libraries*

277 "Is he the butcher?", *The Inter Ocean*, November 20, 1888

physical appearance but why the long-running surveillance? There are clues in Tumblety's own autobiography with talk of nocturnal liaisons with military top brass and state secrets being shared in casual conversation.

Then there were Tumblety's increasingly frequent brushes with the president and senior administration officials like "Billy" Seward. This could have rattled young Pinkerton. Over the years, the persistent detective hinted he was aware of the underground homosexual scene that Tumblety inhabited that included top people. Did Pinkerton view Tumblety as an enabler who emboldened and organised wealthy and powerful gay men creating a network of sodomites within the American establishment?

It should be noted that up until recent times, and especially during the anti-Soviet Cold War period of the 1940s and 1950s, homosexuals were unfairly regarded as a security risk. Not only could they be blackmailed by the enemy, but there was an implicit assumption that homosexuals were, by their very nature, conniving and treacherous. Appalling bigotry of course but that was the conventional wisdom. In the 1950s, nearly a century after the Civil War, the US State Department testified before a sub-committee of the Senate Committee on Appropriations that it had successfully removed ninety-one homosexual employees on security grounds.[278] As if this was some kind of achievement deserving some applause.

Pinkerton never denied his interest in Tumblety:

At that time my duties in Washington were connected with the secret service of the army and my attention was naturally drawn to him a good deal by his military appearance.[279]

278 Judith Atkins, "These People are Frightened to Death. Congressional Investigations and the Lavender Scare", *Prologue Magazine*, Vol. 48, No.2, Summer 2016

279 Ibid: "Is he the butcher?"

But there was also the question of Tumblety's focus on what Pinkerton called "a certain class of complaints", by which he meant venereal disease. This would prove to be the doctor's undoing in the Union army as he distributed illustrated materials on the subject. On being handed a sample of Tumblety's medical texts, General McClellan hit the roof. Pinkerton recounts what happened next:

> *A little inquiry soon showed that he had flooded the army with his handbills and with objectionable books, so much so that General McClellan issued strict orders that the circulation of these books in the army should be suppressed on the grounds that many of the books were calculated to debase the soldiers, their contents being of an immoral character and their illustrations even more so.[280]*

All of which harked back to two episodes in Tumblety's life. His hawking of pornographic literature on the Erie Canal packet boats and his medical apprenticeship under that expert on the French pox, Dr Lispenard. But one could also argue that in the likely absence of any sex education for Union troops, Tumblety was performing a valuable service, keeping healthy soldiers in active service against the Confederacy.

During the war, an estimated 73,000 white troops in the Union forces were treated for syphilis while 109,000 were registered by surgeons as having contracted gonorrhoea. Among African American troops, the incidence was far lower. The situation was so dire that government-sanctioned prostitution was introduced with licensed sex workers inspected and treated by army doctors.[281]

---

280 Ibid: "Is he the Butcher?"
281 "The Civil War: Sex and Soldiers", *Dittrick Medical History Center*, Case Western Reserve University

Pinkerton's description of Tumblety's medical pamphlets plays on the old trope of the incorrigible sexual deviant corrupting the morals of young men. But Tumblety wasn't the only purveyor of sex education to Union troops who could, if they wished, buy contraceptives and sexually explicit material by mail order from various sources. For example, a certain Thomas Ormsby sold his "Private Circular for Gentlemen Only" to Union troops accompanied by "French safes" (condoms) and "sex toys".[282]

However it was the celebrity doctor Tumblety who came to General McClellan's attention, and he was duly drummed out of camp. Billy Pinkerton sighed that this humiliation would only feed the Indian Herb Doctor's PR machine - all publicity being good publicity.

Of course, this military acknowledgment that the doctor existed only caused a still more wide attention to be turned upon him.[283]

Ejected from the Army of the Potomac, Tumblety may yet have enjoyed the last laugh because McClellan's own downfall wasn't far off. The general had always been immensely popular with his troops who nicknamed him "Young Napoleon" and "Little Mac", but there was no love between him and President Lincoln. McClellan derided Lincoln as a coward, an idiot, and "the original gorilla". It seemed to be of no concern if his caustic views got back to the president's ears.

The gorilla insult, with its racist undertow, most likely originated in the Confederacy. It referenced the idea that the gorilla "is an animal that sits upon the branch of a tree, and, when a man is passing under, seizes him around the throat,

---

282 Ibid: "The Civil War: Sex and Soldiers"
283 Ibid: "Is he the Butcher?"

draws him up, and holds him suspended in the air till he is choked".[284] For McClellan to adopt this insult with evident glee was too much for the president. As was his countermanding of Lincoln's repeated orders to attack the forces of Confederate General Robert E. Lee with vigour and speed.

Despairing that McClellan would ever defeat Lee, and getting wind of the general's openly derisive attitude towards him, the president removed McClellan, replacing him with General Ambrose Burnside in November 1862. McClellan would later run for president against Lincoln in the 1864 election on the Democrat ticket but went down to a thumping defeat.

Aside from attending dinner at Arlington House, Tumblety hosted his own soirées for military officers at his suite of rooms. They were strictly male-only occasions. The doctor was open to treating women as patients, but not socialising with them. He preferred to be surrounded by uniformed men where he could don his fake cavalry uniform, playing the role of dashing Hussar covered in gold braid and buttons.

The only female presence were parts of their anatomy - shocking evidence in the 1860s that links Tumblety to the Jack the Ripper case in 1888. This was a grim revelation from a dinner party guest who was taken aback by what he saw in Tumblety's otherwise plush and sumptuous apartment. Objects that should have been in a hospital or mortuary. Totally incongruous in this domestic setting. And raising the question: how did he get hold of these items?

As the evening meal was cleared away, Tumblety proudly displayed the stomach-churning contents of his cabinet of curiosities. He turned the key and opened the creaking wooden doors. In the flickering light, a series of glass jars came into view. Within several of them were the uteruses of unknown women. The doctor stepped back and gestured. He was clearly

---

284 "Correspondence", *The Illinois State Journal*, June 29, 1861

impressed with his collection and expected his guests to show some appreciation. Instead, their faces betrayed disgust and horror.

The guest who described this ghastly vision was Colonel Charles A. Dunham (1832–1900). He claimed in an 1888 interview to have met Tumblety shortly after the Battle of Bull Run. Along with a military colleague, a lieutenant-colonel, Dunham accepted an invitation to a late-night dinner at Tumblety's "cosy and tastefully arranged" residence in Washington DC, which consisted of three rooms: an office and entertaining area on one floor and located a floor above were one or two bedrooms.

This was most likely in mid-1862. The address given by Dunham was H Street, which is half an hour's walk from Willard's Hotel. Either he misremembered the doctor's address or Tumblety had this property at his disposal. Places were set for eight guests, a lucky number for the doctor apparently. Everybody else present was in the military and Dunham knew them all. The colonel declared later that whatever Tumblety's deficiencies as a surgeon, he certainly knew how to be the perfect host. The best caterers in Washington provided the food and drink, served by attentive waiters. The whole event was choreographed to perfection.

Once dinner was finished, two card tables were produced for the gentlemen to play poker or whist. With a lot of fine wine guzzled, the guests got bullish and played for high stakes, though Tumblety affected disapproval, saying he wasn't the gambling type. Then one of the officers committed a major social faux pas. He asked why there were no women present. Tumblety's mood suddenly soured.

His face instantly became as black as a thunder cloud. He had a pack of cards in his hand, but he laid them down and said, almost savagely: "No, Colonel, I don't know any such cattle, and if I did I would as your friend, sooner give you a dose of quick poison than take you into such danger". He then broke into a homily on the sin and folly of dissipation, fiercely denouncing all women and especially fallen women.[285]

Tumblety, still blazing with rage, told the guests to leave the card tables and join him in his office where he would "illustrate his lecture". Everybody obediently followed. One side of this room was covered floor to ceiling in wooden cases the size of wardrobes. These were gigantic cabinets of curiosities. When the doors were opened with a flourish, they revealed tiers of shelves filled with glass jars of all shapes and sizes containing anatomical specimens.

About a dozen of these jars were arranged on the table. Within them were "the matrices of every class of women". Almost half of one of the cabinets contained surgically removed uteruses. Dunham was justifiably unnerved. The Indian Herb Doctor had revealed a much darker side to his character in this inner sanctum. And somehow, he expected his male guests to emerge from this unsettling experience, sharing his abiding hatred of women.

Dunham's testimony has come under fire. He is frequently dismissed as a fraud and a perjurer who made up the entire content of his 1888 interview, though for what reason is unclear. Maybe to insert himself into the Jack the Ripper story, which was why he was interviewed about Tumblety who, at the time, was being held by Scotland Yard in London. However, there is no clear motive for Dunham to have lied about this incident and a re-examination of the facts bears out what he said happened at the dinner party.

His claim to have met Tumblety after the Battle of Bull Run, which took place on 21 July 1861, could present a problem

---

285 "The Missing Tumblety", reprinted from the *New York World* in the *Democrat and Chronicle*, December 3, 1888

because the doctor didn't arrive in Washington DC until the end of that year. However, there were two battles referencing the same location with the Second Battle of Bull Run being fought over a year later, on 28 to 30 August 1862. If this is the battle Dunham is referring to, it allows for Tumblety to not only have been present in Washington DC but well networked into the military by then.

The main argument against Dunham and his story of the uteruses in jars is that he was allegedly a proven liar. This references a chain of events that unfolded during the heightened atmosphere at the closing stages of the American Civil War. Dunham operated as a spy and a journalist in this period. But to assume that somebody who performs either of those roles is then unable to tell the truth, as some appear to argue, is ridiculous. However, to bury this argument once and for all, let's examine why Dunham has been so controversial.

Dunham operated under several aliases as he was engaged in covert operations. Using the fake name Sanford Conover, he was tasked with finding evidence that would link President Lincoln's murder to the Confederate government, as opposed to Booth having acted alone. His testimony at the trial of the Lincoln conspirators in 1865, delivered behind closed doors, implicated the Confederate leadership as being directly involved in Booth's plot.

Dunham claimed in court that, before the assassination, he was present at a meeting in Montreal between Jacob Thompson, head of the Confederate Secret Service, and John Surratt – son of Mary Surratt, a Washington DC boarding house owner, and the only woman to hang as a Lincoln conspirator. Conover (aka Dunham) had apparently worked undercover for a period as a clerk in the War Department in Richmond, the Confederate capital, and was acquainted with Thompson.

Other witnesses, independent of Dunham, saw Booth with Confederate officials at the St. Lawrence Hall on St. James Street

Francis Tumblety in full procession regalia
(Copyright: public domain)

I

*President Abraham
Lincoln – assassinated
in 1865*
(Copyright:
public domain)

*John Wilkes Booth,
assassin of President
Lincoln*
(Copyright:
public domain)

Lincoln received into heaven by George Washington
(Copyright: public domain)

The yard at 29 Hanbury Street where Annie Chapman's body was discovered
(Copyright: public domain)

Lincoln received into heaven by George Washington
(Copyright: public domain)

Annie Chapman on her wedding day in 1869
(Copyright: public domain)

Annie Chapman's murder in The Illustrated Police News, *September 1888*
(Copyright: public domain)

The yard at 29 Hanbury Street where Annie Chapman's body was discovered
(Copyright: public domain)

THE MISSING TUMBLETY

An American Quack Suspected of the Whitechapel Crimes.

HE PROBABLY SEEKS AMERICA

A Braggart and Charlatan—Circumstances Against Him—Details of His Adventurous career—A Rochester Boy. His Life in This City.

Tumblety flees London for New York as he faces Jack the Ripper charges –
Democrat and Chronicle *newspaper, December 3, 1888*

Thomas F. Byrnes, Irish-born New York police chief
(Copyright: public domain)

in Montreal, which was regarded as the de facto Confederate headquarters in Canada.[286] At the billiard table and clearly quite drunk, Booth was overheard proclaiming that "Abe's contract is near up, and... he will get his goose cooked...".[287]

Conover's damning testimony about the secret Montreal meeting placed the blame for the murder of Lincoln squarely at the door of ex-Confederate President Jefferson Davis. Booth could now be depicted as a puppet of Confederate spymasters and even the Confederate President. But the charge against Davis never stuck. The main reason being that Conover's courtroom evidence was undermined – by himself.

Having given his testimony behind closed doors, Conover aka Dunham returned to Canada to secure more evidence to back it up, this time travelling under another false name: James Watson Wallace. He must have hoped to reconnect with Confederate sympathisers in Canada, obtain more dirt on Davis, and return to the relative safety of Washington DC.

But then his courtroom statements appeared in the newspapers. Conover/Wallace/Dunham found himself in Canada, surrounded by disgruntled and defeated Confederates, having to explain himself. His cover had been blown. This put Dunham in a very dangerous place. Now, he rattled off a series of frantic statements claiming he had never appeared in court, that he wasn't Sanford Conover, and that he never met Thompson or Booth in Canada. This was Dunham saving his skin.

Then on returning to Washington DC from a very hostile Canada, he backtracked on all those statements claiming Confederate agents had held a gun to his head and forced him to say such things. This flip-flopping completely undermined Dunham even though his own brother-in-law confirmed that

---

286 Barry Sheehy, *Montreal, City of Secrets: Confederate Operations in Montreal During the American Civil War* (Baraka Books, 2017)

287 Andy Blatchford, "Lincoln assassin John Wilkes Booth's Canadian connection", *The Canadian Press*, October 13, 2014

while in Canada, Confederates had threatened to shoot him like a dog. Dunham's panicked actions left the case against the Confederacy in tatters. So, the administration understandably backed away from him and worse, labelled Dunham a serial liar.

The picture that emerges is of an adventurer who enjoyed a bit of espionage until aggrieved parties turned up to silence him. His testimony more than likely contained nuggets of truth amidst a blitz of propaganda delivered in court to damn the Confederacy. It's hard to imagine that he wasn't directed by people in the administration to implicate Jefferson Davis as the author of the Booth plot. America had spent four bloody years being torn apart and among Union supporters, there was a thirst for revenge at all costs.

It wouldn't be surprising if Dunham had even been coached in his witness statements as, for example, were those testifying against the Lincoln plotter and accomplice of John Wilkes Booth, David Herold, who all used exactly the same phrase - "light and trifling" - to describe Tumblety's former valet. Treason trials have tended to be rigged affairs throughout history and the 1865 prosecution of Herold, Surratt and the others was a foregone conclusion before it even started. Dunham had a role to play but he messed it up.

In 1867, under the name Sanford Conover, Dunham was convicted of perjury in relation to the statements he made in the Lincoln trial. It was impossible now to believe that the Montreal meeting between the Confederate spy chief and Lincoln plotters had happened. This was maddening for newspapers in the Union who wanted to see Jefferson Davis clapped in irons and tried as Booth's handler.

These newspapers vented their spleen at Dunham/Conover. He was "the most deliberate liar this country ever produced" and it was essential to put him prison as it was unsafe "for

Conover to be at large with his arsenal of falsehoods".[288] This kind of reportage has served to trash Dunham's credibility ever since – including his statements decades later about Tumblety.

However, if one is prepared to reappraise Dunham and not assume that he was incapable of ever speaking the truth, then some interesting questions emerge. Here was a man who evidently knew Tumblety well and had met John Wilkes Booth. His description of Tumblety's love of dashing, male military officers, the sumptuously decorated apartments, the immaculate taste in catering, and the gruesome cabinet of curiosities fits with everything others related about the Indian Herb Doctor. By 1888, Dunham was a practising lawyer, and the Civil War was fast receding history. His testimony should therefore not be dismissed out of hand.

Especially when it's backed up from another source. By 1869, Tumblety was in St. Louis, having left Washington DC six years before, and chanced upon a bellboy, James D. Maguire, at the Southern Hotel. Tumblety "took a fancy to young Maguire" and engaged him as his valet.[289] Things soon turned sour, and he left Tumblety's employment returning to his previous post at the hotel.

In an interview twenty years later, when Tumblety was suspected of being Jack the Ripper, Maguire confirmed that his former boss "has always been outspoken, if not a notorious as a woman hater". Maguire claimed Tumblety had avoided any relationships with women for thirty years. "His antipathy to fallen women has been especially marked".[290] And most damningly from Maguire:

---

288 "Sanford Conover again", *Chicago Tribune*, August 13, 1867
289 "Is he Jack the Ripper?", *The Leavenworth Standard*, January 18, 1889
290 Ibid: "Is he Jack the Ripper?"

So long ago as 1861, when in Washington, he had an anatomical museum, in which the chief feature was an unusual number of glass jars containing specimens of the same nature as those which have been carved from the White Chapel (sic) unfortunates.[291]

Maguire was convinced that Tumblety was insane and referencing Lincoln's Surgeon General's views on homosexuality, added: "Time and again he has been forced to leave places because he practiced abominable vices which Surgeon General Hamilton says no sane man can be addicted to".[292]

In short, Maguire supports Dunham's testimony and taking all things into consideration, Dunham is a credible witness. His account of the grim content of Tumblety's cabinet of curiosities should be taken at face value and clear evidence that the Indian Herb Doctor was very likely Jack the Ripper.

---

291 Ibid: "Is he Jack the Ripper?"
292 Ibid: "Is he Jack the Ripper?"

Five

Washington's Clandestine Gay Network

If a gentleman craved same sex encounters in the 1860s, then Washington DC was hard to beat as a city full of male white-collar office workers, actors, waiters, soldiers, and political operators. As with the 20th and 21st centuries, LGBT people were drawn to a big metropolis where they could become their true selves and indulge their passions. The American capital was long recognised for its prevalence of what the police and courts described as obscene and lewd behaviour - little wonder Dr. Tumblety decided to relocate.

Shadowy forms drifted across Lafatyette Square at night. Men who knew that within a stone's throw of the White House, they could get what they wanted. Sometimes just a one-on-one encounter but police records indicate regular incidences of all-male open-air orgies. In one incident, eighteen men were taken into custody in one police swoop for engaging in what can only be described as an act of mass oral sex. [293] Punishments for this kind of activity ranged from fines to imprisonment in the workhouse or penitentiary for up to five years.

293 Jonathan Ned Katz, *Gay American History* (Penguin, 1992)

One gay man observed that most of the sex he enjoyed was with professional types: a doctor; a reporter for the *Washington Herald*; an auditor for the Department of Agriculture; and an office apprentice at the Bureau of Standards.[294] If Lafayette Square proved unproductive, he might head over to Franklin Park, Judiciary Square, or the Washington Monument grounds.

The effects of sodomy were deemed to be potentially earth shattering. In 1860, the year before Tumblety arrived in Washington DC, John Haskell was arraigned for examination after his arrest "caused such intense excitement". Bail was set at $6,000, which is $216,000 in today's value, which Haskell was unable to meet so was kept behind bars. The newspaper assured nervous readers: "All is quiet in the city now".[295]

When it got too cold in the winter months, the action moved indoors. The capital's theatres could accommodate all tastes. In the upper reaches of the main hall, Washingtonians could find whatever they pleased. In the Civil War era, theatres were only just moving from candlelight to gaslight and limelight (a block of lime heated to incandescence then focused with mirrors). So, there were still plenty of murky corners where amorous assignations could go undetected.

Meanwhile, the theatre basements were home to smoke-filled saloons serving alcohol, cigars, and oysters. In 1865, the Park Theatre in Brooklyn was nearly destroyed by a fire that took hold in a basement saloon under the theatre run by Mr George Reckerby. Hot ashes had been carelessly dumped in a basket.[296] These raucous bars were populated by theatregoers, actors, prostitutes, and thieves.

---

294 Brett Beemyn, "The Geography of Same-Sex Desire Cruising Men in Washington DC in the Late Nineteenth and Early Twentieth Centuries", *Left History*, 2004

295 "By Telegraph to the Hartford Daily Courant", *Hartford Courant*, February 29, 1860

296 "Fire under the Park Theatre", Times Union, December 22, 1865

Tumblety was addicted to the theatre. He was hard to miss as he entered any place of entertainment. All six foot of him in his finery with his trusty greyhound trotting alongside. Tumblety would pay five dollars to make sure the dog didn't miss the show.[297] By all accounts he was a discerning canine. "The dog used to lean over the railing and take in the play with great interest".[298] It was reported that this dog was later given by Tumblety as a gift to the United States Secretary of State William "Billy" Seward.[299] He in turn gave Tumblety an Arabian horse.

What the dog saw from its seat in the circle could be very saucy and daring in 1860's Washington DC. One of the most popular stars of the time was a Jewish convert of African American and Creole heritage who took both male and female lovers. Adah Isaacs Menken (1835-1868) became internationally famous for her role in the drama Mazeppa. The climax of the play involved Menken being strapped, seemingly naked, to a real horse which charged up a series of platforms to the top of the stage. The role had previously been played by men and the actor replaced with a dummy for the horse stunt. But Menken was made of sterner stuff. Wearing flesh-toned tights to scandalise the audience, she made a spirited ascent.[300]

Menken counted Charles Dickens among her friends from whom Tumblety would later obtain a glowing testimonial. Or maybe not. We will never know for sure. Though it would be intriguing to imagine that Tumblety gained access to the author of *Oliver Twist* through the bisexual queen of the Washington stage. Just imagine that on one of his many later trips to Europe, he knocked on the door of Charles Dickens with a letter of introduction from Adah Isaacs Menken.

---

297 "Is he the fiend?" *The Buffalo News*, December 1, 1888

298 Ibid, "Is he the fiend?"

299 Ibid, "Is he the fiend?"

300 "The Late Adah Isaacs Menken", *Evening Star*, August 13, 1868

Tragically, she died in Paris, France of "consumption" (tuberculosis or cancer) in 1868 aged only thirty-three years, having gone through several marriages and conducted an affair with Alexandre Dumas, author of *The Three Musketeers*, in Paris. He was thirty years her senior. An American newspaper obituary felt that Paris must have suited the "peculiar genius" of Adah. "She must have felt at home among its scandals and eccentricities".[301]

Another female actress scandalising respectable society was the British dancer and performer Lydia Thompson and her troupe, the Blondes. In the 1860s they brought their theatrical spectacle *Ixion* to the United States, a topical parody mixing ancient Greek myths with contemporary politics. There was lots of cross-dressing between the male and female members of the troupe and their distinctive blonde hair kicked off a brief fashion trend among New York women.[302]

The Chicago Times dared to give the Blondes a negative review. This led to Lydia Thompson, with three female and four male members of her troupe, ambushing the newspaper editor outside his house and attacking him. Thompson "struck him over the head with a raw-hide" while he grabbed her by the throat then applied his walking cane to one of the male dancers. A couple of revolvers were drawn but no shots fired.[303] This certainly gives a flavour of the theatre scene of the day. Reporting on this violent incident, the *Buffalo Morning Express* tore into the bawdiness of the "she-rowdies" known as the Blondes:

> *Do you know what it is they do? They come on the stage naked, to all intents and purposes; padded; painted;*

---

301 Ibid: "The Late Adah Isaacs Menken"

302 Michael Bronski, *A Queer History of the United States* (Beacon Press, 2012)

303 "The News", *Memphis Daily Appeal*, February 26, 1870

powdered; oiled; enameled; and glorified with false hair.
They are coarsely, vulgarly voluptuous… you may hear,
in fifteen minutes, more abject silliness, and more bad
rhymes, and aimless jokes, vulgarity, slang and obscenity,
issue from female lips than ought to be distributed over
the female utterances of fifteen years…[304]

Thompson was a bawdy British import to the American theatre; but it was English actors who also began to bring middle-class respectability across the Atlantic. The likes of Edmund Kean, William Charles Macready, and Charles Kemble. Kean competed for Shakespearian tragic roles against fellow Englishman Junius Brutus Booth, who left his homeland for the United States in 1821. As we know, he fathered the acting trio of John Wilkes, Edwin, and Junius Junior.

Although Booth senior was part of the new wave of higher brow theatre, he was soon infected by the chaotic decadence of American theatreland becoming a hopeless alcoholic and causing havoc onstage. This included an incident where in the role of Othello he began to genuinely suffocate Desdemona, who had to be rescued just in time by other actors.[305] Not content with that outrage, he waited for the curtain to drop before hitting the actor playing Iago with a metal bracket, who retaliated by smashing a pewter pot into Booth's face, permanently disfiguring his nose.

Tumblety was so immersed in the theatre that he ended up becoming part of the on-stage entertainment. In March 1862, the Canterbury Music Hall in Washington DC put on a "roaring farce" titled *Dr Tumblety's First Patient*.[306]

The Canterbury served up riotous burlesque fare for

304 "The Blondes", *Buffalo Morning Express*, February 28, 1870

305 Champ Clark, *Assassination: The Death of the President* (Time Life, 1987)

306 "Dr Tumblety in Trouble Again", *The Hamilton Spectator*, March 20, 1862

a socially mixed crowd who were not expecting anything too high brow. This was staged as part of a relaunch for the Canterbury at a venue formerly known as the Washington Hall with a new manager, George Percival. [307] His eye was firmly fixed on filling seats and winning rave newspaper reviews and it's notable that the subject of Tumblety was regarded as a guaranteed crowd pleaser. The doctor's colourful reputation was clearly well established.

But if Percival thought Tumblety would take this character assassination lying down, he was in for an ugly surprise. Because with maximum publicity in the newspapers, the doctor fired off a writ. He fulminated that this mocking burlesque was career damaging stuff. As a result of the disrespectful play which poked fun at Tumblety's pretensions, the doctor claimed that his business had suffered, and one female patient had ordered Tumblety off her premises. He had even "been treated with disrespect at his boarding house".

An associate of Tumblety went to see the performance in question. Sure enough, there was a man with a flowing moustache on stage followed by two greyhounds singing a song titled *The Doctor*. The likeness to Tumblety was uncanny.

On 8 March 1862, the libel case went to court with an irate Tumblety brandishing a theatre bill from the Canterbury listing its amusements and farces, including Dr Tumblety's First Patient. In a statement, that would have raised eyebrows among mainstream physicians, Tumblety argued that the burlesque performance was an attack on both him and the entire medical profession. At which point he exhibited his diploma proving he was an authorised doctor and a "gold medal testimonial" regarding his professional ability he claimed had been issued by a respected authority in Canada.[308]

---

307 "Canterbury Hall", *The Baltimore Sun*, March 11, 1862
308 "Dr Tumblety", *Buffalo Courier*, March 13, 1862

Percival's defence was that he had no knowledge of Tumblety and had never met him. This seems unlikely. He added that a similar production had been staged in New York months before in October 1861 by a blackface theatrical troupe called Bryants' Minstrels. This was indeed the case and a classified advertisement for the play has now been discovered, performed at the Mechanics Hall on Broadway, New York. [309]

That production was billed as a "laughable burlesque" titled *Dr Tumblety Outdone*. Remember that Tumblety was in New York before Washington DC and this play was beyond any doubt about him. There was only one Doctor Tumblety. In both cities, he was a well-known celebrity figure and a regular fixture in the theatres. The Canterbury had another sister outlet in New York so what more than likely happened was that the burlesque was trialled on Broadway before transferring to Washington DC. In effect, the burlesque followed Tumblety from city to city. Little wonder he was fed up with it.

As ever with the Tumblety story, there was a strange twist. One evening, a well-built man who claimed to be a friend of Tumblety jumped from the audience to the stage shouting, "See here, you infernal scoundrel, Mr Tumblety is a friend of mine, and I will not let such an effigy as you make him ridiculous".[310]

The angry theatregoer "grabbed the mustache of the supposed actor and gave it a vigorous twist, snatched off his cap and pulled his clothes away".[311] At which point, the assailant reeled. Because standing before him was none other than Dr Francis Tumblety himself. The whole episode, including threats of legal action against the Canterbury, was just another of Tumblety's self-promoting PR stunts.

---

309 "Bryants Minstrels", *New York Daily Herald*, October 12, 1861

310 "Fight for Tumblety's Cash?", *The Sun*, June 26, 1904

311 Ibid, "Fight for Tumblety's Cash?"

This anecdote seems a little far-fetched, especially as Tumblety must have incurred some expense taking the theatre to court. Eventually, both sides yielded some ground with Percival promising to drop the skit. The judge dismissed the case. Nevertheless, it clearly wounded Tumblety. He wrote in his autobiography that his two years in Washington DC had been "replete with many delightful reminiscences" with the "exception of the little unpleasant episode brought about by the manager of the Canterbury Hall".[312]

After Tumblety left Washington DC in 1863, there were promotional advertisements and posters for Grover's Theatre on Pennsylvania Avenue, near Willard's Hotel run by Leonard Grover, who was also the director of the Grand German Opera. This seemingly high-class entertainment was being staged by Percival who had changed his name to Grover. It seems he didn't emerge unscathed from the skirmish with the doctor.

Tumblety's tussles with theatreland didn't end with the Canterbury episode. In January 1863, the following year, there was a review at Carr's Melodeon in Buffalo entitled *Dr Tumblety's Laughing Gas*.[313] This would have been at around the same time Booth and Tumblety were hanging out together in that city. Despite the doctor's love of the theatre, he was a subject of derision, and his foibles were lampooned.

After Lincoln's assassination, the doctor featured in a song written by Tony Pastor (1837–1908) who is often hailed as the father or "dean" of Vaudeville. His Civil War era on-stage act combined humorous songs, "stump speeches", burlesque orations, and witty monologues. The style of comedy was observational, political, and resolutely pro-Union and anti-slavery. Songs included *The Stage-Struck Irishman*, *The Wife that Wears the Breeches*, *A Gay Little Dandy*, and *The Wooden-*

---

312 Ibid: *A few passages in the life of Dr. Francis Tumblety*

313 "Carr's Melodeon", *Buffalo Evening Post*, January 13, 1863

Legged Widow. His '*Carte de Visite* album' mentioned both Tumblety and Booth in the same verse and associated them with other notorious criminals:

> *Then famous Doctor Tumblety*
> *The knight of pill and pestle*
> *Stuck in a corner there you'd see*
> *Along with Madam Restell*
> *Young Booth just by young Cora Hatch*
> *He cuts a pretty figure...*[314]

Tumblety is seated next to one of the most infamous abortionists of the day: Madam Restell. Her real name was Ann Trow Lohman (1811–1878), dubbed in the press as "the abortionist of Fifth Avenue" and "the Wickedest Woman in New York".[315] This linkage is intriguing and suggests that Tumblety may have continued to perform illegal abortions despite the earlier police sting against him in Canada.

Like Tumblety, Restell bought a huge amount of classified advertising in the newspaper to sell her cures. These included Preventative Powder at five dollars and abortions at twenty dollars for lower income women and $100 for society ladies. Equally, like Tumblety, Restell experienced terrifying brushes with the law, spending astronomical sums on legal representation to avoid imprisonment.

Restell was suspected of performing a fatal abortion on Mary Rogers, whose tragic story was adapted by the horror novelist Edgar Allen Poe in his tale, *The Mystery of Marie Rogêt*.[316] In

---

314 Tony Pastor, *Tony Pastor's Book of Six Hundred Comic Songs and Speeches* (Dick & Fitzgerald, 1867)

315 "Madame Restell, Sketch of the Wickedest Woman in New York", *The Cincinnati Times* quoted in The Tennessean, October 30, 1868

316 Karen Abbott, "Madam Restell: The Abortionist of Fifth Avenue", *Smithsonian Magazine*, November 27, 2012

1847, she was sentenced to a year in prison. But like Tumblety, bounced back from this indignity and by 1868 could be found in a stunningly sumptuous Fifth Avenue mansion provoking one newspaper to sneer that its décor was vulgar with "gilt and gaudiness... visible from cellar to garret".[317]

That year, her estimated income was $30,000, which in today's value would be over $600,000 per annum. Like Tumblety, she felt her wealth validated her and excused any character or moral shortcomings:

The Madame has no society – she is a perfect pariah in New York – but she seems to enjoy herself and grow as fleshy as if she had the approval of a good conscience and lived a life of innocence and good deeds.[318]

Tony Pastor puts two people, Restell and Tumblety, both accused of performing illegal abortions, chatting in the corner. In the very next line, the "pretty figure" of the now-dead Booth is sitting with the well-known spiritualist of the day, Cora Hatch – born Cora Lodencia Veronica Scott (1840–1923). This pokes fun at a conspiracy theory, then prevalent among Confederate sympathisers, that Booth wasn't dead. Cora may have succeeded in summoning him up from the grave or he had miraculously escaped death and survived.

Tumblety was clearly well known to the public and theatregoers but what about his claimed friendship with the president? In his autobiography, Tumblety wrote that not only did he get to know Lincoln during his time in Washington DC, but their relationship blossomed. It was, he declared, "of the most gratifying character". Tumblety then experienced "a decline of health of an alarming character which induced me

---

317 Ibid: "Madame Restell, Sketch of the Wickedest Woman in New York"
318 Ibid: "Madame Restell, Sketch of the Wickedest Woman in New York"

to abandon my project of entering the army, and seriously contemplate a trip to Europe".[319] He informed Lincoln of his plans and the president "kindly furnished me with letters"[320] including an introduction to the US ambassador in London. But "circumstances" forced Tumblety to change his mind and head for St. Louis.

Taking Tumblety's account at face value for now, this would either have happened in 1863 when the doctor left Washington DC, facing the prospect of vice-related charges, or around 1864 when he moved to St. Louis. There is a year that Tumblety skips over which is the period that he spent in Brooklyn between leaving Washington DC in 1863 and arriving in St. Louis in 1865. It was in his Brooklyn pharmacy that he employed one of the Lincoln plotters: David Herold.

Tumblety's claim to have enjoyed frequent access to President Lincoln is usually met with loud harrumphs. But from his appearance on Lincoln's inaugural procession through New York and during his two years in the American capital, this exposure to Lincoln is plausible. How far it went is the real question.

Compared to a US President in the 21st century, Lincoln and his predecessors were surprisingly approachable. Presidents Andrew Jackson (1767–1845) and Martin Van Buren (1782–1862) often rode unaccompanied through the streets of Washington DC. President John Tyler (1790–1862) with his "enormous nose, was familiar to all, from the frequency with which it was seen in public".[321] And President Buchanan, in office immediately before Lincoln, was often seen without any security around Washington.

In a November 1862 article titled, "The Assassination of

---

319 Ibid: *A few passages in the life of Dr. Francis Tumblety*

320 Ibid: *A few passages in the life of Dr. Francis Tumblety*

321 "The Assassination of the President", *The Indiana State Sentinel*, November 24, 1862

the President", three years before it actually happened, *The Indiana State Sentinel* bemoaned the newly introduced armed guard at the gates to the White House and "the care taken to keep strangers outside of the approaches to the building".[322] The introduction of an armed guard for Lincoln as he left in a carriage seemed "ridiculous" to the newspaper.

Though it conceded, through gritted teeth, that there had already been attempts on Lincoln's life including one as he rode towards the Soldiers' Home. A man had fired twice from behind a fence on the side of the road. Lincoln was unharmed but his horse was wounded. The would-be assassin was whisked away to "one of the many Government prisons, where the order to commit is not required to name the cause of arrest".[323]

Despite attempts on his life and the revelation of plots, security precautions for the president, even as the Civil War raged, were regarded by many as a monarchic affectation. The argument ran along these lines. No sane person would ever assassinate the President of the United States. The American Republic had never required an army to compel the people to obey the US Constitution. And the president should trust the American people to ensure his security.

> *Let us hope that this armed guard of Mr. Lincoln is only a passing show, got up for the amusement of a gaping crowd, and that it has not and never has any foundation, in a fear by the President or any of his friends, that he was in danger of assassination.*[324]

When Tumblety arrived in Washington DC in 1861, he

---

322 Ibid: "The Assassination of the President"

323 Ibid: "The Assassination of the President"

324 "Extraordinary precautions – a military guard in the White House – the assassination of the President", *The Hamilton Spectator*, December 4, 1862

could reasonably expect to get into the White House, Congress, and Union military headquarters. He just needed to deploy his customary chutzpah and make some thorough plans. The first move was to base himself at Willard's Hotel, right opposite the White House and within a stone's throw of the president.

Lincoln was the ultimate prize. There is an intriguing paragraph in his autobiography where Tumblety offers an account of his first meeting with Lincoln. This was written after Booth had fired the fatal bullet:

Through a distinguished officer with whom I became acquainted in Boston, Massachusetts, I was introduced to the late lamented President, with those gentle and genial manners I was charmed, and for whom, until the day of his ruthless assassination, I entertained feelings of the warmest respect and admiration, even as I now, and ever shall, reverence his memory.

At the time of Lincoln's murder, Tumblety was still only thirty-five, while Lincoln was twenty years older. By all accounts, the doctor was a striking figure who inspired strong feelings among both men and women. He possessed bags of charisma, as confirmed by journalists, as well as handsome features and a certain presence. Wouldn't it be possible that Lincoln's careworn eyes alighted on the celebrity doctor at the presidential *levées*? It's hard to imagine how he could have missed him.

Those who cannot conceive of such a thing "are blind to Lincoln's same-sex inclinations in part because of a personal aversion to male homosexuality, but more importantly because they fail to perceive the vast differences between the sexual culture of antebellum America and that of our own time".[325] The question is: if Lincoln and Tumblety did enjoy the intimacy

---

325 Michael Ferguson, "Was Abraham Lincoln gay?", *National Library of Medicine*, National Center for Biotechnology Information, 2010

that the doctor claimed, why was he also consorting with those plotting to kill the president?

After spreading material in the US Army deemed to be indecent, Tumblety was put under greater official scrutiny. As a result, his cruising activities in the capital soon came to light and according to Billy Pinkerton, he was all but driven away from Washington DC well before the assassination as a "suspicious character".[326]

Leaving Washington DC, he firstly headed up to Philadelphia, which at the time was the second largest city in the United States. This would be a short and dramatic stay with the doctor required to perform another hasty disappearing act, before moving on to Brooklyn.

Tumblety rented an office on the second storey of a building at 333 Chestnut Street, a 17th century thoroughfare drenched in history with the Liberty Bell located at one intersection. The doctor was staying at Girard House, a ten-year-old hotel that encompassed the Broadway Oyster House and Noonan's Bowling, Billiard, and Shuffle-Board Rooms. Another ideal location for vigorous networking.

From the moment he set foot in Philadelphia, Tumblety was being trailed (or "piped" to use their parlance) by two detectives: Detective Callahan and Detective Carlin. It's not known whether Pinkerton tipped off local police to keep tabs on Philadelphia's new resident. The duo followed Tumblety as he appeared in the streets "dressed in a fantastic costume, cavalry boots, and spurs" riding a "spotted horse" and commanding the usual popular attention. He was officially classified as a "suspicious person" but despite their best efforts, the detectives were unable to pin anything on Tumblety.[327] More than likely because he was aware of being under surveillance.

---

326 Ibid: "Is he the Butcher?"

327 "The Philadelphia Adventures of Dr. F. Tumblety", *Daily Missouri Republican*, May 14, 1865

But then on 21 May 1863, a clearly agitated Indian Herb Doctor entered the Central Police Station insistent on reporting a crime against his person. The affidavit that followed was recorded at the front desk in "Mr Bulkley's blotter". Again, the scenario described has a sad ring of familiarity. He had been robbed of a gold medal presented to him by the grateful citizens of Montreal several years before. The value, Tumblety claimed, was about $800, which would be just under $20,000 today. The thief was a man referred to as "St Clair" and he had stopped by at the Girard where Tumblety showed him the medal at which point St Clair ran off with it.

It doesn't take a wild leap of imagination to piece together a credible sequence of events that fits with the doctor's previous behaviour. He had picked up St Clair in the cruising grounds, taken him back to the hotel, enjoyed some fun in the bedroom, then boastfully shown the impressionable young man one of his costly trinkets to dazzle his new conquest, who might have ended up as a valet if he hadn't proven to be so light fingered.

A warrant was issued for the arrest of St Clair by Alderman Beltler. It fell to detectives Callahan and Carlin to go and apprehend the villain. He was arrested the following day, taken to the same station where it emerged his real name was Joseph Aspinwall. But as happened before and would occur again afterwards, the capture of one of Tumblety's criminally inclined bedfellows would prove to be his undoing. Once again, the actual crime took second billing as the doctor's private life came to the fore.

Philadelphia's chief of police, Benjamin Franklin (named after the Founding Father), acted on a "lingering doubt" in Callahan's mind about Tumblety's story regarding the medal. Franklin wrote to the authorities in Montreal asking if they had indeed awarded such a prestigious item to the Indian Herb Doctor for his services. The answer came back: no. Furthermore,

Montreal still regarded Tumblety as "an impostor, a charlatan, and a suspicious person".[328]

At which point, Tumblety showed up at the police station informing the front desk that the stolen medal had been slid under the door of his office on Chestnut Street. Aspinwall was immediately released from the police cells and now became the victim, not the suspect. Even described as being of "good character", which was doubtful. It was now Tumblety in the dock again.

Franklin, holding the incriminating response from Montreal in his hands, blew up at the doctor. The accusations from Canada were repeated to his face and he was condemned for putting an innocent young man behind bars. Tumblety returned fire defending his reputation. But as happened with Charles Whelpley and other young men who dipped into Tumblety's wealth for their own gain, it was the Indian Herb Doctor who was going down in flames.

Things got so heated between the two men that the station's fire marshal, Dr. Blackburn (yet another Blackburn in the story, confusingly), came to the assistance of his boss using language that was "respectful but decidedly emphatic". Tumblety was given twenty-four hours to leave Philadelphia. Just in case the doctor had any second thoughts about staying, Franklin added that he suspected Tumblety was a Confederate spy. An astonishing remark given that Confederate forces were at that moment massing near the city to attack. Did he really think Tumblety was linked to the Confederacy or was it just a heavy-handed tactic to run this character out of town?

Whatever the truth, Tumblety must have been terrified by this accusation. It did carry the death penalty after all. In June 1863, the Confederate General Robert E. Lee invaded

---

328 Ibid: "The Philadelphia Adventures of Dr. F. Tumblety"

the state of Pennsylvania in the Gettysburg Campaign and began marching on the state capital, Philadelphia. There was a large pro-South presence in the city and a growing air of resignation to being conquered by the Confederacy. It took until July for the Army of the Potomac to defeat Lee's forces but by then, Tumblety had sped north to what he must have believed was a safer location.

It seems that he crossed the border back into Canada for a short period setting up in Sherbrooke, a city in southern Quebec, just under a hundred miles from Montreal. This was incredibly risky given the outstanding manslaughter charge in Canada from which he had so brazenly absconded after attempting to steal the victim's heart and liver.

For whatever reason, Tumblety then skipped back into the United States basing himself in Brooklyn with a store on the south-west corner of Fulton and Nassau streets. Business then boomed once more for Tumblety. He was reported to be making $100 a day out of his herb preparations, which would be over $2,000 at today's value. This was deposited at the Brooklyn Savings Bank.[329]

It would be during this time in Brooklyn that the Indian Herb Doctor made a very unfortunate choice of valet. Tumblety was seen processing through Brooklyn followed by a young, impressionable man who within eighteen months would be executed for his role in the assassination of President Abraham Lincoln: David Edgar Herold.

On 7 July 1865, Herold sobbed uncontrollably as a cap was placed over his head.[330] Minutes later, his lifeless body dangled from the end of a rope. As he breathed his last, he reportedly wet himself. It seemed somehow pathetically fitting. The most feeble-minded of the Booth gang that killed President Lincoln

329 "The Whitechapel Murders", *The Courier-Journal*, November 24, 1888
330 "Execution of Payne, Herold, Atzerott, and Mrs Surratt", *Valley Spirit* (Weekly), July 12, 1865

had sought adventure but instead met his own miserable end at the age of just twenty-three.

Herold studied at the Washington Seminary, a Jesuit-run Catholic school, before going on to Georgetown College where he obtained a certificate in pharmacy. He qualified in 1860 and took up posts at several pharmacies in Washington DC. While working at Thompson's Pharmacy in 1863, he delivered a bottle of castor oil to the White House and, incredibly, handed it in person to President Lincoln.[331]

In the very same year, Herold met Lincoln's killer, John Wilkes Booth. The actor had developed a tumour on his neck and his theatrical manager, Matthew Canning, insisted on taking the tempestuous thespian to a surgeon. Dr. John Frederick May recommended an operation when his assistant was present but Booth, flying into one of his hissy fits, demanding action straight away.

Here is Canning, who will be your assistant… now cut away.[332]

This wasn't one of Booth's better ideas as blackened blood gushed out. Canning nearly fainted at the sight. The actor's skin turned a sickly white as he reeled uncontrollably, falling out of the chair. The tumour was largely removed but it was a scene of carnage. Canning later said he thought Dr. May was trying to cut Booth's head clean off. This reckless surgery left Booth with a scar that helped identify his corpse after he was shot in the aftermath of the Lincoln assassination.

Booth's first encounter with Herold was very likely because he needed drugs for the pain his neck tumour was causing. The introduction was possibly made by John Surratt, the son

---

331 Andrew Haynes, "The pharmacist who helped Lincoln's assassin", *The Pharmaceutical Journal*, March 27, 2015

332 George Alfred Townsend, "Interview with Matthew Canning", *Cincinnati Enquirer*, January 19, 1886

of Mary Surratt who would hang alongside Herold. They had both trained at the Charlotte Hall Military Academy in the late 1850s. Booth would then introduce Herold to Tumblety who employed him at his Brooklyn pharmacy in 1864.

When the doctor then had to depart Brooklyn in haste over new vice allegations, Herold went back to Washington DC to become fatally enmeshed in Booth's assassination plot. Although Tumblety wasn't in the capital, we know from Captain Cavanaugh's testimony that he knew Booth on an "intimate" basis and employed the co-conspirator, David Herold, as well as introducing Booth to another conspirator who would hang – Mary Surratt. The key question is whether Tumblety knew Herold was leaving his employ to get involved in Booth's suicidal mission to assassinate the president.

In photographs taken in the days before his execution, Herold looks confused, overwhelmed by the enormity of what was about to happen. At his trial, nobody had anything positive to say about him. An eternal boy. A lost soul. Incapable of becoming an adult. Fixated on boys and men. What wasn't mentioned at the trial, but did get coverage in the newspapers, was his association with Tumblety.

This presents us with a conundrum. Tumblety insists he had a close and intimate friendship with Lincoln. He tells us of his grief on hearing about the president's murder and he attended Lincoln's funeral, mourning the great man's loss deeply if we are to believe his autobiography. So, why was he also associated with Lincoln's killers?

The link between Booth, Herold and Tumblety was exposed in the newspapers after Lincoln's murder thanks to statements to the police given by Booth's teenage errand boy. The day after Lincoln was shot by Booth, the errand boy went on the run. Terrified for his life, he disappeared into thin air. The police eventually apprehended him in Court Street, Brooklyn, five days after Booth was shot dead. In a Washington DC police station, it emerged that the boy had been with Booth over a period of several months.

His subsequent confession connected Booth, Tumblety, and Herold in a murderous triangle. Booth was a friend of Tumblety and had introduced him to Herold who then became his employee. *The Brooklyn Daily Eagle* led with the story claiming that Herold worked for Tumblety at his office in Brooklyn in the immediate run up to the assassination:

Just before going to Brooklyn, he became acquainted with Booth in Washington, through whom he made the acquaintance of Harrold (sic). *The latter was then out of employment, and having some knowledge of drugs, was engaged by Tumblety to go to Brooklyn as his assistant. Harrold remained with Tumblety until, for some reason not stated, the latter found it prudent to break up his Brooklyn establishment.*[333]

After leaving Tumblety's employment, Herold returned to Washington DC and was next heard of as Booth's accomplice in the assassination of Lincoln. Tumblety, meanwhile, had run into a spot of patient trouble, plus the usual cruising issues, in Brooklyn and hastily packed up his office, making off for St. Louis. However, if Tumblety had any knowledge of the plot to kill Lincoln, were his movements dictated by that as opposed to his perennial problems around picking up young men?

The errand boy was interrogated by the police in Washington DC on 4 May 1865. The very next day, Tumblety was arrested as a suspected Lincoln plotter. There was also another charge against the doctor over an alleged Confederate plot to spread yellow fever that will be detailed further in the next chapter. But the paperwork for his jailing at the

333 "Arrest of Dr. Tumblety as an accomplice in the assassination", *The Kingston Daily News*, May 8, 1865

Old Capitol Prison, obtained from the US national archive, specifically states the assassination of President Lincoln as being the reason for his detention on the director order of Secretary of War, Edwin Stanton.

Why was Booth's errand boy so scared that he went on the run? Part of the reason may be the fury that was unleashed by news of the president's assassination. Indicative of this was an incident where a man from New Jersey, Mr Stevens, was arrested by police because he looked like Booth. Once at the police station, with a mob baying for his blood outside, it became obvious he wasn't Booth. The "stupid detectives", as one report described them, ordered the crowd to disperse. But they refused – with one man insisting that Stevens "ought to be shot anyhow".[334]

But the errand boy's fear seems to have been more grounded in the belief that his life was in danger from Booth's associates, including Tumblety, than the police or any mob. Like the doctor, Booth employed these impressionable young men "as a sort of valet or errand boy".[335] Under interrogation, the teenager confirmed what Cavanaugh would state decades later, that Tumblety and Booth "were on very intimate terms". Did the errand boy really believe that Tumblety might kill him – or networks to which he was attached? The evidence shows that he certainly thought his life was in danger.

The errand boy's testimony is so incriminating that some have sought to undermine it. One claim being that he wasn't Booth's errand boy but a publicity-seeking young thief, which seems rather implausible. It's a very convoluted way to get off a theft charge and risk arrest for being part of the Booth plot – which carried the death penalty. Imagine the idiocy of trying to deflect from a petty theft charge by stating: I am not a thief

334 "Mob Justice", *The Wheeling Daily Register*, May 5, 1865

335 "Booth's Errand Boy arrested in Brooklyn", *Detroit Free Press*, May 7, 1865

but I was party to a conspiracy to murder the President of the United States.

Another theory advanced to pull apart the Booth-Tumblety-Herold axis of evil is the claim that Herold, as Tumblety's valet, was a case of mistaken identity. The man that journalists thought was Herold was in fact Mark Blackburn, Tumblety's long-term soulmate and assistant. However, given the enormity of the Lincoln story, it beggars belief that a newspaper like *The Brooklyn Daily Eagle*, which very much owned this story and ran with it, would have conducted no fact checking or interviews with witnesses. Plus, any journalist covering the Lincoln treason trial knew exactly what Herold looked like. He was one of the most recognisable faces of the time.

The government, police, and newspapers had no doubt that Herold worked for Tumblety in Brooklyn and Booth had undoubtedly introduced Herold to Tumblety. Everybody on Main Street in Brooklyn had witnessed the regular Tumblety processions with the doe-eyed man child Herold in tow:

> *About a year since, it will be remembered, Fulton Street was put into a state of the most feverish excitement by the appearance of a very tall muscular man, of rather handsome and imposing appearance, with a huge black moustache, who was in the habit of promenading the street every day between ten o'clock and twelve and sometimes in the afternoon.*[336]

The Brooklyn Daily Eagle described disdainfully how Herold attached himself to both Tumblety and Booth with "a womanish sort of admiration". So weak was Herold's character that he "seemed to ape almost unconsciously all the airs of his master", adopting a very deferential stance towards Tumblety. Two newspapers described the Tumblety-Herold relationship:

---

336 "The Assassination", *The Brooklyn Daily Eagle*, May 4, 1865

Harold – who was a pale faced, large eyed, poetical looking boy – was with Tumblety constantly. He seemed a compromise between friend, companion, and servant to the doctor.[337]

Whenever he appeared on the street he was accompanied by a valet and two greyhounds. His valet was known as Harold and was implicated with Booth in the assassination of President Lincoln.[338]

Tumblety had a three-room suite near Nassau Avenue consisting of a bedroom for himself and two business areas – a similar configuration to what Dunham described in Washington DC. His two employees were a contrasting and recognisable pair. One short, stout man looked after the piebald horses, while the other, taller figure was his "confidential valet". This was Herold.

At the trial of the Lincoln conspirators in 1865, Herold's character was dissected as he faced the death penalty for his role in the assassination. The identical term "light and trifling" was used by at least two witnesses. Francis Walsh described Herold as "more like a boy than a man" and considered him "boyish in every respect".[339] Another character witness, James Nokes, said he had known Herold since he was born. He described Herold's family as consisting of about seven children who were still living, all of them female except for young David who was unreliable, rather superficial, and influenced by those around him.

William Keilotz was a neighbour:

I consider his character very boyish. I see him often with boys; he is very fond of their company, and never associates with men.[340]

337 "Oh! Dr. Tumblety", *The New North-West*, December 21, 1888

338 "Jack, the Ripper, Ubiquitous", *The Bottineau Courant*, December 6, 1888

339 Benn Pitman, Philip Van Doren Stern, *The Assassination of President Lincoln and the Trial of the Conspirators* (Philip, Funk & Wagnalls, 1956)

340 Ibid: *The Assassination of President Lincoln and the Trial of the Conspirators*

Yet another witness, Dr Charles W. Davis, echoed the boy theme, having known Herold since childhood:

I do not know that I can describe his character in better terms than to say that he is a boy... there is very little of the man about him... I should think that his age is about twenty-two or twenty-three, but I consider him far more of a boy than a man.[341]

Herold's mind was stuck somewhere around sixteen years of age. He shared this immaturity with another plotter, also hanged, George Atzerodt. The two had been buddies for years going to the circus, bars, and "leg shows" at the Canterbury Hall in Washington DC.

Both had been teased as children and had used humour to disarm their tormentors. Neither had outgrown the habit, or the immaturity; a bout of flatulence might have them chuckling intermittently for half an hour.[342]

Prior to working for Tumblety, Herold had been with a pharmacist named Dr Samuel McKim of Washington DC. Their six-year acquaintance hadn't left a good impression on McKim. Again, referring to Herold as a "boy", he was unable to trust the Lincoln conspirator with any prescription for a patient in case he tampered with it as a "joke". "In mind, I consider him about eleven years of age".[343]

Given that Tumblety displayed no obvious Confederate sympathies and waxed lyrical in admiration of Lincoln, the

---

341 Ibid: *The Assassination of President Lincoln and the Trial of the Conspirators*

342 Michael W. Kauffman, *American Brutus* (Random House, 2005)

343 Ibid: *The Assassination of President Lincoln and the Trial of the Conspirators*

question must be posed how he came to be so closely associated with at least two of the Lincoln plotters, David Herold and John Wilkes Booth, and possibly Mary Surratt as well.

The snickering tone of the coverage by journalists and use of words like "womanish" and "adoration" echoes the phrasing of reports on vice-related police and court cases involving gay men. The adjectives were always loaded and coded.

It intimates that there was something sexual in the relationship between Tumblety, Booth, and Herold. As for the errand boy, he was very likely their catamite.

Six

The Killing of Lincoln

On 6 May 1864, Tumblety appeared before the police court in Brooklyn accused of "kicking a white man downstairs".[344] The aggrieved party was a patient, Fenton Scully, who had come to see the doctor all the way from 21 Bethune Street, near Greenwich Village in New York. Ship passenger records suggest Scully was British born, arriving in New York from Liverpool on Boxing Day, 1851 aboard the steamship, *Constitution*.[345]

Police officer Riggs from the 41st precinct introduced Scully to the court. He had come to see the doctor, "attracted by the fame of the medicine man". Scully was an asthmatic and the usual remedies, recommended by mainstream physicians, had been ineffective. Won over by Tumblety's claims in the newspapers to succeed where conventional medicine failed, he sought out the Indian Herb Doctor.

---

344 "The Indian Doctor on the War Path", *The Brooklyn Daily Eagle*, May 6, 1864

345 Arriving Passenger and Crew Lists for Castle Garden and Ellis Island for 1820-1957 accessed via *Ancestry.com*

Asthmatics were poorly served by the medical profession. Those afflicted were often recommended to smoke tobacco without inhaling; drink strong coffee to stay awake for as long as possible; glug down lots of alcohol in the belief it would "shock" the nervous system into stopping an asthma attack; or even smoke Indian hemp. Chloroform and opium were also on occasion prescribed.[346] In fairness to Tumblety then, any of his herbal medications would have been a marked improvement, and arguably less harmful, than other dire remedies on offer to asthmatics.

Tumblety promised Scully he could cure him for twenty dollars but took fifteen dollars on account and then prescribed a "liberal supply of medicine".[347] He was going to need a large amount because Tumblety specified "a wine glass full" to be taken every five minutes until he felt better. "Scully's asthma obstinately resisted the deluge and indeed got worse".[348] With just about enough breath left in his body, the patient struggled back to the doctor's office and demanded an explanation.

The Indian Hippocrates told him that his case was hopeless, and recommended resignation.[349]

Scully suggested that as his asthma was nowhere near cured, Tumblety should refund the fifteen dollars as promised. The doctor thought differently. The patient was shown the door but was unwilling to exit. "Scully like his asthma was obstinate and wouldn't go".[350]

---

346 John Bottrell, "Check out these 19th century asthma remedies", *Health Central*, December 18, 2009

347 'The Indian Doctor in Court', The Brooklyn Daily Eagle, May 10 1864

348 Ibid: "The Indian Doctor on the War Path"

349 Ibid: "The Indian Doctor on the War Path"

350 Ibid: "The Indian Doctor on the War Path"

The Doctor then tried a course of physical treatment on the refractory patient with the most signal success. The prescription read: Patient taken vigorously by the collar; well shaken after taken; sole leather promptly applied to the base of the dorsal vertebrae; result, prompt evacuation – of the premises by the patient.[351]

This alleged assault led to Tumblety finding himself before Justice Perry at the police court, who had issued a warrant for the doctor's arrest. He arrived with his legal adviser and friend Mr Parmenter who got the case postponed. As an aside, it was noted in the newspapers that Tumblety's dog had gone missing so no canine in attendance. [352]

His choice of dresswear in court that day consisted of a very dapper, butternut-coloured suit with exceedingly wide accompanying pantaloons offset by the brevity of his coat tails. Atop his head was a pork-pie cap and a stout yellow cane in hand. A couple of days later the case was dismissed when witnesses testified that Scully had been the ill-behaved party. "The herbalist departed rejoicing".[353]

In early 1865, Tumblety set up in the city of St. Louis applying the usual modus operandi. He based himself in the busy commercial district on Olive Street living at the recently built and ostentatiously lavish Lindell Hotel that boasted its own barber and Turkish bath.[354] It would burn down two years later.

Tumblety hired a local newsboy to hand out leaflets advertising his business at the foot of the front steps of his office dressed as a native American, "his head adorned with long

---

351 Ibid: "The Indian Doctor on the War Path"

352 Ibid: "The Indian Doctor in Court"

353 "The Indian Doctor Acquitted", *The Brooklyn Union*, May 10, 1864

354 "Lindell House Burns", *The Daily Gazette* (Davenport, Iowa), April 1, 1867

feathers". The doctor, meanwhile, took to the streets in his usual garish take on a cavalry officer riding his circus horse with the greyhounds running alongside.[355]

Only this time, it proved too much for the local Provost Guard. Tumblety was arrested ostensibly for impersonating a military officer. The provost took him into custody where he was subjected to lengthy questioning. This story is often regarded as yet another example of Tumblety's fraudulence. But in fact, what it illustrates is the overreaching powers of the provosts, already a subject of concern at the time, and their infringement of basic civil liberties during the war.

The system of provosts was a kind of military police and intelligence function copied from something similar in the British armed forces and introduced on both sides, Confederate and Union, in the American Civil War. The intention was to enforce discipline within the army but as the war dragged on, civilian politicians became concerned that the provosts were extending their powers to the public in areas like controlling the right of movement and inspecting passes. For example, a Confederate provost took it upon himself to interrogate the wife of General Robert E. Lee, Mary Anne Custis, as she journeyed to meet her husband, causing widespread indignation.[356]

They also became increasingly involved in policing vice acting as police, judge, jury, and jailers. Provosts kept a watchful eye on incidences of drunkenness, prostitution, or any conduct between soldiers deemed to be unbecoming. In this context, it's easy to see why the Indian Herb Doctor would be an obvious focus of interest when he crossed their path in his military splendour.

From a modern perspective, where criticism of police conduct in many countries is rife, one can sympathise with

---

355 "The Indian Herb Doctor", *The Brooklyn Daily Eagle*, May 10, 1865

356 John Wenner, "Military Intelligence: The Civil War Provost Guard", *Warfare History Network*

Tumblety's protest that he was victimised for not dressing in a 'normal' manner. His arrest was a rather pathetic example of police harassment to which the doctor had every right to be annoyed. He responded with some wit to his predicament:

> I have been charged with eccentricity in dress, but I presumed, as this is a free country, that so long as a person does not outrage decency or propriety, he has a perfect right to suit his own taste in the color and fashion of his garments. It seems, however, that I was mistaken, and even my partiality for a fine horse and a handsome dog – weaknesses which must be constitutional in my case, as I am happy to know they are in many amiable individuals in this and every other country – has, in connection with the cut of my apparel, furnished sufficient foundation, in the estimation of the might-is-right party, to annoy and persecute me.[357]

Tumblety's Barnum-esque costumes weren't usually a genuine attempt to impersonate a member of the armed forces. The only exception being when he swanned around military bases in Washington DC pretending to be a military surgeon. Normally though, this cosplay was just about drumming up business through spectacle.

Especially if one considers that his costume frequently changed during the street processions, sometimes on the hour, with the doctor metamorphosising from a cavalry officer to an English sportsman and on to a Scottish highlander. Nobody in their right mind believed the doctor was a real cavalry officer, least of all Tumblety himself. As he stated, the overriding influence on his approach to public relations was the equally stunningly dressed, P.T. Barnum.

---

357 Ibid: *A few passages in the life of Dr. Francis Tumblety*

Yet Tumblety was arrested for his outlandish appearance and it's hard not to share his anger at what was bullying, intimidation, and one might even say, in modern parlance, institutional homophobia. Though that concept was one hundred and fifty years in the future.

The provost's men apprehended Tumblety as he was viewing some land with a view to building a property in Carondelet, Missouri, just outside the city of St. Louis. The fuming Indian Herb Doctor was kept in a cell for two days. According to his own account of the incident, the officers sneered that he had been "putting on foreign airs", which included "riding fine horses, dressing in semi-military style, with a handsome robe, high patent leather boots, and spurs".[358] Keeping a large greyhound and sporting a black moustache were also cited by the Missouri law enforcement officers.

In short, as one of my gallant captors affirmed: "You're thinking yourself another God Almighty, and we won't stand it".[359]

Fortunately, as was often the case with Tumblety, he happened to be in the company of an "influential friend" that day who got him out of jail. The presence of these influential friends at key moments was a hallmark of the doctor's life. Just as the prison doors were opening, an important person would step forward to save Tumblety's skin. On other occasions, he would simply have to make himself scarce. But whenever he could, his networks were summoned to the rescue.

The furious doctor demanded an explanation from the local police chief for his treatment and was told that "medical rivals" had pressured the police to incarcerate him. This echoes previous

---

358 Ibid: *A few passages in the life of Dr. Francis Tumblety*
359 Ibid: *A few passages in the life of Dr. Francis Tumblety*

brushes with the law where mainstream physicians did their utmost to get this unqualified charlatan out of their community. Not least because he was sometimes showing them up.

The American Civil War was grinding to its bloody close. Between 620,000 and 750,000 soldiers were dead and an unknown number of civilian casualities.[360] Both sides were weary of the conflict though feelings of anger and desire for revenge were still strong. One actor declared he would soon astonish the world. "What are you going to do?" - asked his listener jokingly, "kill Jeff Davis, take Richmond, or play Hamlet a hundred nights?"[361]

John Wilkes Booth remained silent. He was certainly not going to murder the Confederate President Jefferson Davis. Taking Richmond was now unfeasible at this stage of the war. As for playing Hamlet a hundred times or more, his brother Edwin had walked off with that honour a long time ago. No, John Wilkes was going to slay Abraham Lincoln in what he thought would be the performance of a lifetime. Some cruel wags later sneered it was the last desperate scene of a ham actor.

So much promise squandered for so little gain. The gay poet Walt Whitman had high hopes for John Wilkes and was certainly enamoured by him: "I can still hear the clank and feel the perfect hush of perhaps three thousand people waiting. A shudder went through every nervous system in the audience. It certainly did through mine. His genius was to me one of the grandest revelations of my life, a lesson of artistic expression".[362]

If John Wilkes felt that his brother Edwin's acting was more highly appraised by the critics, he could have been consoled by

360 Guy Gugliotta, "New Estimate Raises Civil War Death Toll", *The New York Times*, April 2, 2012

361 Gene Smith, *American Gothic: The Story of America's Legendary Theatrical Family – Junius, Edwin, and John Wilkes Booth* (Simon & Schuster, 1992)

362 Stefan Kanfer, "John Wilkes Booth acted out the tragic downfall of a brilliant, afflicted family", *The Baltimore Sun*, October 11, 1992

his own much larger bank account. By 1865, he had become the "highest paid and most gaudily dressed" actor in America.[363] Little wonder he hung out with the Indian Herb Doctor given his sartorial taste and wealth. The two had been seen together in Buffalo in 1863 by Cavanaugh, and the doctor had employed Booth's co-conspirator David Herold at his Brooklyn pharmacy through 1864. He may also have introduced Booth to another plot conspirator, Mary Surratt. So, they were the firmest of friends.

But Tumblety was now in St. Louis and Herold had joined Booth for the last tragic chapter of his life, to be played out in his hometown, Washington DC. Lincoln, meanwhile, sensing victory in the Civil War, was running for re-election in 1864 against his former military chief of the Army of the Potomac, General McClellan. The very general who had run Tumblety out of camp for circulating immoral literature among Union troops. Eleven southern states didn't participate in the election as they were still part of the increasingly embattled and soon-to-be-defeated Confederate States of America.

Lincoln won a second term. Plenty of people were upset about that. Radicals to the left thought the president was too soft on the now ex-Confederacy and wanted the southern states to suffer for their act of rebellion. To the right were those seeking peace terms with the Confederacy and still hostile to the emancipation of African American slaves. In August, Lincoln was downbeat about the chances of winning, but the capture of Atlanta and other Union victories assured him the presidency.

Booth seethed like a venomous Prima Donna. He had formed his little cabal of plotters including David Herold and Mary Surratt. The original plan had been to kidnap Lincoln and force renewed prisoner exchanges between the Union and Confederacy, that would benefit the south. But most Booth

---

363 Ibid: "John Wilkes Booth acted out the tragic downfall of a brilliant, afflicted family"

biographers are of the opinion that he was a psychopathic, vainglorious narcissist bent on murder from the outset.[364] Something about Lincoln had got right under the actor's skin. A source of homicidal irritation that went beyond his full-throated declarations of support for the Confederacy backstage to his fellow actors.

Was there more to Booth's angst than his political views on slavery? Lincoln flirted with Booth several times and was publicly rebuffed. But for how long could the actor have held out against the express wishes of the head of state? The president was no dictator, despite Confederate claims to the contrary, but to snub his invitations repeatedly would have been unbecoming, even for the impetuous Booth. Better to give the president a little of what he wanted, keep him off guard, and treat what might transpire in the White House as an intelligence gathering exercise for the eventual killing.

Lincoln in bed with Booth seems too fantastic to imagine. Yet the president had form in that department and one 20th century psychologist was convinced that Lincoln favoured same sex relations. The president was undoubtedly bisexual if not homosexual, according to Kinsey scientist Clarence Arthur Tripp (1919–2003). Tripp's research papers are held at The New York Public Library and in relation to Lincoln's relationships with several men, including Speed and Derickson, he noted sarcastically that the only thing separating homoeroticism from outright homosexuality was an orgasm. The idea that Lincoln got under the covers with these men so often and nothing happened was absurd to Tripp as it should be to anybody today.

Tumblety infers very strongly that he got amorous with Lincoln plus the doctor enjoyed what Cavanaugh described as an "intimate" relationship with Booth - the two behaving like love struck teenagers. Could we dare to close the triangle and

---

364 Ibid: *American Brutus*

have Lincoln, Tumblety, and Booth locked, for a period no matter how short, into a clandestine homosexual love triangle? Not a ménage à trois, but Lincoln taking both men as partners.

Let us be very clear about the facts when making such an audacious statement. The homosexuality of Tumblety is simply beyond doubt. He didn't need the burgeoning science of psychoanalysis to give his urges a name. He just got on with it. As for Lincoln, the litany of bed sharing with men provoked gossip at the time and comment from biographers in the decades after his assassination.

Which leaves Booth. More than likely he and Tumblety first met in Washington DC's theatreland, which combined entertainment space, drinking hole, and pick-up joint. The doctor was so well known in the theatres of the American capital that he was being lampooned on stage. Booth was the most handsome and richest actor of his day and struck up some kind of relationship with Tumblety. So much so they met out of town and the doctor, intentionally or not, even assisted the Lincoln plot by introducing Mary Surratt to Booth and giving Herold a job. So, just how intimate was the giggling duo spotted by Captain Cavanaugh in 1863? If there was a sexual link between all these men with cross currents of love and hatred, could it have played a role in Lincoln's assassination?

Colonel Dunham perjured himself trying to paint Booth as a puppet of Jefferson Davis. His testimony fell apart. Let's assume that the Davis connection to Booth was indeed fictional - and any meaningful link to the Confederate government. That leaves us with a largely personal vendetta by Booth against Lincoln dressed up in Confederate colours. A petulant Prima Donna who despite all the fame and money made in theatres under Union control, wasn't number one in Washington's gay pecking order. That position belonged to the president.

And then there is the question of syphilis. The incurable wrecker of lives that drove men and women to insanity and blighted the prospects for their children. Lincoln's law firm partner, friend, and first biographer was sure the president was a sufferer. It's an open and shut case that Tumblety had contracted the pox as his future health regime, to be detailed, will prove. If Booth's wild promiscuity had left him free of venereal disease, it would have been almost a miracle for that time. But imagine if Lincoln had been the source of his infection. Syphilis was an agonising death sentence with no cure. The beautiful actor would experience physical disfigurement and madness, most likely ending his days in an asylum - a fate that befell Lincoln's widow for a short period. What better motive to plant a bullet in the president?

On 15 April, 1865, a man later described in the newspapers as "handsome and extremely well dressed" sauntered into Ford's Theatre in Washington DC. He exchanged greetings with the staff who knew him well. Basil Moxley, the doorkeeper at Ford's, ushered him through. The clerk selling tickets chatted to the strikingly good-looking man about President Lincoln attending that night's performance, most likely with General Ulysses S. Grant, who had by now led the Union armies to victory in the recent Civil War.

The man, of course, was Booth. Seen regularly propping up the bar, cigar in hand, surrounded by doting, intimate friends who referred to him as "pet",[365] The actor was an incorrigible sex maniac. His carnal relationships encompassed friends, fellow actors, prostitutes, and fans. But that day, murder dominated his mind, not sex.

Booth left the theatre making his way to some nearby stables hiring a saddle horse, a "high strung, fast, beautiful bay mare", that he would pick up later. Then he strolled over to the Kirkwood Hotel where he asked the front desk to send a message up to Vice President Andrew Johnson asking if he was

---

365 "Green Room Talk", *The Anaconda Standard'*, February 3, 1895

busy. It turned out he was. Booth then skulked away, irritated by the rebuttal.

Meanwhile in the White House, Lincoln was told that Grant wouldn't be accompanying him to the theatre. He sat chatting to the Speaker of the House of Representatives, Schuyler Colfax until Mrs Lincoln burst in asking testily, "Well, Mr Lincoln, are you going to the theatre with me or not?". Almost reluctantly, he rose, and the presidential party made their way to a performance of the popular farce, *Our American Cousin*.

When President Lincoln got to Ford's Theatre, they were late. The carriage was driven by their regular coachman, Francis Burns, while Charles Forbes, footman to the president, sat alongside. On arrival at the theatre, they were greeted by John F. Parker of the Washington Metropolitan Police. Parker wasn't held in high regard as a law enforcement officer:

> *Good men were hard to get in wartime, but the local police force reached a new low when it appointed Parker to the White House staff as one of the President's guards. He had been in trouble several times, and as the events of the evening were to show, he was certainly not the man to be entrusted with the life of the President of the United States.*[366]

Lincoln, victor of the Civil War and the 1864 presidential election, sat in a rocking chair to watch a very undemanding play that would permit him a couple of hours to unwind and relax. Members of the audience glanced upwards at the main attraction of the evening, ignoring the antics on stage. While Booth ascended the stairs that he knew very well up to the box with a concealed Derringer pistol. What passed for security that evening was easily circumvented with a nod of recognition and a smile.

---

366 Ibid: *The Assassination of President Lincoln and the Trial of the Conspirators*

During the third act, the crack of a pistol was heard followed by Booth leaping from the presidential box to the stage bellowing, "*Sic semper tyrannis*", then making his escape. Many of the audience, stunned at first, wondered if this was part of the performance until Mary Todd began screaming for help. As Booth scampered off, his leg badly injured, some shouted, "Hang him!".[367]

Lincoln had been shot through the head with some of his brain "oozing out". The president was immediately conveyed to a private residence where leading figures in the administration and army medics gathered around the mortally wounded head of state. In vain, the physicians tried to save his life. But early the following morning, Lincoln expired.

The rest of the plot fell apart in a grim comedy of errors. David Herold went with Lewis Powell to "Billy" Seward's house with the intention of assassinating the Secretary of State, but Powell botched the attempt, leaving Seward with some flesh wounds. Fellow plotter George Atzerodt was supposed to kill Vice President Andrew Johnson but lost his nerve and got drunk instead. Booth would be killed in a shoot-out with government forces, while Herold, Powell, Atzerodt, and Mary Surratt would swing from the gallows together on 7 July 1865.

On 6 May 1865, just three weeks after the president had been killed, Tumblety was arrested in St. Louis as a suspected member of Booth's gang of assassins. Booth was already dead at this point, but Herold wouldn't hang for another two months. The doctor must have been terrified. In the first edition of his autobiography, published a year later when he was in Cincinnati, he wrote of his feelings on hearing what Booth had done:

The news of the assassination of President Lincoln was flashed along the telegraph wires, and spread an (sic)

---

367 "Assassination of the President", *Evening Star*, April 15, 1865

universal gloom over the length and breadth of the land. I,
who had known and esteemed him for his many amiable
and social qualities, felt, I am sure, the great national loss
as keenly as any; and from an innate respect to the man,
and in sacred reverence to his memory, I attended his
obsequies at Springfield Illinois...[368]

Tumblety, therefore, was at Lincoln's funeral on 4 May 1865, just two days before his arrest. The train carrying Lincoln's body retraced the route he had taken for his inauguration back in 1861 through seven states and the cities of New York and Albany, where Tumblety and Booth had seen him respectively. Millions of Americans lined the route with the train crawling at a snail's pace and taking a fortnight to reach its destination: Springfield, Illinois.

The doctor joined the deceased Lincoln at Springfield though not without a jarringly cold-hearted grumble about how much money he was losing. An odd observation for somebody who claimed to be grief stricken. In his autobiography, Tumblety calculated that attending the funeral was going to hit him financially as his practice was earning $300 a day net of expenses, which is about $5,500 at today's value. But, he added, it was worth it as he got to meet old friends from the White House.

Almost the first person I met on my arrival at Springfield
was the steward of the late President's household, who
knew me at once, for he had frequently seen me at the
White House, and bursting into tears, he caught my hand,
exclaiming: "O, Doctor, this is a sad time for us to meet!"[369]

---

368 Ibid: *A few passages in the life of Dr. Francis Tumblety*
369 Ibid: *A few passages in the life of Dr. Francis Tumblety*

His respects paid, Tumblety returned to St. Louis. As he got back, a drama was unfolding in Brooklyn that would directly impact the doctor in a very life changing way. As mentioned earlier, Booth's errand boy had gone on the run after the assassination, fleeing Washington DC. The boy was quickly tracked down to Brooklyn, where Tumblety and Herold had only recently been working together.[370] The frightened youngster was described as "a sort of valet or errand boy" for Booth who police picked up on Court Street, opposite Montague Hall in Brooklyn. His statement to police focussed the attention of the authorities on Tumblety.

The very next day the doctor was arrested and detained initially in St. Louis by the Provost Marshal. Tumblety had only recently been taken into custody by his subordinates in the Provost Guard over his alleged military attire. This time, no influential friend would spring him from custody. An order to arrest him had come from the very top: the Secretary of War, Edwin Stanton. Tumblety was powerless to act as his office and apartment, in his own words, were "searched, ransacked, and plundered". Every portable item was whisked away along with a large amount of money.

Tumblety fumed, believing that law enforcement had lined their pockets with some of his wealth. Very likely this was true. There is evidence in the US National Archive that Tumblety spent years petitioning the government for compensation. Given the gravity of the crime for which he was imprisoned, it seems unlikely he would have chased the authorities for his money unless he genuinely believed he had been robbed by corrupt law enforcement. In truth, given his reputation, Tumblety was an easy target for police officers who, like his valets, could always get away with stealing from him by dredging up his sexuality.

---

370 "Booth's errand boy arrested", *The Pittsburgh Gazette*, May 5, 1865

After a couple of days under lock and key in St. Louis, Tumblety was transferred to the Old Capitol Prison in Washington DC, which in 1865 was a large, fifty-year-old brick building standing where the Supreme Court is today. Half a century before it housed the US Congress, relocated after the British burned down the US Capitol in 1814. During the Civil War, it became a prison for Confederate troops, spies, blockade runners, and Union army officers guilty of insubordination.[371]

What must the Indian Herb Doctor have been thinking as he sat in a prison cell knowing that the American public wanted to see the guilty swing at the end of a rope for the murder of their beloved president? Even a man as resourceful as Tumblety will have wondered if this time, no amount of money or connections would prevent his execution. His mind raced as he figured out how to explain being seen so often with David Herold on his Main Street processions and hoping that nobody had spotted him in the company of John Wilkes Booth.

Tumblety languished in the Old Capitol Prison with others accused of being involved in the Lincoln assassination including, at one point, John Wilkes Booth's brother, Junius Brutus Booth Junior.

A document from the Washington Provost Marshal's office in Washington DC to the prison governor, signed by Colonel T. Ingraham on 10 May 1865, makes it very clear in writing why Tumblety was being incarcerated at the Old Capitol Prison:

You will receive and confine in the prison under your charge, until further orders, the person of Francis Tumblety charged with complicity in assassination (sic) of the Pres. To be held for Orders of Sec. of War thru Col. Wells.[372]

---

371 Robert Brammer, "The Old Capitol Prison and the United States Supreme Court", *In Custodia Legis Law Librarians of Congress*, January 24, 2020

372 Document sourced from the US National Archive

Outside the gates of the Old Capitol Prison, in the hotel bars, salons, and corridors of power, pleading voices worked to ensure that Tumblety didn't find himself standing on the scaffold with his former valet, Herold. His networks had to work hard on his behalf. Because not only was Tumblety being implicated in the plot to assassinate President Lincoln, but also an early example of biological terrorism against military and civilian targets.

In the summer of 1864, there was a flurry of reports that a Kentucky-born physician, Dr. Luke P. Blackburn, was spearheading a plot to infect northern cities and the Union army with yellow fever. Infected clothes and rags were to be circulated among target populations. Somehow, it came to be believed that Blackburn and Tumblety were in fact the same person. How this confusion arose is anybody's guess. In his autobiography, Tumblety emphasised the yellow fever plot charges over the assassination related allegations to distract from his association with Booth and Herold. Also, the yellow fever plot charge really was entirely without foundation.

In the 1860s, it wasn't yet realised that yellow fever is transmitted by mosquitoes. That revelation would come from research conducted in Cuba during the Spanish-American war forty years later. In the months after Lincoln's murder, the assassination plot and the Yellow Fever Plot became curiously intertwined in the climate of paranoia that gripped the nation.

At the 1865 trial of Herold, Surratt, Powell, and other plotters, the yellow fever angle was explored as an earlier unsuccessful attempt to kill Lincoln. Instead of putting a bullet in his head, the plan was to sneak yellow fever into the White House and bring Lincoln down by exposing him to the deadly disease. But how had Dr. Blackburn and his yellow fever plotters hoped to achieve this?

An English prosecution witness, Godfrey Joseph Hyams, told the trial that in December 1863, he had met Blackburn at the Queen's Hotel in Toronto and was aware of his Confederate leanings. Blackburn took Hyams upstairs and pledged his friendship as a Freemason, extending his hand. He then promised Hyams a fortune of at least $100,000 if he would "take a certain quantity of shirts, coats, and underclothing into the States and dispose of them by auction".[373] Hyams was to choose markets frequented by Union troops.

If successful with his operation, Blackburn gushed, Hyams might make "ten times $100,000".[374] The Englishman picked up the deadly cargo with Spanish language markings which Blackburn had shipped from Bermuda, where yellow fever was rampant. Some of the rags had also been infected with smallpox and other contagious diseases, just for good measure. There was also a briefcase, a "valise", with items similarly infected to be sent directly to President Lincoln. Hyams refused to be associated with that part of the plot but believed it was sent to the White House later.

Blackburn asked whether Hyams had ever contracted yellow fever. The answer was no. Blackburn advised him to chew camphor and "get some strong cigars, the strongest you can get, and be sure to keep gloves on when handling the things".[375] Blackburn then gave Hyams some cigars he claimed were bought in Havana. Hyams went to Hamilton, Ontario while Blackburn travelled to Montreal. As the poisonous materials began to be circulated, Hyams asked for some of the promised money, but Blackburn disappeared off back to Bermuda.

After a great deal of nagging, Hyams got a measly fifty dollars to tide him over. He did eventually manage to catch up with

---

373 Ibid: *The Assassination of President Lincoln and the Trial of the Conspirators*

374 Ibid: *The Assassination of President Lincoln and the Trial of the Conspirators*

375 Ibid: *The Assassination of President Lincoln and the Trial of the Conspirators*

Blackburn in person and demanded the hundreds of thousands of dollars the Confederacy had promised to reward him - but he was met with a wall of obfuscation. Other witnesses confirmed the clothing, which looked new, was indeed sold but the hoped-for mass infection failed to materialise for reasons we now understand.

Hyams betrayed the plot to the United States two days before Booth shot Lincoln. He then appeared as a witness in the Lincoln trial but Blackburn, arrested in Canada, managed to avoid extradition due to insufficient evidence. For years, he laid low operating as a bona fide doctor before entering the political fray back in the United States and, incredibly, being elected Governor of Kentucky in 1879. By which stage, it was long realised that there was no connection whatsoever between Governor Blackburn and Doctor Tumblety.

After three weeks in the Old Capitol Prison, Tumblety was released. He stepped out into the open air, a dishevelled figure, furious at his treatment but also painfully aware that he now had a major public relations problem. His reputation was in tatters. Not only had he been accused of complicity in the killing of a beloved president (on the Union side), but he'd also been drawn into a plot to spread disease. Hardly a good association for a medical man boasting of his unparalleled ability to cure people.

The case of mistaken identity between himself and Dr. Blackburn was a stick with which to beat the establishment and especially Lincoln's Secretary of War, Edwin Stanton. Tumblety created a fog of bluster and righteous indignation focussing attention away from the Lincoln murder and on to the failed act of biological terrorism.

In a letter dated 9 June 1865, published in *The Washington Star*, and republished in his 1866 autobiography, he made hay over the Blackburn confusion:

...I have been unconditionally and honorably released from confinement by the directions of the Secretary of

War, there being no evidence whatsoever to connect me
with the yellow-fever or assassination plot, with which
some of the Northern journals have charged me of having
some knowledge. My arrest appears to have grown out
of a statement made in a low, licentious sheet, published
in New York, to the effect that Dr. Blackburn, who has
figured to unenviously in the hellish yellow-fever plot, was
no other person than myself.[376]

He didn't know this "fiend in human form" and had never
met him in his life. With a characteristic Tumblety flourish,
he added that hundreds of distinguished people in American
life could be brought forward to vouch for the veracity of his
statement as well as certificates from "innumerable numbers of
gentlemen in high official positions".[377]

One reason Tumblety may have been confused for the future
Governor Blackburn was the continued involvement of his
friend and valet Mark Blackburn in his business. Whatever the
reason, the doctor made maximum capital out of this cock up by
the authorities. However, he was eventually forced to comment
on the alleged links to the Lincoln plotters - especially David
Herold. Tumblety realised he had to nip that story in the bud:

While in imprisonment (sic), I noticed in some of the New
York and other Northern papers, a paragraph setting forth
that the villain Herold, who now stands charged with
being one of the conspirators in the atrocious assassination
plot, was at one time in my employment. This, too, is
false in every particular, and I am at a loss to see how it
originated, or to trace it to its origin.[378]

---

376 Ibid: *A few passages in the life of Dr. Francis Tumblety*
377 Ibid: *A few passages in the life of Dr. Francis Tumblety*
378 Ibid: *A few passages in the life of Dr. Francis Tumblety*

He then asserted that for the five past years, there had only been one man in his employment: the dutiful Mark Blackburn. But we know this isn't true. In 1861, for example, Tumblety was in court in New York fighting a fraudulent valet, Charles Whelpley. This valet had access to Tumblety's bank accounts and allegedly forged cheques using his employer's signature. Other valets had followed with similar consequences.

A disclaimer from the editor placed under Tumblety's letter stated that Herold had been identified beyond any doubt as Tumblety's valet in Brooklyn though sometimes gave his name as Farrell. Then a remarkable revelation that Herold sometimes adopted the name – Blackburn. Following his release from prison, the newspapers publicly accepted the doctor's innocence with regards to the Lincoln plot but weren't going to back down on the fact that Herold worked for Tumblety.

In the same letter, Tumblety responded to claims that were circulating in the aftermath of the assassination that the doctor knew Booth in some capacity:

Another paper has gone so far as to inform the public that I was an intimate acquaintance of Booth, but this too is news to me, as I never spoke to him in my life, or any of his family.[379]

Fifty years before Cavanaugh talks about Tumblety having an "intimate" relationship with Booth, the doctor himself references a contemporary article in the 1860s making exactly the same accusation. Not only were journalists in 1865 aware that the doctor had employed Herod as a pharmacy assistant, but they knew he was a good friend of John Wilkes Booth. Or, as Tumblety put it in his rebuttal, "an intimate acquaintance".

---

379 Ibid: *A few passages in the life of Dr. Francis Tumblety*

There is a bizarre postscript to Tumblety's period of imprisonment following Lincoln's murder. A man of genteel manners from Louisville, Kentucky approached the Indian Herb Doctor claiming that while Tumblety had been in prison, he had assumed his identity and made a staggering sum of money from patent medicines. For once, the flamboyant medical entrepreneur was lost for words. The sheer impudence of this self-confessed fraudster left him flabbergasted.

He might have assaulted this individual in the same manner as Fenton Scully the asthmatic, but Tumblety wrote that after his time in the "Washington Bastille", as he now called the Old Capitol Prison, his "robust physique" was no more. Three weeks inside had destroyed his hardy constitution. He was simply not up for a physical altercation.

At first the visitor complimented the Indian Herb Doctor then condemned Edwin Stanton, but Tumblety barked at him to get to the point. He was in no mood for small talk. "All in good time", came the reply. Then the confidence trickster detailed what he had done:

> You see, that hearing, as I have remarked, of your arrest, and knowing the great reputation you have acquired as the Indian Herb Doctor, I thought it a pity that such first-rate capital should be lost to the world; and moreover, being under the impression that, in consequence of your having got into Stanton's clutches... I determined to step into your shoes, which I did, and as you will fully concede, to pretty good purpose.[380]

Tumblety asked him flat out: have you been impersonating me? "Keep cool," he replied. Believing that Tumblety was doomed after being charged with such devastating crimes, this fraudster

---

380 Ibid: *A few passages in the life of Dr. Francis Tumblety*

went to Louisville, where Tumblety had never set up shop, and pretended to be him. He played the role with such conviction that very soon he was unable to service the large number of clients.

> *I believe that I have about played myself out; however, I made hay while the sun shone, and here is the result.*[381]

He brought out a pocketbook and took out a bank draft for $8,000, about $146,000 in today's value. Tumblety was shocked: "I was dumb with astonishment at the cool impudence of the fellow, and indignation at the trick he had played upon the public in my name". The man now asked whether he could be taken under the doctor's wing as an apprentice if he handed over the $8,000.

But the doctor didn't need his money, nor his contrition. Just his departure:

> *...I regarded him as the most unblushing impostor that had thus far ever crossed my path, I pointed to the door, a gesture which he at one comprehended. Nevertheless, he walked toward it with the most provoking composure, bowed with admirable sang-froid, and disappeared, since which I have never seen his face.*[382]

It was almost as if Tumblety had met his own reflection.

381 Ibid: *A few passages in the life of Dr. Francis Tumblety*
382 Ibid: 'A few passages in the life of Dr. Francis Tumblety'

Seven

Tumblety after Booth and Lincoln

The Indian Herb Doctor was in and out of New York most of his life. As the biggest city in North America, it presented a vast market for patent medicines. It was also a honeypot for men seeking other men. The now-wealthy boy from the Rochester ghetto was free to indulge his lusts and passions provided he could avoid the long arm of the law. For poorer LGBT men, life in New York could be perilous.

Some sank into prostitution, as the American social reformer and clergyman Charles Henry Parkhurst (1842–1933) discovered. He was once shown around the Golden Rule Pleasure Club on West 3rd Street by a police detective. The basement was divided into cubicles. In each, sat a young man or boy wearing make-up and "affecting the airs of a young girl, a high falsetto voice, and a girl's name". The guide explained to the Reverend Parkhurst what they did for money whereupon the shocked reformer "fled in horror".[383]

On the streets, young men were cruised by older gentlemen. The sight of rent boys being picked up by gentlemen clients was

383 Milton Rugoff, Prudery and Passion (G.P. Putnam's Sons, 1971)

familiar to anybody living and working in the downtown area of the city, regardless of their own sexuality. From the 1840s, it became a talking point in weekly newspapers aimed at sporting chaps. Reports brimmed with simultaneous disgust and fascination:

> THE SODOMITES – *We hope that in presenting to our readers a sketch of some of the inhuman enormities that a set of fiends bearing the form of men are nightly in the habit of disgusting nature with their monstrous and wicked acts; our excuse must be, that we have undertaken to rout from our city these monsters... We know them all by sight, and most of them by name. They are nearly all young men of rather genteel address, and of feminine appearance and manners; among this herd of beasts is one or two old and lecherous villains whom we know well...*[384]

One witness to the Tumblety way with men was Clement R. Bennett, the "well-known" stenographer of the Circuit Court in New York. His speedy shorthand was the talk of the town. This may seem an incongruous route to celebrity, but Bennett was hailed as "one of the fastest writers and readers of shorthand in the country",[385] commanding fees for court work that ran to tens of thousands of dollars at today's value.[386]

Bennett first met Tumblety in 1870 at the Jerome Park races, five years after the killing of Lincoln. The Indian Herb Doctor was accompanied by a "flashily dressed man", who was clearly a recent conquest. The doctor stopped Bennett in the street and began quizzing him about the wealthier residents in the district, clearly prospecting for business. Tumblety pointed to the "magnificent summer houses of the

---

384 "Sodomites", Whip 1, no. 6, reprinted in *Horowitz*, Attitudes towards Sex in Antebellum America 137-8

385 "Shorthand Study", *San Francisco Chronicle*, April 6, 1890

386 "Maslin's Report", *San Francisco Chronicle*, February 19, 1891

metropolitan capitalists" and gestured with "a jockey riding whip, the head of which appeared resplendent with jewels". He wanted to know who lived in each house.

The dash and hauteur of the man made such an impression upon me that afternoon... that I have never forgotten him.[387]

In 1874, Tumblety was staying at the Northern Hotel on Cortlandt Street where he had an opulent suite of rooms "the floors of which were covered with well-worn leather trunks, valises and bags". Bennett was still in Tumblety's social circle and saw for himself the male harem assembled by the doctor:

He cordially invited any young man whom he fancied, wherever he met them, in the parks, squares or stores, to call upon him at this hotel, where he was wont to say he would them 'an easy road to fortune'. By his suavity he was successful beyond comprehension in enlisting and securing the attendance, at certain hours of the day and evening, of good-looking young men and boys, greenhorns to 'walk into my parlour'.[388]

How or why the stenographer came to be in Tumblety's suite isn't explained. But he was clearly impressed by the doctor's ability to attract the male talent. There is also evidence of Tumblety's undoubted wealth and the way he 'flashed the cash', to coin a modern phrase, to dazzle his young charges.

On yet another occasion, Tumblety showed off his medals to Bennett given to him allegedly by the British and a collection of written testimonies from "English noblemen". Bennett was convinced of their authenticity. "The papers were apparently

---

387 "Dr. Tumblety", *San Francisco Chronicle*, November 20, 1888
388 Ibid: "Dr. Tumblety"

official and genuine, as they bore the coats of arms, the crown, etc of the donors, the peculiar aristocratic chirography in signature, etc."[389]

On the streets of New York, Tumblety cut an imposing figure at over six feet in height; weighing 180 pounds; clean-shaven red cheeks; and a thick, black, curly moustache. Bennett marvelled at his many costume changes, including a double-breasted, buttoned-up pea-jacket, light pantaloons, flashy necktie, cloth gaiters on his English box-toe shoes, a military or university cap with a gold cord, and some "loud jewelry".

Sadly, by 1879 when Bennett last saw Tumblety, things had changed dramatically with the Indian Herb Doctor looking "shabby, careworn, lame, appeared to be living a dissolute and dissipated life, and was begging for a night's lodging".[390] The glory years of Washington DC in the 1860s seemingly far behind him. But in just under ten years, he would be back in the global headlines.

In 1866, a year after Lincoln's murder, Tumblety had relocated to Cincinnati, where he published the first edition of his autobiography taking aim in print at those who had him imprisoned after the assassination with most of the venom aimed at Lincoln's Secretary of War, Edwin Stanton. The doctor liked to get his side of the story in print and distributed as widely as possible. Only in the past, he had used the letters pages and classified advertisement columns of the newspapers but now he issued an autobiography. Events demanded something more substantial. This would go through several editions over the years including one attempting to rebut the allegation that he was Jack the Ripper.

The 1866 first edition of the autobiography set out to prove that he and Lincoln had been incredibly close, and that the

---

389 Ibid: "Dr. Tumblety"
390 Ibid: "Dr. Tumblety"

late president had shown him nothing but tender kindness. So why had he been imprisoned? Tumblety presented the incident as an inexplicable personal vendetta against him by Lincoln's Secretary of War, Edwin Stanton.

The doctor's salvo was well timed as there was growing criticism of the draconian measures that had been enacted by Stanton and other radical Republicans after Lincoln's death. Stanton was among those who wanted to punish the southern states and crush any lingering dreams of rebellion. But a growing constituency of public opinion felt that many arrests were "arbitrary", going far beyond protecting the internal security of the Union.

Despite the barbs from his opponents, Stanton retained his position as secretary of war under Lincoln's successor, President Andrew Johnson, but disliked what he perceived as his boss's soft treatment of the South. The president and the secretary of war became bitter enemies, with Stanton supporting an unsuccessful attempt to impeach Johnson in 1868. Maybe Tumblety hoped that by taking potshots at Stanton in his autobiography, he might redeem himself with the White House. But in truth, Washington high society had moved on from the Indian Herb Doctor.

While in Cincinnati, Tumblety followed his usual tactic of basing himself at the most prestigious hotel: Burnet House, described as "the finest hotel in the world", by the London Illustrated News.[391] This impressive hulk was erected in 1850, five storeys of mid-century grandeur topped off with an impressive dome, forty-two feet in diameter. The well-heeled guests and visitors enjoyed splendid views of the surrounding landscape, helped by the hotel being located on top of an ancient Indian burial mound.[392]

391 "Burnet House Menu", *cityclubapartments.com*

392 Jeff Seuss, "Our history: Spirit of history alive at Burnet House site", Suess, Jeff, *Cincinnati Enquirer* (online edition)

Abraham Lincoln had been a guest twice, the second time on the way to his inauguration. On 20 March 1864, General Ulysses S. Grant (1822-1885) and William Tecumseh Sherman (1820-1891) met on the second floor, maps spread out before them, to hammer out a plan to end the American Civil War. And in Tumblety's final years, one notable guest at Burnet House was the gay poet and author, Oscar Wilde (1854-1900), during his year-long tour of Canada and the United States in 1882. Over those months, Wilde delivered an impressive 141 lectures and although Tumblety never mentions Wilde by name, it would certainly be out of character if the Indian Herb Doctor had not attended at least one of these highly publicised events and what an intriguing thought that he buttonholed him.

Tumblety's "parading through the Burnet House" wasn't appreciated by all the staff.[393] A reception clerk said the doctor had signed himself in as 'Twomblety' and nobody knew anything about him, other than he didn't have a room at the hotel and had no reason to be there. They were all aware however, that his strange figure was "a kind of patent medicine man… who sold some off-colour medicine".[394]

Not long after arriving in Cincinnati, Tumblety fell gravely ill with typhoid fever and was admitted to St John's Hospital on 3rd and Plum Streets, an institution managed by the Sisters of Charity. He was attended to by Dr Minor and Dr Haile, the latter commenting years later that Tumblety's condition had been "feeble", so he stayed until the epidemic abated in the city. Haile was impressed by the patient's "fierce black mustache" and "erect, stately walk".

He had diamonds as big as Alvin Joslyn's and used to be

393 "Is he the fiend?", *The Buffalo News*, December 1, 1888
394 Ibid: "Is he the fiend?"

followed around by an immense Newfoundland dog.[395]

Alvin Joslyn was a fictional theatrical character played by actor Charles Davis, who made a fortune on the stage and invested it in huge diamonds, which he wore very ostentatiously. While the doctors marvelled at Tumblety's jewels, he gave up all hope with Cincinnati as an outbreak of cholera ensued. Haile remembered the Indian Herb Doctor announcing loudly that he would be leaving this "accursed city".

Dr Minor added that Tumblety was the "first man who ever brought English coach dogs to the city" and that "he fairly coined money". His Midas touch clearly hadn't departed him. Though, in a moment of candour, Tumblety confessed that "all his pills, powders, and tonics were made of tanbark".[396] This magic ingredient, tanbark, was the bark of trees used in the leather tanning industry. The fact that this unpromising ingredient was recognised as both a medicine and foodstuff by some native American tribes lent a tiny amount of credence to Tumblety's sales patter that his medical knowledge came from tribal herbalists steeped in ancient wisdom.[397]

Flouncing off after his attack of typhoid and narrow escape from cholera, Tumblety went to Pittsburgh, where he got involved in the coal business. Just as California had its gold rush, Pittsburgh was a magnet for fortune seekers after 1860 with its seams of black gold. America's iron and steel industry was hungry for coke, a fuel derived from coal, and the Pittsburgh mines increased production dramatically.

How the doctor tapped into this boom and why is a mystery. Maybe he was growing disenchanted with medicine and thought coal could be a new route to riches. Not long

---

395 "Dr Tumblety's Career", *The Cincinnati Enquirer*, December 5, 1888
396 "Dr Tumblety", *The Buffalo Sunday Morning News*, December 16, 1888
397 "Herb: Tanbark Oak", *naturalmedicinalherbs.net*

after disappearing off to Pittsburgh, Tumblety returned to Cincinnati with several barges of coal. He was no stranger to the transporting of cargo by water, having observed this activity while selling smut on the Erie canal packets. Inexplicably, Tumblety decided to sink the barges shortly after arrival. During this operation, he fell off one of the barges into the water and ended up at St John's Hospital again, only this time with pneumonia.

Tumblety was in and out of Cincinnati over the years and interestingly, there is a small announcement in *The Cincinnati Enquirer* on 14 February 1872, noting that Deputy Marshall Butts had arrested a man "as a suspicious character" and ended up taking him before Mayor Simon Stevens "S.S" Davis (1817–1896).[398] When the Mayor found himself looking over at Tumblety, he immediately ordered his release.

This story has those familiar elements that recur in Tumblety's life. Being arrested as a suspicious character in his case was a euphemism for cruising men in public places. Being hauled before the mayor was probably at his own request because the city's top political figure was very likely in one of the doctor's protective networks and the tactic worked.

Mayor S.S. Davis may have got to know Tumblety as a client or the doctor had contributed at some point to his political campaign fundraising. Possibly the two met through the politician's Civil War era charity work for hard-up soldiers through organisations like the Home of the Friendless and Foundlings and the Relief Union.

While speculating in coal in Pittsburgh, a poem about Tumblety was published in the local newspapers, almost certainly penned by himself. It's reminiscent of the dire verses of the Victorian poet William McGonagall (1825–1902), mocked in his lifetime and ever since. It gives an insight into

---

398 "Covington", *The Cincinnati Enquirer*, February 14, 1872

the mind of the doctor who "knew their disease without telling; whether by seeing or only by smelling".

Ode to the Indian Herb Doctor went as follows:

Cures he has wrought of each disease,
With healing herbs and barks of trees;
Simples culled from mountain and glen,
Plucked from the moor or dragged from the fen;
The mandrake, elm, and bitter bog bean –
Sarsaparilla and horehound, I ween –
Butternut, colt's foot, and Irish moss,
The bark of the willow and garlic sauce –
With these the Doctor's wondering skill,
Each killing disease was sure to kill,
Gouts, consumption and shivering ague,
Deathly diseases – complaints that plague you;
All things nasty, for which physic's given,
Out of you soon by these herbs will be driven;
See certificates – given galore –
Citizens all, at least three-score,
Blind and lame, who walk and see,
Given up by the doctors, twenty-three,
All grown sound and healthy by taking
Medical potions of Tumblety's making.[399]

Tumblety's fortunes seem to have see-sawed during the years after the Civil War. At times, he appeared to be as fantastically wealthy as ever, but on other occasions, he was clearly on the verge of destitution. For example, in 1869 a distressed Tumblety placed a small advertisement in the *New York Daily Herald* announcing that a savings bank book issued by the Provident Institution for

---

399 "Ode to the Indian Herb Doctor", *The Pittsburgh Daily Commercial*, August 8, 1867

Savings had been stolen on 8 February.[400]

This Jersey City-based bank primarily serviced the needs of "humble workers" and immigrants.[401] Not exactly the kind of blue-chip financial institution one might associate with the flamboyant and ostentatious doctor. The robbery occurred in his hotel room on Cortlandt Street in lower Manhattan, still a reasonably prestigious location.

Eighteen months after this advertisement was placed, Francis Tumblety was being given another four months stay at a workhouse in Pittsburgh at his own request. This was a way of obtaining free board and lodging through the cold winter months at the public expense.[402] Either Tumblety had become exceedingly thrifty, with no regard to his public reputation – as this was announced in the newspapers – or, more likely, he had fallen on hard times.

Given his endless capacity for making money, why would he suddenly be on his uppers? One possible explanation is the doctor's own health. As would become clear, it's very likely that Tumblety had contracted syphilis. With the limited treatments and therapies then available, he would have experienced periods of respite in between episodes of physical and mental decline, and even incapacity.

Fears over his longer-term health might explain why Tumblety shuttled increasingly between the United States and Europe, evidencing a new wanderlust and maybe a sense of his own mortality. Ship passenger lists show him crossing the Atlantic repeatedly. For example, on 22 December 1869, he was aboard the steamship *Champion* making his way from New York to Liverpool. That port city in the north-west of England

---

400 "Savings Bank Book Stolen", *New York Daily Herald*, May 8, 1869

401 "Provident Bank. Jersey City Past and Present", *New Jersey City University*, 2021

402 "At his own request", *The Pittsburgh Daily Commercial*, December 16, 1870

was both an exit point for immigrants from all over Europe leaving for a new life in America and for those coming in the opposite direction to live and work in Britain.

Like many people of Irish descent, Tumblety had family who had emigrated to Liverpool during the famine, settling in the Scotland Road dockside area of the city. The doctor rarely mentioned his extended Irish family, but one assumes some level of contact was maintained, especially as several relatives would be beneficiaries in his will decades later. These relatives could be found in Liverpool, Ireland, Rochester, and near San Francisco.

We do get one rare glimpse of a brother and sister living in California in 1870. The brother lived at Alameda in the San Francisco Bay Area and was referred to locally as "Crank" Tumblety. Like Francis, he was unmarried and shared "his brother's aversion to women".[403] By some mysterious means, he made a small fortune, sharing his brother's capacity for money making. One newspaper referred to Crank as "a modified counterpart of the doctor".[404]

While in San Francisco, the herb doctor's finances went through another inexplicable rough patch, so he set up once more in the "pimple curing" business amassing a considerable sum in a short period of time and leaving about $900 on deposit at the Hibernia Bank, after which he once more upped sticks for another city. That's about $20,000 at today's value.

During the years between the Lincoln assassination arrest and the Ripper murders, Tumblety was sighted in both American and European cities. Colonel James L. Sothern was a Chicago lawyer who witnessed the Indian Herb Doctor processing through the streets of London - a vision of camp flamboyance at the very heart of the British Empire:

---

403 "Is he Jack the Ripper?", *The San Francisco Examiner*, December 16, 1888
404 Ibid: "Is he Jack the Ripper?"

I have met that fellow all over America and Europe. The first time I saw him was in London. It was along about 1870, I believe, and he was dressed up in the most startling fashion. I never saw anything quite equal to it. He had an enormous shako (tall cylindrical military cap with a metal plate on the front and a plume) *on his head, an overcoat, the front of which was covered in decorations; earrings in his ears.*[405]

Tumblety was accompanied by a black companion, "fantastically got up in a particolored dress that appeared to be a blending of the flags of all nations". A large, bemused crowd of Londoners trailed behind gawping at this spectacle in their midst. Incredible to think that eighteen years later he would be in London again but this time keeping a much lower profile and accused of one of the worst crimes of the 19th century.

Billy Pinkerton ran into Tumblety in England in 1874. These were "accidental" encounters, he claimed, that took place in Liverpool and London. Pinkerton's other criminal detective work did indeed require him to visit Europe. For example, in 1873 he followed a gang that had robbed the Third National Bank in Baltimore over to London where they absconded with their ill-gotten gains.

On that occasion, he happened to bump into two notorious American forgers – Austin Byron Bidwell and George McDonnell – in a fashionable tailor shop. He immediately directed London police to tail them as they would be planning some criminal endeavour in the British capital. So, it's entirely possible that Pinkerton's eagle eyes chanced upon Tumblety in London while working on a completely different case. But these chance sightings of the Indian Herb Doctor were a suspiciously regular occurrence and journalists still seeking the latest on

---

405 Ibid: "Is he the fiend?"

Tumblety knew that Pinkerton would always have some juicy morsels of information to share.

While in London, Tumblety filed a police complaint that followed the by now predictable pattern. The doctor had employed yet another young man who took his fancy. As ever, he expected total compliance from his new charge. Instead, Tumblety was robbed and left out of pocket. Then, unwisely, he sought redress from the authorities, at which point the accused played the only card he could, implicating the older man as a pederast and sodomite.

Pinkterton recounted that the watch was an impressive piece of bling. A very showy item attached to a thick gold chain that Tumblety wore wrapped twice around his neck. Tumblety had "picked up" the boy in Liverpool and taken him to London as his valet. At some point, he made off with the watch. The police treated the crime as a run-of-the-mill robbery, recovering the item from a pawnbroker and arresting the thief.

In custody, the boy confessed to his crime but then made a statement to the police which caused a warrant to be issued for the doctor's arrest. Tumblety had told the London police he was an American citizen. So, a certain Superintendent Shaw turned to Pinkerton for more information about his fellow countryman:

I told him that the boy had undoubtedly told the truth, as the vile character the boy gave of the Doctor was just the character that he had a reputation for in the United States.[406]

Unsurprisingly, Tumblety didn't appear at the police station to take back his very expensive watch and big gold chain. Instead, Pinkerton discovered the doctor had fled to Paris, sensing the

---

406 Ibid: "Is he the Butcher?"

legal net was closing in on him. Years later, when accused by Scotland Yard of being Jack the Ripper, Tumblety would jump bail and make for France again. Crossing any border to evade the long arm of the law was a well-worn tactic of the Indian Herb Doctor.

Tumblety spent an increasing amount of time in the United Kingdom but without neglecting his American business. Various valets of differing quality and trustworthiness were left to run his affairs in the United States while he set up shop across the Atlantic. Tumblety was able, so he claimed, "to move in the highest circles" in England by brandishing a letter of introduction from the late President Lincoln.[407] On the assumption, of course, that his arrest in 1865 as an accomplice of Booth had been forgotten by most people.

In the mid-1870s, Tumblety set up an office in Liverpool, England, beginning a homosexual relationship with a local twenty-one-year-old writer, Thomas Henry Hall Caine (1853–1931). Hall Caine, as he was known, was on the verge of becoming the Victorian world's top-selling author realising millions of sales for his novels that touched on the raciest themes of the day including infanticide and illegitimacy.

He even managed to incur the wrath of England's growing Muslim community, as well as the Ottoman sultan who was Islam's global caliph at this time, with an ill-judged play. This was a four-act historical drama about the life of the Prophet of Islam, titled *Mahomet*, which included input from the *Dracula* author, Bram Stoker (1847–1912) and the famous actor he managed, Henry Irving (1838–1905). It was banned in the British Empire by the Lord Chamberlain who was the official theatre censor. Britain had no wish to create a diplomatic incident over a theatre production.

Hall Caine's father was a blacksmith from the Isle of Man,

---

407 "Personal", *The Pittsburgh Daily Commercial*, April 17, 1872

while his mother was a seamstress from Cumberland. Nothing in his background pointed to wealth and fame, but these were the things Hall Caine craved. Tumblety more than likely seduced Hall Caine with his larger-than-life tales of being on intimate terms with President Lincoln and then thrown into jail by that brute Edwin Stanton on trumped up charges. How could the aspiring novelist not be impressed by that torrid tale?

The Indian Herb Doctor took the slightly built Liverpudlian under his wing and nurtured his burning ambition. Hall Caine shared his despairing view of Liverpool as a place where "manners lack something of the delicacy, cordiality, and geniality which not even the robustest Johnsonian temperament can afford to dispense with".[408]

Tumblety put Hall Caine's florid writing skills to use updating his autobiography. By 1875, the doctor was shuttling regularly between Liverpool and London and the two wrote to each other with updates on progress. Some of that correspondence has survived. In one very unusual letter, Tumblety wrote to Hall Caine: "You have proved yourself feminine and I feel under a great obligation and hope some time to be able to make some recompense".[409] Quite what the doctor meant exactly is unclear.

Hall Caine suffered from an anxiety disorder and the Indian Herb Doctor attempted to treat him.[410] This created a degree of dependency on the part of the writer towards the doctor for most of their relationship, with Tumblety very much the dominant partner. Business drew the doctor increasingly to London with its wealthier clientele, but he was also forced to return periodically to the United States to deal with financial issues and rogue valets who had been left in charge during his absence.

---

408 "Mr T. H. Hall Caine on Intellectual Life", *The Liverpool Daily Post*, May 19, 1879

409 Vivien Allen, *Hall Caine. Portrait of a Victorian Romancer* (Sheffield Academic Press, 1997)

410 Hall Caine, *My Story* (William Heinemann, 1908)

This put a strain on his relationship with the novelist. In his letters, the doctor tried to get Hall Caine to relocate to London by describing the sights and attractions. On 29 March 1875, he was singing the praises of the Crystal Palace, Sanger's Circus, and the funfair at Cremorne Gardens.[411] Then he proposed that the two go into the patent medicines business together, as there were huge commercial opportunities in England that it would be foolish to ignore. But talk of sharing the risk and cost must have set alarm bells ringing in Caine Hall's mind.

Tumblety then changed tack urging Caine Hall to leave Britain altogether and journey with him to the United States. "Your genius and talent will be appreciated in America", he wrote from London to Hall Caine, still in Liverpool and refusing to leave that city. Tumblety pleaded that he could facilitate introductions to "newspaper people" and "literary gentlemen" in the United States, furthering Hall Caine's career.[412] The doctor could undoubtedly have done this though equally, he may have reduced Hall Caine to yet another in a long line of valets trailing behind his circus horse in a silly costume.

Tumblety became frantic with a blizzard of letters and telegrams deluging Hall Caine in Liverpool, but nobody likes a needy lover. The ties between the two men began to loosen at the writer's instigation. His confidence was growing and his rise to national prominence as an author, who would soon be outselling Charles Dickens, was underway. However, in one notable incident, Tumblety's brother-in-law in Liverpool – a man named Brady, married to the doctor's sister, Bridget – got in touch with Hall Caine to say he had been down to London and Tumblety hadn't been seen at his lodgings for fifteen days.

This tells us two things - that the doctor had a sibling in Liverpool and that he was enlisting his family to save his flagging

---

411 Ibid: *Hall Caine. Portrait of a Victorian Romancer*
412 Ibid: *Hall Caine. Portrait of a Victorian Romancer*

homosexual relationship. It also reveals Tumblety's ability to disappear off the radar for periods with nobody – family, valets, or lovers – knowing where he was. As often happens at this stage of a dying relationship, misery turned to anger. Tumblety re-emerged on 14 May and fired off a furious missive from the Midland Hotel in Birmingham on 4 August, demanding money from Hall Caine. This evidenced the very ugly side of the doctor's character:

Dear Caine, Don't trifle with my patience any longer. Send me two pounds to the above address no more nor no less a paltry amount than two pounds and our friendly correspondence shall go on, independent of the little financial matters. Nobody else knows anything about it, there is no fraud being committed on you as I am not in the habit of telling people my private affairs. I got your letter this morning and felt a little surprised at finding an excuse in it instead of two pounds. I am stopping here for 3 or 4 days don't fail to send a p.o. (by which Tumblety meant postal order).[413]

Incredibly, Hall Caine sent the money. However, this left a bad taste in the writer's mouth. He felt used. Given the enormous wealth Tumblety was rumoured to have in various banks and his extravagant lifestyle, with constant travelling from one continent to another, it's hard to understand why he needed to press Hall Caine for a mere two pounds.

By the end of August 1875, Tumblety was sailing back to New York, urging his one-time boyfriend to join him. Then he wrote from New York a couple of times and from San Francisco. "It gives me infinite pleasure to hear from you and I should dearly love to see your sweet face and spend an entire night in your

---

413 Ibid: *Hall Caine. Portrait of a Victorian Romancer*

company." On 31 March 1876, he wrote a letter from St. Louis that included a cutting from an English newspaper indicating that Tumblety was in an American prison for some offence.

Fed up at being pestered, Hall Caine transferred his affections to Dante Gabriel Rosetti (1828–1882), the great artist and founder of the Pre-Raphaelite movement, who was twenty-five years his senior and in failing health. He also formed a closer friendship with Bram Stoker, who dedicated his novel *Dracula* to Hall Caine.[414]

The real-life author of *Dracula* has long been believed to be gay but deeply repressed and agonised on the subject. As with so many Victorians, Stoker's mental state was compromised by a childhood scarred by disease, including a period of paralysis. His homosexuality was given some limited outlet in his correspondence with the American poet Walt Whitman, friendship with Oscar Wilde, and "slavish adoration" of the actor Sir Henry Irving - often seen as a model for the Dracula character.[415]

In a letter from Stoker to Hall Caine dated 23 February 1897, he explained that the dedication at the beginning of the forthcoming Dracula novel would read: To my dear friend Hommy-Beg. This was a nickname for Hall Caine used between the two of them. Stoker concluded: "If the book is ever worth remembering it will be well understood what is meant".[416]

In 2008, the New York Times bestselling American author James Reese imagined an encounter between Bram Stoker and Tumblety in his book, *The Dracula Dossier*.[417] The premise of

414 Bram Stoker, *Dracula* (Archibald Constable and Company, 1897, London)

415 David J. Skal, *Something in the Blood: The Untold Story of Bram Stoker* (Liveright, 2016)

416 "Letter from Bram Stoker to Hall Caine", *Manx National Heritage Library*, February 23, 1897

417 James Reese, *The Dracula Dossier: A Novel of Suspense* (William Morrow, 2008, New York)

his thriller is that as Jack the Ripper terrorises London's East End, Stoker has figured out his real identity. This is after his dear friend, Thomas Hall Caine, introduces him to Tumblety, just as Stoker accidentally cuts himself with an exotic knife. The *Dracula* novelist takes an instant dislike to the Indian Herb Doctor, but nevertheless they are both initiated into an occult society, the Order of the Golden Dawn.

Realising Tumblety is the Whitechapel serial killer, Stoker is unable to tell the police because the doctor has an incriminating stash of correspondence proving his illicit homosexual affair with Hall Caine that would ruin him – as it did Oscar Wilde, who also features in the novel.[418]

In real life, the paths of Tumblety and Hall Caine diverged dramatically in the years that followed their affair in Liverpool. Hall Caine was made a Knight of the British Empire in 1918 for his patriotic writing during the First World War and a Companion of Honour in 1922. He became a pillar of society. Tumblety, in contrast, would gain global notoriety as a suspect in the Jack the Ripper murders.

While in Liverpool courting Hall Caine, Tumblety got himself implicated in a second case of manslaughter in January 1875. This was fifteen years since his previous manslaughter charge in Saint John, New Brunswick. Either Tumblety was very lucky in the intervening period not to accidentally kill anybody with his potions, or deaths weren't traced back to his negligence. Alternatively, he paid off the families of patients who died while on his books. Another scenario is that Tumblety was a serial killer who knew, most of the time, how to mask his tracks.

This manslaughter case concerned a patient, Edward Hanratty, of 91 Athol Street in Liverpool. Hanratty had begun to feel unwell and was put under the care of a local family doctor, Dr. John Bligh, for seventeen weeks. When his condition didn't

---

418 Colette Bancroft, "Killer Uncloaked", *Tampa Bay Times*, October 5, 2008

improve, he caught sight of Tumblety's classified advertisements and put himself into the hands of the Indian Herb Doctor, showing up at his office at 177 Duke Street. With so many fellow Liverpudlians claiming to have been cured of everything from cancer to dyspepsia, Hanratty looked forward to a full recovery.

Tumblety agreed to help for the princely sum of fifty shillings. For this, he prescribed some pills and medicine in liquid form. Hanratty took a tablespoon of this medicine and promptly died the same night. Tumblety did himself no favours by refusing to issue a death certificate. More than likely, he was reticent to specify the exact cause of Hanratty's death.

Manslaughter charges were pressed. Tumblety offered up a spirited defence and the verdict was equivocal enough for the doctor to emerge a free man, able to continue his practice. The jury decided that Hanratty had died of natural causes. Whether this had been "accelerated by unskilful treatment", they left as an open question though Tumblety was censured for "administering medicine, he being in total ignorance of his patient".[419]

Keeping track of Tumblety in the 1870s and 1880s is a challenge. He was traversing the full breadth of the United States from San Francisco to New York and then journeying around Europe and spending an increasing amount of time in Liverpool and London. He also claimed to have visited the diamond mines of South Africa as well as British-ruled India and far-off China. This encompassed a spell as an army doctor in the Franco-Prussian War and an audience with Pope Leo XIII. One can take much of this with a pinch of salt though Tumblety should never, of course, be underestimated.

While Hall Caine had been an intellectual equal, Tumblety was about to revert to type with a more disagreeable relationship in New York that would end up once more in the courts and

---

419 "The Great American Doctor", *The Yorkshire Herald and the York Herald*, January 30, 1875

newspapers. The doctor just couldn't resist the allures of teenagers on the streets, and they couldn't resist his bank balance. Now in his forties, Tumblety was transforming into a more obviously depraved, lecherous figure.

Around 1877, Tumblety was in New York trying to put Hall Caine out of his mind. While cruising for sex on the Battery, he had a chance encounter with a young man.[420] There was nothing unusual in this. Other chaps nearby were up to the same thing. Since the 1820s, the Battery had transformed from a military fortress to a pleasure garden. Castle Clinton was leased by the US Army to the New York City government and converted into a theatre and area for promenades. Though the castle would be converted later into an immigration centre, the surrounding gardens remained popular with fun-seeking gentlemen.

The doctor approached a fine-looking chap, fresh from college and seeking employment. Tumblety wasted no time bringing the youth under his wing, manifesting his usual controlling tendencies, and giving the attractive lad responsibility for looking after his investments. This consisted of $100,000 mostly invested in government bonds and kept under lock and key in a downtown safe-deposit company. Truly a recipe for disaster.

The young man became what was described as an 'amanuensis', essentially a glorified secretary taking dictation from Tumblety. One report suggested the doctor needed somebody in that role as he was barely literate himself. The evidence does not support this slur as it's very clear that Tumblety was both literate and numerate and more than aware of the assets he owned.

On 23 April 1878, Tumblety left his office at 77 East 10th Street and set off for a trip to Europe on board the Guion line steamer, *Montana*. He gave his handsome assistant, only so recently picked up on the Battery, full power of attorney. While

---

420 "The Missing Tumblety", *Democrat and Chronicle*, December 3, 1888

on his travels in Europe, Tumblety wrote a considerable number of letters to his fetching valet in which he warned him repeatedly of the dangers of "lewd" women. The correspondence revealed the usual desire, on Tumblety's part, to control and direct his valets as well as his obsessive misogyny.

He put an extraordinary level of trust in this valet and showed a chronic inability to learn from past experience. In Tumblety's absence, his valet helped himself to the doctor's investments. A considerable number of South Carolina railroad bonds were disposed of without Tumblety's permission, and the proceeds pocketed by the young man and his mother, a certain Mrs Lyons. Tumblety returned to find the young man had vanished. Enraged by this theft of his wealth, he brought a suit against Mrs Lyons for grand larceny of $7,000 worth of bonds. The case was considered at the Tombs Police Court.

Mrs Lyons took on the services of a young but intensely ambitious Irish-born attorney, William P. Burr (1856–1930). Tumblety brought in a more seasoned lawyer, James Dodds McClelland (1848–1919), a future state senator. He might as well have saved his money. Burr proved to be a Rottweiler in court, tearing Tumblety to pieces. Yet again, it was the doctor on trial while the valet's mother sat back and enjoyed her opponent's utter humiliation.

Burr enjoyed needling Tumblety, asking mockingly, "what institution had the honour of graduating so precious a pupil"?.[421] Tumblety refused to answer, saying it would incriminate himself, but the lawyer pressed him for an answer. According to the court reports, something snapped inside Tumblety. He made as if to lunge at Burr but managed to exercise restraint at the last minute. Maybe McClelland held him back.

The case fell through, and Mrs Lyons walked free. But now her son, emboldened by his mother's triumph, reappeared.

---

421 Ibid: "The Missing Tumblety"

The ex-college student alleged an "atrocious assault" and the evidence presented "was of the most disgusting sort".[422] This was all code for gay sex, and everybody knew it. To strengthen his allegation against the doctor, he produced a page from the *Police Gazette* as an exhibit that featured a portrait of Tumblety with some unflattering biographical details. These all related to previous charges for gross indecency.

The case was suddenly dropped. But the aggrieved doctor dusted himself off and went on the attack again. This time mounting a suit against William P. O'Connor, the broker who had disposed of the bonds. There seems little doubt that Tumblety was convinced he had been defrauded and the only reason he was failing to get satisfaction was his own character, blameless in his eyes. Lawyers for the brokers and two detectives from Brooklyn, Charles Frost and Charles Chambers, presented a "great mass of evidence" against the doctor.[423] Tumblety's case duly crumbled.

Burr later commented on the character of Tumblety, at the time he was arrested in London as the suspected Jack the Ripper. Rather vindictively, he clearly relished the thought of Tumblety dangling from a rope in London's Newgate prison. Burr certainly didn't hold back. His damning insights related solely to Tumblety's homosexual conduct.

I had seen him before that time hovering about the Old Post Office building, where there were many clerks. He had a seeming mania for the company of young men and grown-up youths.[424]

At the start of the 1880s, two unthinkable things happened. Another President of the United States was assassinated, and

422 Ibid: "The Missing Tumblety"
423 Ibid: "Is he Jack the Ripper?"
424 *New York World*, December 2 1888

Francis Tumblety somehow managed to cross paths with the perpetrator in the lead up to his murderous deed. Journalists were astounded that the Indian Herb Doctor could find himself in the proximity of yet another presidential slayer.

President Garfield's killing seemed inexplicable. Of all the four American heads of state murdered during their term in office, his homicide is still the most baffling. More astounding news couldn't have come, declared one newspaper. Garfield was a president, it continued, of noble and amiable qualities that even a revolutionary nihilist would have struggled to find a reason to shoot him.[425] Yet somebody conjured up the motivation.

President James Garfield (1831–1881) was the second American head of state after Lincoln to be assassinated. Unlike Lincoln, he managed to linger for nearly three months after being shot by Charles J. Giteau (1841–1882) in 1881 and died mainly due to the medical team using unsterilised instruments and poking their filthy fingers into his wound.

The shooting happened at the Baltimore and Potomac Railroad Station in Washington DC and by a sad coincidence, Lincoln's son – Robert Todd Lincoln – was on the train platform when Giteau struck. That meant he had been in the vicinity of two presidential assassinations. He went on to make that a hat-trick in 1901 as he was visiting the Pan-American Exposition in Buffalo when President William McKinley was killed by the anarchist, Leon Czolgosz.

Tumblety also got himself associated with both the Lincoln and Garfield assassinations. In 1881, he was in the same hotel as Giteau where both men found themselves equally unwelcome on account of their respective oddball behaviours. The fact their paths crossed was remembered by journalists in 1888, when Tumblety was arrested as Jack the Ripper. What was it about

---

425 "President Garfield Shot!" *Springville Journal*, July 9, 1881

Francis Tumblety that murder and manslaughter seemed to follow him around?

An in-house detective at the Fifth Avenue Hotel in New York, James Pryor, never forgot his first sighting of Tumblety in full self-promotional garb:

> He had an army officer's cap, a big cape, and light-coloured trousers. He was a dandy, then, I tell you. You couldn't find a finer made man in this town. He had a big black mustache, one of the blacking-brush kind, black eyes, a good complexion, and a walk like he had just been elected Alderman.[426]

A "thick-set young man" walked about twenty paces behind the doctor as a kind of hired, handsome heavy. Tumblety never spoke to this person who shadowed him into the hotel every day as a bodyguard. Pryor was approached by "gentlemen" guests who didn't want Tumblety "so near them". Eventually, they impressed on Pryor the need to remove the doctor. Something about Tumblety unnerved them and he had to go.

But there was also another problematic guest at the hotel. A "wild-faced little fellow sat cross-legged on the floor, sometimes with a drab hat pulled down over his eyes, scribbling feverishly". He claimed to be writing speeches for the Republican presidential hopeful, James Garfield, who was running in the 1880 primaries campaign. This manic whippet behaving strangely was Giteau.

His upbringing had been unorthodox to put it mildly. Born in Illinois in 1841, his father had sent him off to join a utopian community in Oneida, upstate New York. Believing that Jesus had already returned, they felt it was their duty to make the world free of all sin. They also practised free love and rejected monogamy, though the female cultists avoided Guiteau as he

---

426 Ibid: "Is he the fiend?"

was deemed to be too ugly. What this did for his self-confidence one can only imagine. Cult members also indulged in group sessions where one member would have all his or her faults laid bare in stark terms. Guiteau got such a hammering from everybody on one occasion that he fainted.[427]

His life was a sad tale of serial failure. Jailed as a debt collector for pocketing the money. A marriage that collapsed because he beat his wife, preferring the company of sex workers. Unable to get his head round the complexities of being an insurance salesman then spending periods in shabby clothes hanging around hotel lobbies for shelter, which was undoubtedly how he found himself in the Fifth Avenue Hotel in New York with the Indian Herb Doctor processing through the same lobby.

Giteau proved to be utterly delusional. Convinced he had been promised a consular role in another country representing the US government from one of its embassies as a reward for the powerful speeches he had penned in praise of Garfield.

He pestered Garfield's team for an overseas ambassadorship that they had no intention of ever giving him. In short, Giteau was regarded as a complete crank. But Pryor was concerned enough at this young man's behaviour that he warned local political bigwigs that Giteau would "hurt somebody someday" and this proved to be prescient.

One morning I went into the reading-room and there he was writing a speech in his bare feet. He had taken his shoes off and thrown them aside. I had a tough time getting him out, because he didn't want to go.[428]

Tumblety and Giteau were both ejected from the hotel. Three months later Giteau assassinated President Garfield.

---

427 Owen Dwyer, *The Garfield Conspiracy* (Liberties Press, 2021)
428 Ibid: "Is he the fiend?"

Years later in 1888, when Tumblety was arrested on suspicion of being Jack the Ripper, it was claimed he had been "often seen" with Giteau at the hotel.[429] But there is no evidence that the two knew or spoke to eachother or had any kind of relationship.

Unsurprisingly, some thought that given his track record of being arrested as a Lincoln plotter, Tumblety might also have been working with Giteau to kill Garfield. But to what end?

One unsubstantiated theory is that the heterosexual Giteau killed Garfield as he had witnessed a homosexual triste between the president and a man named James Harrison Rhodes (1836–1890) many years before when they were young men and this had somehow traumatised him.[430]

It's difficult to see any motive for Tumblety being involved in Garfield's untimely death other than a desperate but highly dangerous PR stunt and this seems fanciful. In contrast to the Lincoln episode, the doctor never claimed to be intimate in any way with Garfield or members of his administration and certainly not with Giteau.

A cartoon at the time of the assassination had a demonic Giteau surrounded by draft speeches. One speech was titled, 'Anything for Notoriety'.[431] One might observe this was an appropriate comment on both Giteau and Tumblety.

---

429 "Oh! Dr. Tumblety", *The New North-West*, December 21, 1888

430 'American People: Volume 1, Search for my Heart', Kramer, Larry, Farra, Straus and Giroux, 2015, ISBN: 978-0374104399

431 'From Grave to Gay', Nast, Thomas (cartoonist), Harper's Weekly, December 1881

Eight

Becoming Jack the Ripper

B y the year 1888, Tumblety was in his fifties and getting on a bit by the standards of the 19th century. Any youthful lustre had long departed. His method of business operation had once involved high-profile arrivals in big American cities with plenty of gaudy razzmatazz. Now he skulked unseen by ship between the United States and Britain. The shameless theatricality and self-promotion of his earlier years had given way to a more secretive demeanour. A certain gloom seemed to be descending on this once exuberant personality.

1888 would see an atmosphere of terror engulf London as the world's first modern and recognisable serial killer stalked the British capital. Jack the Ripper carried out a series of extraordinarily brutal murders on several women in the Whitechapel district of the city. Incredibly, the man implicated in the Lincoln assassination would find himself a suspect in the Ripper killings. Tumblety would therefore be linked in his own lifetime to the two greatest crimes of the 19th century.

One of the Ripper murders in particular ties Tumblety to the case as a very credible suspect - the butchering of Annie Chapman (1840-1888). The manner of her death and the location of two items taken from her body point strongly to the Indian Herb Doctor. He was irrefutably in the city at the time and Scotland Yard thought they had their man. Yet, as will be seen, he got away.

Between 5.15am and 5.30am on 6 September 1888, nature called for Albert Cadosch. The carpenter needed to use the back yard lavatory of a rundown property at 27 Hanbury Street. This was a typical flat-fronted house built two hundred years before for the Spitalfields weavers with large windows to admit light. It had since degenerated into a doss house for about seventeen lodgers. On his way to relieve himself, Cadosch heard a woman's cry: "No, no!". Then something fell against the rickety fence separating numbers 27 and 29. Half dazed with tiredness he thought nothing more of it. There was always some kind of drama being played out in London's East End.

Just forty-five minutes later, the mutilated body of Annie Chapman was discovered by one of the other occupants of the house, a Spitalfields Market porter named John Davies. This would be the second "canonical" murder by the killer who came to be known globally as Jack the Ripper. The canonical murders are those recognised by most experts as being by his hand. There were other brutal slayings of women before and after the canonical ones that bore certain similarities, but where the link to Jack the Ripper is disputed.

Davies immediately roused everybody in the house and then sped down to the Commercial Street police station to report the crime. He went nowhere near the body as he related in a statement:

I did not examine the woman when I saw her. I was too frightened at the dreadful sight. Our front door at 29 Hanbury Street is never bolted, and anyone has only to push it open and walk through to the gate at the back yard. Immoral women have at times gone there.[432]

432 Ibid: "East End Outrages", *The Western Times*, September 10, 1888

The inference being that Annie was just another "immoral woman" who took that night's pundit to the back yard at a property she knew well. Davies clearly regarded the victim as a prostitute murdered by a deranged customer. But Annie's friend Amelia Farmer, a fellow lodger, insisted that Chapman had a boyfriend of sorts, Edward "Ted" Stanley, and "she had not been in the habit of frequenting the streets, but had made antimacassars for sale".[433]

When the police arrived, they surveyed the gruesome scene. The killer had taken his time as he mutilated her with disturbing precision, leaving the victim's heart and liver on her shoulder.

It was obvious both from the marks upon the body and of the splashes of blood upon the palings which separate the dwellings one from the other, that the woman while lying down had her throat first cut and then was ripped open and disembowelled.[434]

Hanbury Street is now at the heart of a revitalised East End but in 1888, it was the home of the poorest in London including a large Jewish community who were often the subject of discrimination. The Jewish residents were the latest of waves of immigrants preceded by the French Huguenots and succeeded by Bangladeshis in the 20th century. In 1888, 29 Hanbury Street was owned by a certain Amelia Richardson who rented it out to lodgers looking for somewhere to sleep. Some of them were long-term residents having been there for up to twelve years.

At the front basement level was a "cat's-meat shop"[435] – which, despite the misleading description, was selling horse meat from knacker's yards to pet owners. There was also a packing case

433 "The Fiendish Murder", *Reynold's Newspaper*, September 16, 1888
434 Ibid: "East End Outrages"
435 Ibid: "East End Outrages"

business being run from the premises. Richardson described her lodgers as "poor but hard-working people" mostly employed in the fish market at Spitalfields. Some went out to work as early as 1am in the morning. None had noticed the body in the back yard until Davies chanced upon Annie Chapman.

Though Annie was often characterised as simply a sex worker who got unlucky one night, this picture dehumanises a woman who slid from semi-respectability to a street-level existence in Whitechapel. She had been married to a veterinary surgeon in Windsor but had lived apart from him for four years. He died eighteen months before the murder. That terminated the ten-shillings weekly allowance she received from him.[436] Already living in East End lodging houses, this woman in her late forties faced a bleak future.

It was a fate that could befall anybody, male or female, in a society that had no welfare safety net. For thousands in the East End, the dawn of each day was the commencement of a battle for survival at the end of which one might have some pennies for a bed. Then the whole ghastly cycle was repeated over and over until death came as a relief.

The back yard of 29 Hanbury Street, as witnesses told the subsequent inquest, was often used for paid sexual encounters. Amelia Richardson's son, John, who worked at the packing case business confirmed this. As did another witness, Elizabeth Long, who saw Annie talking to a man aged over forty at around 5.30am by her reckoning. They were sober. He said, "Will you?" She replied, "Yes". This was such a commonplace that Long didn't find it remotely unusual. The man, she observed, "looked like a foreigner" and was "shabby genteel".[437]

By today's standards, Annie was short at about five-feet-two in height. Fair brown wavy hair, blue eyes, and a large, flat nose.

---

436 Ibid: "The Fiendish Murder"

437 "The case of Annie Chapman", *Lloyd's Weekly Newspaper*, September 23, 1888

She was found wearing a skirt, bodice, and two light petticoats. The manager of a lodging house on Dorset Street, Timothy Donovan, remembered Annie and that two years before, she had stayed there with a man named Jack Sivvy, a sieve maker. This had earned her the nickname locally, "Annie Sivvy".

She was quiet and reserved. Possibly Annie had two children, one a disabled boy at a charity school in Windsor and the other a girl believed to be in a circus troupe travelling around France. She had previously been teetotal, according to the man in Dorset Street but had embraced the demon drink by the time of her murder. As Donovan told the inquest: "She was generally the worse for drink on Saturdays".[438] While another witness said, "She was very industrious when sober and was a very clever little woman. I have seen her the worse for drink; but I don't think she could take much without being drunk. She had been living a very irregular life for five years, especially since her husband's death".[439] Like thousands of other women in the East End, she did whatever it took to keep her head above water.

It was initially claimed that there was no sign of Annie having struggled as she was overpowered and struck with the murderer's knife. Police noted that the pool of blood which flowed from her slashed throat fell close to the step where she lay. "She does not appear to have moved an inch after the fiend struck her with the knife."[440] Annie's corpse was taken to the mortuary at the corner of Eagle Street. The lumps of flesh and organs removed by Jack the Ripper were placed back in her body. One organ, however, was missing. Annie's uterus had departed with her killer.

There was a possible sighting of the murderer just under two hours after his crime. Step forward Mrs Fiddymont, wife of

---

438 "The Whitechapel Murder", *The Morning Post*, September 11, 1888
439 Ibid: "The Whitechapel Murder"
440 Ibid: "East End Outrages"

the landlord of the Prince Albert public house, half a mile from 29 Hanbury Street. At 7am on 6 September 1888, the pub was already open for business and serving pints of draught beer. As Mrs Fiddymont was gossiping with another woman at the bar, in walked a man "whose rough appearance frightened her".[441] He wore a brown stiff hat, a dark coat, and no waistcoat. The hat was pulled down over his eyes. He asked for a half pint of ale. As Mrs Fiddymont drew the pint, she noticed blood spots on the back of his right hand. His shirt was also torn.

The other woman, Fiddymont's friend Mary Chappell, remembered his shirt was a light blue check pattern and torn badly around the right shoulder. This certainly suggests that Annie didn't die without a fight - assuming he was the killer. Chappell also observed a narrow streak of blood under his right ear and dried blood between the fingers of his hand.

The strange man, realising he was being watched, downed the beer with a single gulp and left. Both women urged a local builder, Joseph Taylor, to follow him. At one point, Taylor came alongside and was able to estimate his age at between forty and fifty. Tumblety at this time would have been somewhere between fifty and fifty-five. "He had a shabby genteel look, pepper and salt trousers which fitted badly, and dark coat."[442]

This could easily have been Tumblety down on his luck, but elements of the physical description are not an exact fit with the Indian Herb Doctor. He had a moustache, but it was ginger, and his hair was sandy coloured. Though, Tumblety was no stranger to hair dye. In later life he would blacken his hair and rouge his cheeks. The suspect's height was put at five-feet-eight inches, which is below the six feet usually ascribed to the doctor though one does shrink a little with age.

Many of the statements about the Jack the Ripper killings

---

441 Ibid: "East End Outrages"
442 Ibid: "East End Outrages"

are contradictory and, at the time, newspapers reported that the reliability of witness statements had to be set against how much alcohol had already been drunk that morning.

Martha Tabram (1849–1888) was the first victim in a spate of horrific killings that created a climate of terror in Whitechapel for about three years from 1888. However, unlike other women killed with equal brutality in the same area of London, she isn't considered as one of Jack the Ripper's 'canonical' victims. The canonical five, almost universally accepted as being killed by the Ripper, are Mary Ann Nichols, Annie Chapman, Elizabeth Stride, Catherine Eddowes, and Mary Jane Kelly, all killed in the second half of 1888.

Tabram's exclusion from the canonical five can seem rather arbitrary and rests in part on the police view at the time. One of the criteria for not including Tabram was that the thirty-nine wounds on her body were inflicted by stabbing, as opposed to slashing – which was the Ripper's signature approach. But even at the time, the pathologists noted similarities between Tabram's wounds and those on Annie Chapman.[443]

The canonical victims were attacked using "strong bladed" instruments. Chapman had been cut open by "a very sharp knife, probably with a thin, narrow blade, at least six inches to eight inches in length, probably longer". There was very little bleeding from the arteries considering the severity of the wounds, suggesting the Ripper cut the throat first and then set to work on the abdomen.[444]

Robbery wasn't a motive. The canonical cases all indicated little sign of a struggle. And in the view of the pathologists, the murderer had some degree of anatomical knowledge. Sex was ruled out as the main motive. Jack the Ripper seemed focused on the brutal dissection of the women he butchered. By far the

---

443 Ibid: "The Whitechapel Murders. Resumed Inquest on Mrs Nichols", *The Morning Post*, September 24, 1888

444 Ibid: "The Whitechapel Murders. Resume Inquest on Mrs Nichols"

worst example of this was the killing of Mary Jane Kelly (1863–1888). Whereas the Ripper's victims tended to be middle-aged, Kelly was only twenty-four years of age at her death on 9 November. She was murdered indoors, allowing the killer free rein to complete his ritualistic, pseudo-medical dismembering. The newspapers spared their readers no details:

> *The examination revealed a state of things never equalled in the annals of crime. The head was not lying apart from the body but was hanging by a mere thread. Both ears and the nose were cut off. All the flesh was stripped completely off the thighs, and the woman was not only disembowelled, but the womb and other parts were taken away similar to the previous murders in this locality.*[445]

Police, journalists, and crowds of sightseers descended on the scene: a bleak, barely furnished room on the ground floor of 26 Dorset Street, opposite St Stephen's church in Spitalfields. This was a typically narrow road in Whitechapel with barely enough room for two vehicles to pass each other. There were numerous "courts" – dark alleyways – leading off the street, each packed with lodging houses where a night's rest might be obtained for a few pennies. Nearby was a poster put up after a previous Ripper murder: "A Hundred Pounds Reward – Whitechapel Murder".

One young woman, Mrs Pannier, sold roasted chestnuts on the corner of Widegate Street, about two minutes' walk from where Kelly had been slain. She offered an intriguing piece of evidence. A man had approached her the following day at around noon. He was "dressed like a gentleman" with a black moustache; a black silk hat; black coat and speckled trousers. In his hand was a "shiny bag" about a foot in depth and a foot and a half in length. He strode up to Pannier:

---

445 "Another fearful crime. A woman cut to pieces and disembowelled. Terror in London", *Reynolds's Newspaper*, November 11, 1888

I suppose you have heard about the murder in Dorset Street?

The chestnut vendor replied that indeed she had. The man grinned and staring into Pannier's face added:

I know more about it than you.

He bounded off down Sandys Row but for one short moment, glanced back - then vanished. Pannier asked other women locally whether they had seen this man. Three of them had been accosted as well. When one of the women asked what the gentleman had in his bag, he leered. "Something that the ladies don't like."[446]

Tumblety would later admit to journalists that not only was he in London at the time of the Whitechapel murders, but he joined the grisly tide of voyeurs that flocked to the district. If he was the sinister individual who had spoken to Pannier, then the absence of an American accent wouldn't have been unusual. The doctor had spent enough time in England to affect a London or Liverpool brogue.

On 7 November 1888, Tumblety was taken into custody by London police over four acts of gross indecency involving four different men: John Doughty, Arthur Brice, Albert Fisher, and James Crowley. These incidents seem to have taken place over several months, possibly July to November that year, and the likelihood is that the doctor was arrested either after a period of surveillance or because of one verifiable offence but then he somehow implicated the others, maybe by carrying their written details on his person.

Like the poet Walt Whitman, Tumblety could have kept a diary of his conquests or contact details for a replay. Whitman's

---

446 Ibid: "Another fearful crime. A woman cut to pieces and disembowelled. Terror in London"

notebooks from 1862 to 1863, now in the Library of Congress, give a flavour of what a gay man might have had in his pocket that a police officer would have found incriminating:

Jerry Taylor (Oct 9, 1863; Washington, D.C.), N.J. of 2d dist. Reg't slept with me last night.

David Wilson night of Oct. 11, '62 walking up from Middagh - slept with me - works in a blacksmith shop in Navy Yard - lives in Hampden st. - walks together Sunday afternoon & night - is about 19.[447]

After his arrest on 7 November, Tumblety was released on police bail which gave him the window of opportunity to murder Mary Jane Kelly before appearing in court over the gross indecency charges.[448] During that period, Scotland Yard's inquiries brought the realisation that the doctor could indeed be Jack the Ripper. For Kelly, that was too late.

The charges Tumblety faced for his homosexual acts with four men stemmed from new legislation targeting the exploitation of underage girls. It also had a bearing on the Ripper murders. The toughening of laws governing sexual crime were the direct result of a series of newspaper articles in *The Pall Mall Gazette* revealing the grim extent of prostitution and child exploitation in Victorian London. Through the summer of July 1885, under the title The Maiden Tribute of Modern Babylon, *The Pall Mall Gazette* related harrowing accounts of human trafficking and slavery, mainly of young girls.

The newspaper's editor, William Thomas Stead (1849–1912), procured a thirteen-year-old girl, Eliza Armstrong, to evidence how working-class girls were being traded to middle-

447 Jonathan Ned Katz, *Gay American History* (Avon Books, 1978)

448 Stewart Evans, Paul Gainey, *Jack the Ripper: First American Serial Killer* (Arrow Books Ltd, 1996)

class gentlemen. She apparently cost Stead about five pounds from her two male abductors, with two pounds of that amount to be handed over subject to a so-called "certificate of virginity". A certain Madame Mourey, who specialised in such verifications for the price of one guinea, conducted an examination of Eliza as she had done other girls.

So moved was the playwright George Bernard Shaw by Eliza's plight, that thirty years later he would name the main protagonist in *Pygmalion* after her. Newspapers around the world carried the news that London was a sink of corruption and vice. A shocked American newspaper stated that England had "long enjoyed the reputation of sustaining a higher standard of morality than any other country in Europe" but that now lay in ruins. The sex scandals coming out of Britain revealed "the lowest grade of immorality among a class of people from whom decency at least ought to have been expected".[449]

The pretense of superior virtue on the part of England will not henceforth be received with the same respect as heretofore.[450]

Newsagents in London decided their customers needed to be shielded from the truth. *The Pall Mall Gazette* was removed from sale. W. H. Smith took the newspaper off their railway bookstalls, as did a couple of other large retailers. But the public hungered for the gruesome details. Street vendors with copies responded by upping the price and pocketing the difference. Many readers were horrified, not by the revelations, but by the newspaper daring to print such disturbing material. Comments from the letters page of *The Pall Mall Gazette* of 9 July 1885, give a flavour of this disapproval:

449 "Probabilities", *The Kansas City Star*, July 23, 1886
450 Ibid: "Probabilities"

Anything more disgusting I never read. I consider it a disgrace that such matter should ever be allowed to be published in any newspaper that calls itself respectable. (Name indecipherable, 63 Aldersgate Street)

You will strengthen and stimulate and encourage the very vices you abhor! (Mr Lewis Miles)

My own opinion, after twenty-five years' experience in London, is that the vice is much exaggerated, but I may be mistaken. (Dr John Harvey, Chapel-place, Cavendish Square)

The result of the newspaper's crusading journalism was the passing in the same year of the Criminal Law Amendment Act, referred to as the Stead Act in honour of the editor of *The Pall Mall Gazette*. Among other things, the legislation raised the age of consent for sex between men and women from thirteen to sixteen. There were calls for vigilance associations to ensure its provisions became a reality on the streets. "Crime must be met by pains and penalties; vice by moral forces. The great cure for this evil was publicity." But cleaning up London and other British cities wasn't going to be an overnight process.[451]

All over the country the reports continued to pour into the offices of *The Pall Mall Gazette* of unending vice. A Manchester girl aged fifteen, Elizabeth Ann Kearns, abducted and then forced into prostitution in nearby Liverpool. Hundreds of obscene publications seized in Birmingham and summons issued to the vendors. A desperate woman in Nottingham who dumped two unwanted babies in a hamper, placing them on a train unattended.[452] While it was an achievement to toughen the

---

451 "The National Vigilance Association – the Treasury Prosecution", *The Pall Mall Gazette*, September 5, 1885

452 Ibid: "The National Vigilance Association"

legislation on child sexual exploitation, Stead found himself in court. He was now stood accused of the very vice he had set out to extinguish through the power of campaigning journalism.

It was alleged that Stead had conspired with Eliza's abductors to remove the girl illegally from her parents.[453] There is no doubt that today, Stead's modus operandi would be viewed as unacceptable and abhorrent. To reveal the reality of child prostitution, he had knowingly permitted a thirteen-year-old girl to be knocked out with chloroform, taken to a brothel, drugged again, inspected for her virginity, and not returned to her parents. The judge's summing up expressed what many Victorian gentlemen throughout London had felt about having the city's seedy underbelly brought to light:

You deluged for some months our streets and the whole country with an amount of filth which, I fear, tainted the minds of children you were so anxious to protect, and which, I do not hesitate to say, has been and ever will be a disgrace to journalism.[454]

Stead was imprisoned for three months though he became a celebrity behind bars. In 1912, he would go down with the Titanic in the north Atlantic ocean, drowning with over 1500 other people.

It was in this atmosphere of heightened tension around sex-related crime that Tumblety was taken into custody with reports on his arrest making a linkage to the *Modern Babylon* newspaper articles and resulting legislation.

In a later exclusive interview to an American newspaper, Tumblety made an oblique reference to a homosexual scandal that rocked London in the following year, 1889. This story

453 "The abduction of Eliza Armstrong", *The Guardian*, September 8, 1885
454 Trial report, *The Times*, November 11, 1885

gripped the British capital and reflected a new kind of aggressive journalism prepared to take down establishment figures. It also showed that the police were becoming surprisingly well versed in the new sciences of psychology and psychoanalysis, being more aware of homosexuality - though in a very negative context. .

The Cleveland Street scandal bubbled to the surface on 4 July 1889, with a post office messenger, Charles Swinscow, found in possession of a large amount of money - more than he could have earned in the day job.[455] Under police interrogation, he admitted to having sex with other men at 19 Cleveland Street, just off Tottenham Court Road in London's West End. Another messenger, Alfred Newlove, had introduced Swinscow to the easy money that could be made selling their bodies to senior army officers, business tycoons, and aristocrats at this gay brothel.

On 7 July, Newlove was arrested, and the full facts tipped into the newspaper columns. The house was run by George Hammond and assisted by the self-styled "Reverend" George Veck. Clients included dukes, financiers, and senior military figures. The police officer put in charge of the investigation was Inspector Frederick Abberline who led the police operation in Whitechapel to find Jack the Ripper.

When police arrived at Cleveland Street, they found the brothel had shut for business. Hammond had escaped just in time to France and would end up in Seattle. The whole matter was referred to the Director of Public Prosecutions, Sir Angus Stephenson on 25 July.

On 29 July, some of the post office messengers working at the brothel were taken to Piccadilly and lined up outside the gentlemen's clubs that stretched down Pall Mall. They were instructed by police to point out any of their aristocratic

---

455 H. G. Cocks, *Nameless Offences: Homosexual Desire in the Nineteenth Century* (I.B. Tauris Publishers, London, 2009)

clients they saw leaving a club. A couple of days later, the Commissioner of the Metropolitan Police, James Munro reported to Stephenson that one of the aristocrats identified by the "telegraph boys" was Lord Arthur Somerset, equerry to the Prince of Wales.

What followed was an attempted cover up of the affair with the Prince of Wales and the Prime Minister intervening behind the scenes to protect Lord Somerset. Newlove and Veck stood trial on 18 September but by then, Somerset had fled to Europe and showed no signs of returning from the continent. Although he did return at the start of October to attend his grandmother's funeral but astonishingly was able to abscond once more.

London's newspapers had a field day kicking the establishment over the whole scandal and for the first time, began to include sordid details previously excised from vice-related stories. For this, they were accused by establishment voices of being no better than common blackmailers and of promoting sodomy. All homosexual activity in the 1880s was illegal, no matter where it was conducted and with whom. Yet the aristocracy felt it could live by a different moral code to the great unwashed. However, the emergence of the popular press proved to be a great leveller in that regard.

Having taken Tumblety into custody on gross indecency charges with four men, police in London reached out to counterparts in the United States to find out more about the doctor. Police Superintendent Campbell in Brooklyn received a cable dispatch from Robert Anderson, Assistant Commissioner of the London Metropolitan Police. Displaying some of his old-style bravura, Tumblety assisted Anderson in getting the correct information from Campbell. In the dispatch, Anderson wrote:

He says he is known to you, chief, as Brooklyn's beauty.[456]

There was also a "considerable telegraphing" between police departments in London and San Francisco gaining information about the doctor who was active on the west coast from 1870 with an account at the Hibernia Bank. San Francisco police offered to get samples of Tumblety's handwriting from the bank for Scotland Yard. Anderson fired off a dispatch:

P. Crowley, Chief of Police, San Francisco Cal.:
Thanks. Send handwriting and all details you can of
Tumblety.
ANDERSON
Scotland Yard

As reports arrived in London of Tumblety's imprisonment in 1865 over the Lincoln assassination; charges of manslaughter and illegal abortion; the long record of vice-related arrests, and his very publicly stated hatred of women – Scotland Yard came to view that Tumblety was beyond any doubt Jack the Ripper. After months of being mocked by the newspapers, the police could finally declare they had the serial killer in their grasp.

American newspapers confirmed Scotland Yard's suspicions with a blizzard of articles reminding their readers about Tumblety and his long record of immoral behaviour and crime. Most damning was the overt misogyny and the bizarre collection of uteruses - the very body part removed by the Ripper in the Annie Chapman murder.

Tumblety has been notorious as a woman-hater. In all that
is known of his life in the last thirty years he has never made
himself the companion of females. His antipathy to fallen

---

456 "Jack, the Ripper, Ubiquitous", *The Bottineau Courant*, December 6, 1888

women has been especially marked. As long ago as August 1861, when in Washington, he had an anatomical museum in which the chief feature was an unusual number of glass jars containing specimens of the same nature as those which have been carved from the Whitechapel victims. He was continuously denouncing women at times flying into a fury when the subject was mentioned.[457]

It's very striking that there was little comment about Tumblety in the British or Canadian press. But the American newspapers gleefully seized on the opportunity to demolish the one-time celebrity doctor. Fortunately for journalists, there was no problem getting old acquaintances to come forward and trash Tumblety's already toxic reputation. Going right back to his childhood days in Rochester, everybody was agreed that the Indian Herb Doctor had the psychological make-up of a serial killer.

One rather arresting visual detail that emerged in the coverage surrounding his arrest in the American press related to his Brooklyn store in the 1860s where the now long-dead David Herold had worked as a valet. In the shop window, some remembered a large array of tubes "in all conceivable shapes through which a red-colored fluid was constantly flowing".[458] Despite this lurid, possibly gynecological display, the store had been a "rendezvous of many prominent Brooklyn ladies" seeking cures for their ailments.

A small minority disagreed that the doctor was the Ripper, stating that he was just a vain, preening narcissist with eccentric habits. Some argued that the whole Whitechapel affair was just another publicity ruse by the Indian Herb Doctor with one newspaper warning that he was placing himself in considerable

457 "Tumblety Facts in the History of the Supposed Whitechapel Fiend", *St Louis Globe-Democrat*, January 5, 1889
458 "Dr Tumblety in Brooklyn", *The Evening World*, November 24, 1888

danger with this self-promotion using the Jack the Ripper killings.[459] It could all end with a rope around his neck.

Most interviewees from his past, though, believed he was indeed Jack the Ripper. They were prepared to state on the record that the doctor was a dangerous misogynist with a violent criminal record who detested women, especially sex workers. And the manner of the murders offered further proof that Tumblety had wielded the bloody knife:

> *Tumblety has some surgical skill, without doubt. Charlatan though he undoubtedly is, he has been practising medicine for the last thirty years in all parts of the world, and he has naturally acquired some knowledge and dexterity in the use of a knife. He is a tall, heavy man, and quite strong enough to do all that the Whitechapel murderer has done.[460]*

In recent years, less had been heard of him "until now, a man passed middle age, he looms up as the notorious fiend of the century".[461] This would be a fitting end to his story: Tumblety finally convicted of a great crime and unable to wriggle away as he had done before. But what could have motivated him to commit the Whitechapel murders?

In considering him as the serial killer, we need to avoid the worn out old homophobic cliché of the homicidal homosexual in literature, plays and films of the past.[462] In the late 19th century and into the modern era, the trope persisted of the homosexual or bisexual being more likely to display

---

459 "Dr Tumblety", *The Buffalo Sunday Morning News*, December 16, 1888
460 Ibid: "Tumblety Facts in the History of the Supposed Whitechapel Fiend"
461 Ibid: "Is he the fiend?"
462 Jordan Schildcrout, *Murder Most Queer: The Homicidal Homosexual in American Theater* (University of Michigan Press, 2014)

"Dark Triad" traits than heterosexuals. That is the triad of psychopathy, Machiavellianism, and narcissism. This has reflected heterosexual fears of homosexuals being out to seduce them or destroy the family and societal power structures.

While one doesn't wish to lend this view any credibility, the description of the Dark Triad in practice by one psychologist sums up Tumblety brilliantly:

The traits may enable fast life history strategies that allow people to pursue selfish social and sexual agendas that impose costs on those around them. [463]

As mentioned previously, President Lincoln's US Army Surgeon General during the Civil War, William Alexander Hammond, went on to be a top neurologist writing extensively on sexuality in the last decades of the 19th century. Like most medical opinion of the time, he viewed homosexuality as a mental illness where an underlying cause rooted in some trauma had to be identified through therapy and then brutal cures administered, including ice-cold showers and large doses of bromide. When Tumblety's arrest as Jack the Ripper was reported in the American press, some wondered if Hammond's now mercifully outdated and discredited analysis of homosexuality was being vindicated.

Tumblety is believed to be insane. Time and again he has been forced to leave places because of abominable vices. Surgeon General Hammond, one of the best modern authorities on such subjects, holds that men addicted to such vices are undoubtedly insane. More than that, before

---

463 Peter K. Jonanson, Severi Luoto, "The dark side of the rainbow: Homosexuals and bisexuals have higher Dark Triad traits than heterosexuals", *Personality and Individual Differences*, October 2021, Vol. 181

Tumblety was suspected Dr. Hammond gave his opinion that the murderer when found would be a man of that class.[464]

Setting aside Hammond's outdated homophobia, something could have been happening to Tumblety that was unbalancing his mind, driving him to lash out violently. The murder of Kelly, for example, saw pieces of her body thrown around the room in a deranged manner. Then there was the ghastly harvesting of uteruses. At one moment, this brutal monster was making a careful incision into Kelly's body, as if conducting a surgical procedure, then tearing her apart like a demented butcher. What drove such a visceral fury?

Insanity driven by a crippling disease perhaps? There is compelling evidence that Tumblety, like Lincoln and Booth, had syphilis. Before the discovery of modern antibiotics, this was a slow death sentence - a long and agonising descent into physical and mental decay, which could be slowed but not stopped. As will be seen, the personal health regime that the doctor embarked on before his stay in Whitechapel, and would resume once he returned to the United States, fits a man seeking to arrest the inevitable progress of the pox.

There is a growing body of medical research to support the idea that a syphilitic can experience acute psychosis and Intermittent Explosive Disorder. In a recent study, one patient who had previously been "easy going" and "laid back" became physically violent, displaying erratic and aggressive behaviour until they received a modern treatment that would have been unavailable to Tumblety in the 1880s.

This patient, like others in the same condition, heard voices, became furious, and struck out. Syphilis can be latent for a long period of time and is sometimes described as "the great imitator"

464 Ibid: "Tumblety Facts in the History of the Supposed Whitechapel Fiend"

because it presents as different illnesses on the surface. But ultimately it can result in very disturbing personality changes. In effect then, Tumblety could have lost control of himself and become utterly psychotic.[465]

The association he would have made between prostitutes and the spreading of venereal disease is straight forward enough. But given he was likely to have contracted the disease from a rent boy or casual sex with any number of males over the years, one must wonder why his victims were female, instead of male? Yet all his most savage comments throughout his adult life were reserved for women. Plus, there was his claim to have been married unknowingly to a female sex worker and the gory display of uteruses that chimed so forcefully with the Whitechapel murders.

Tumblety isn't the only Jack the Ripper suspect said to have committed the multiple murders over an abiding hatred of prostitutes spreading incurable venereal disease. Prince Albert Victor (1864–1892), son of Queen Victoria, has been a long-running candidate to be Jack the Ripper, as he had contracted gonorrhoea and was enraged, the theory runs.[466] During his lifetime, he was also rumoured to be involved in the Cleveland Street scandal, thus making him bisexual or homosexual. But with regards to the Ripper case, he was at Balmoral in Scotland when Elizabeth Stride and Catherine Eddowes were murdered. This would seem to rule him out.

Aside from her uterus, something else was absent from Annie Chapman - two or three cheap imitation gold rings she was known to wear on a single finger. One was more than

465 Harneel S. Saini, Matthew Sayre, Ishveen Saini, Nehad Elsharkawy, "Neurosyphilis Presenting as Intermittent Explosive Disorder and Acute Psychosis", *Cureus*, 2019, Vol.11, Issue 12

466 Euran McLelland, "Jack the Ripper suspect Prince Albert Victor is revealed to have been suffering from gonorrhoea – most likely caught from a prostitute", *Mail Online*, February 26, 2016

likely her wedding ring while the other would be a 'keeper' ring, designed to keep the favoured ring in place. They were missing when Annie's body was found. Scotland Yard was sure that if they could find the rings, they would be able to confront Jack the Ripper. These rings, as will be seen, tie Tumblety to that one Ripper killing and from Annie Chapman, arguably to the rest of the victims. As one report stated:

Great weight is attached to the statement as to the rings which were on the murdered woman's hand before the murder was committed, but which had been wrenched off by the wretch before he had good his escape.[467]

A pawnbroker in Mile End believed he might have the rings, which turned out to be fake gold. Another chance to unmask Jack the Ripper failed. The cheap jewellery was still somewhere out there.

Every pawnbroker in the metropolis has been warned and should the murderer's needs or his lack of knowledge induce him to produce his plunder in a London pawnshop, his immediate capture is assured.[468]

But the rings remained elusive.

The inquest into Annie Chapman's death was held in the Alexandra Room of the Working Lads' Institute. A woman named Eliza Cooper was questioned. She had quarrelled with Annie in the days before she was murdered over a bar of soap Eliza had given to Annie's boyfriend as he went to use her outdoor lavatory. Eliza then expected Annie to return the soap, but she refused, offering a derisory halfpenny instead. This

---

467 Ibid: "East End Outrages"
468 "The Whitechapel Murder", *The Morning Post*, September 11, 1888

argument continued to a local public house called Ringers, where Annie slapped Eliza around the face and got a black eye in return. The inquest wanted to know more from Eliza about that night at Ringers. The questioning went as follows:

Q: *Was she wearing rings?*
A: *Yes, she was wearing three rings on the third finger of the left hand. They were all brass. She bought them from a black man.*
Q: *Had she ever a gold wedding ring to your knowledge?*
A: *No; not since I have known her.*[469]

Edward Stanley was also asked about her rings:

Q: *Was she wearing rings when you saw her?*
A: *Yes, I believe two. I could not say on which finger, but they were on one of her fingers.*
Q: *What sort of rings were they? What was the metal?*
A: *Brass, I should think. They were of the colour of brass.*[470]

In the Coroner's summing up and verdict, the killing was deemed to have been carried out by somebody "who had considerable anatomical skill and knowledge".[471] The incisions were precise and the uterus was removed by somebody who knew where to find it and how to cut it out in one piece so that it wasn't damaged. This would have left an anatomical specimen like the uteruses found in Tumblety's cabinet of curiosities.

As Tumblety was investigated by Scotland Yard, a Chicago newspaper caught up with Billy Pinkerton to ask the veteran detective, as he was by then, about his recollections of Tumblety.

469 Ibid: "The case of Annie Chapman"
470 Ibid: "The case of Annie Chapman"
471 "The Whitechapel (Hanbury-Street) Murder", *The Morning Post*, September 27, 1888

Walking along Clark Street with a reporter, he feigned some confusion over the doctor's name. "Tumblety! No, that's not it. Something like that, though. Tumbledy. No! Twombley! That's more like it." It's hard to believe that Pinkerton really couldn't recall the right spelling though at the time, the London police had arrested the doctor as Twomblety and some reports initially referred to him as "Kumblety".[472]

Pinkerton had been trailing Tumblety from the 1860s onwards. He knew perfectly well this Ripper suspect was the Indian Herb Doctor arrested over the Lincoln assassination and implicated in so many valet-related court cases, as well as arrests and surveillance over gross indecency. Why he was being coy with the reporter is uncertain.

But then he perked up recalling that the doctor was "the very same man that I met in Washington long ago". He told the reporter about his first glimpse of the Indian Herb Doctor as a teenage rookie investigator. "He was then a man of about thirty years of age, six feet high, well built, had very dark hair, and very long mustaches (sic), dyed coal black. In fact, his mustaches grew into his beard, or rather the beard lengthened out his mustaches until the latter spread down over his shoulders."

The detective moved on to Tumblety's circulating of obscene material in the Union army, followed by how his various vices were used to drive him from Washington DC after which Pinkerton claimed he next met Tumblety in Baltimore, then New York, then San Francisco, and Chicago in 1869, where Pinkerton now divulged that Tumblety had been forced to leave the windy city over some more obscene behaviour on the streets.

Pinkerton described how he bumped into Tumblety "accidentally" in Liverpool and London in 1874. "People familiar with the history of the man always talked of him as a brute, and as brutal in his actions. He was known as a thorough

---

472 "Billy Pinkerton's Points", *The Inter Ocean*, November 20, 1888

woman-hater; and as a man who never associated with or mixed with women of any kind." The reporter then asked Pinkerton the question on everybody's lips:

And what do you think are the probabilities of his being the man who committed the Whitechapel murders – murders committed apparently without any object in view? Do you consider that the Doctor was insane?[473]

Pinkerton referenced the work of Lincoln's Army Surgeon-General in his answer:

Yes, I do. I think a man guilty of such practices as those I have referred to must be insane; and Dr. Hammond – Surgeon General Hammond – some time ago, when asked as to whether or not he thought that that Whitechapel murderer was an insane man, said that when the murderer of those women was discovered he would undoubtedly be found to be a woman-hater and a man guilty of the same practices which I have described Dr. Twombley, or Tumblety, as being guilty of, and that such men were crazy and as likely as not to murder women.[474]

All the canonical Jack the Ripper victims were murdered in a timeframe that allowed Tumblety to be the perpetrator:

Mary Ann Nichols – 31 August, 1888
Annie Chapman – 8 September, 1888
Elizabeth Stride – 30 September, 1888
Catherine Eddowes – 30 September, 1888
Mary Jane Kelly – 9 November, 1888

---

473 Ibid: "Billy Pinkerton's Points"
474 Ibid: "Billy Pinkerton's Points"

There were non-canonical victims of Jack the Ripper including Emma Elizabeth Smith on 3 April 1888; Martha Tabram on 7 August 1888; Alice Mackenzie on 17 July 1889; and a woman found murdered in Pinchin Street on 10 September 1889. The last body was anonymous because the head and legs were missing. However, the later murders are harder to attribute to Tumblety as he was no longer in London, but the canonical murders could all have been from Tumblety's hand.

Tumblety was committed for trial and granted police bail to the amount of $3,000. Two "bondsmen" came forward with the amount of $1,500 each. This money had been forwarded from Tumblety's account at the Clewes Bank in New York. At Marlborough Street Police Court, he was remanded on £300 bail over the indecency charges. But this was now a far lesser charge. What he was facing was the trial of the century as the suspected Jack the Ripper.

Not since 1865 had Tumblety confronted such a perilous situation having narrowly avoided joining David Herold and the other Lincoln plotters on the scaffold that year. Now, he faced another date with the noose over the murders in Whitechapel.

He had done his utmost to cultivate support networks in London but maybe nowhere near as effective as those in the United States. Staring out over the grey streets of London, the doctor decided to repeat what he had done so many years before in Canada, when faced with a manslaughter charge.

Then, he had fled on a horse across the border avoiding almost certain imprisonment. Now, he resolved to make for a port and board a ship to France. Hurriedly, he packed his belongings and sneaked away. From France, he would board another vessel bound for New York and once again, he would save his own skin.

The next day, London police could find no trace of Tumblety. The Indian Herb Doctor had vanished. An incredulous Scotland Yard tracked down the two hapless bondsmen who claimed to have only known Tumblety for a few days prior to his arrest.[475] They had no idea where he had gone.

The doctor had disappeared into the ether.

---

475 "The Missing Tumblety" *Democrat and Chronicle,* December 3, 1888

Nine

Death and Annie Chapman's Rings

A shaken but certainly not chastened Francis Tumblety stepped off the transatlantic steamship, *La Bretagne* from Le Havre, France on to terra firma in New York after a journey of just over a week. One local newspaper welcomed him back guardedly:

> *We have in our midst once more here in New York that unique personage known as Dr. Tumblety. The man is not a criminal in the ordinary sense, but the suspicion that he is one in some extraordinary sense makes him interesting. He is big, tall and brawny. His heavy mustache exudes black hair dye. He is on the sunny side of 60 and by no means unprepossessing.*[476]

The voyage from Le Havre to New York was not unfamiliar to Tumblety. Ship records show that in September 1875, he made the same journey from Le Havre to New York on board a ship called *Greece*. These records prove that Tumblety's claims

---

476 "Gotham Gossip", *The Times-Picayune*, December 10, 1888

to have visited Europe on several occasions were not fictitious. So, he would have known how to abscond from London to the French port and make his way back home before Scotland Yard could catch him.

It's assumed that Tumblety disembarked alone. But he arrived in the company of a Texan valet named Jack. This mysterious individual, described by a private detective who regarded Tumblety as a friend, was soon viewed as a Ripper suspect. The theory being that he was somehow manipulated in a Svengali-like manner by the Indian Herb Doctor into committing the Whitechapel murders - and other killings. He may also have been the bodyguard shadowing Tumblety when he rubbed shoulders with Giteau.

Despite being a fugitive from British justice, Tumblety was not deported back to London. Pause and reflect on this for a moment. A suspect in one of those notorious murder cases in criminal history was able to walk freely from the city port and make his way to downtown lodgings without being stopped, questioned, detained, or sent back. How could that happen?

There were extradition protocols in place between the United States and United Kingdom going back to the Jay Treaty of 1794 and the Webster-Ashburton Treaty of 1842, that specifically dealt with the surrender of alleged murder offenders. Between 1846 and 1868, the UK made fifty-three extradition requests of the US and there were thirty-six in the opposite direction. Indeed, the US was up for broadening the number of offences covered in the latter treaty.[477] But with regards to Tumblety, no extradition took place.

Over the next couple of years, not only did Tumblety evade extradition over the Ripper murders, but he would avoid conviction in the United States over further crimes in which he was implicated and a copycat Ripper murder that gripped New

---

477 Rebecca Rideal, "Extradition – a very brief history", *The History Vault*, Issue 10

York in 1891. The protection and shielding he received came from the very top of the New York Police Department and the New York District Attorney.

Thomas F. Byrnes (1842–1910) was head of the NYPD. Born in Dublin, Ireland less than ten years after Tumblety's believed birth date, he had emigrated to New York as a child. Byrnes had been aware of Tumblety's existence for at least two decades given the doctor's high-profile presence in the city with various court cases and arrests on vice-related charges. Although repeatedly claiming to have Tumblety under surveillance, he also declared that he had no interest in the doctor's movements.

When Tumblety bolted for Chicago briefly to avoid journalists hounding him over the Ripper killings, they turned to Byrnes and asked him what he was going to do. Wasn't Byrnes concerned that Tumblety might vanish? The NYPD chief affected total disinterest. "I don't know where he is and to tell you the truth, I don't care."[478]

If Tumblety thought that Scotland Yard had forgotten him, then he was soon disabused. Detectives from London followed him to New York. Though their attempt to blend in and be circumspect failed miserably as one newspaper mocked their efforts:

An English detective, whose stupidity was noticeable even among a class not celebrated for their shrewdness, came over to shadow him, and scores of reporters tried in vain to see him.[479]

As soon as Tumblety disembarked, he made a beeline for the house of a certain Mrs McNamara at 79 East 10th Street. This old Irish woman had known the doctor for many years and remained

---

478 "Tumblety on the way to Chicago", *Ashland Weekly News*, December 12, 1888

479 "They suspected his hat", *The Dayton Herald*, February 23, 1889

doggedly faithful. McNamara fended off the journalists and detectives so effectively that "if it were not for the fact that the doctor voluntarily came forward and made his own statement, no one would have ever known whether he was in New York city or New Zealand",[480] as one newspaper put it. Tumblety decided to relate his own version of events. He began producing yet another edition of his autobiography and gave an interview for the press.

Tumblety chose the *New York World* newspaper to tell all. This was a deft PR move calculated to get his story to a wide audience. The *New York World* was a punchy title pioneering what came to be known as "yellow journalism", playing fast and loose with the truth. Its leading reporter was a spirited newshound, Nellie Bly (1864-1922), who penned blistering exposés of life in the New York slums.

Most importantly to Tumblety, the newspaper was friendly to Irish Catholics in New York, as potential readers, and it specialised in crime stories. So, feeling he was in good hands, Tumblety invited a *New York World* journalist into McNamara's house to give his first post-Ripper interview. The journalist found Tumblety in a feverish state, talking "in a quick, nervous fashion" with a "decided English accent". Remember that Mrs Pannier, the chestnut vendor in Whitechapel who had a chance encounter with a man she suspected was Jack the Ripper, said the stranger who addressed her had an English accent.

When describing how the London police had treated him, Tumblety rose from his chair and paced the room.

> *My arrest came about in this way. I had been going over to England for a long time, ever since 1869, indeed, and I used to go about the city a great deal until every part of it became familiar to me.*[481]

---

480 Ibid: "They suspected his hat"
481 New York World article quoted in *The Dayton Herald*, February 23, 1889

Tumblety stated that along with thousands of other Londoners, he visited the Whitechapel district to gawp at the murder scenes. By his own admission, he did not dress appropriately for the occasion being a little too fancy for that economically depressed area. One can imagine the anger he may have provoked attending a murder scene in the very height of fashion. With little hope of blending into the crowd, he drew unwelcome attention to himself, not just from the rubberneckers, but Scotland Yard as well:

I was interested by the crowds and the queer scenes and sights and did not know that all the time I was being followed by English detectives.[482]

The journalist asked Tumblety why the police would have been tracking his movements if he was an innocent man. Tumblety advanced several theories. The first was the notion circulating among Londoners that Jack the Ripper was an American:

Then it is the universal belief among the lower classes that all Americans wear slouch hats; therefore, Jack the Ripper must wear a slouch hat. Now, I happened to have a slouch hat and this, together with the fact that I was an American, was enough for the police. It established my guilt beyond any question.[483]

Then he moved swiftly to his next theory. Tumblety produced from an inside pocket of his coat, two magnificent diamonds. One was thirteen carats and the other, nine carats. "Both of the purest quality, and a superb cluster ring set in diamonds". The

---

482 New York World article quoted in *The Dayton Herald*, February 23, 1889
483 New York World article quoted in *The Dayton Herald*, February 23, 1889

police, he said, took him into custody with the sole purpose of getting their hands on his jewels. Having dragged him into the station, they could force Tumblety to surrender the priceless diamonds.[484]

When asked how he viewed the London police, Tumblety repeated what many Londoners thought at the time. Victorian middle-class opinion regarded the British capital's police as inefficient and useless. In April 1870, the *Saturday Review* blasted that "in the centre of civilization... society has almost returned to its primitive condition, in which men can find safety only in their own strength, and women can find safety nowhere". *Punch* magazine published mocking anti-police cartoons while letters to *The Times* complained that the police were spending too much time on the case, allowing other crimes to flourish.[485]

Tumblety added his derision, fulminating that the London police "stuff themselves all day with potpies and beef and drink gallons of stale beer, keeping it up until they go to bed late at night, and then wake up the next morning heavy at head". As a result of their dreadful lifestyle, the doctor continued, they all have dyspepsia:

Then their heads are as thick as the London fogs. You can't drive an idea through their thick skulls with a hammer. I never saw such a stupid set.[486]

Now in his stride, Tumblety declared that there hadn't been a scintilla of evidence against him except this absurd notion about the slouch hat, for which he had been implicated as the perpetrator of the world's first recognised slayings by a serial killer. This was not true. Scotland Yard had regarded him as a

484 New York World article quoted in *The Dayton Herald*, February 23, 1889

485 Letters, *The Times*, October 11, 1888, original newspaper owned by the author

486 New York World article quoted in *The Dayton Herald*, February 23, 1889

suspect because of what their American counterparts relayed about his past brushes with the law and that collection of uteruses.

If only Inspector Byrnes of the New York Police Department had been in London, Tumblety added, he would have found the Ripper in no time. This was a calculated grovel to a fellow Irish American in New York. Byrnes led the NYPD from 1880 to 1895 and has been credited with inventing the terms "rogues gallery" and "third degree".[487] He also appears as a fictional character in the novel, *The Alienist* later adapted into a Netflix drama series.[488]

Tumblety was then asked about his reported hatred of women. "I don't care to talk about the ladies," he responded tersely. But then offered a deliciously camp morsel to illustrate how women were apparently attracted to him. It involved an aristocratic lady who fell for the doctor's charms while he was in England.

I had received a letter of introduction to a lady of rank, a duchess, who was then at Torquay, which is several hundred miles from London. I presented my letter and was invited to breakfast with her.[489]

The letter would have been one the many testimonials Tumblety always carried on his person from the likes of Abraham Lincoln and the author Charles Dickens. Evidently capable of playing the role of gentleman suitor, Tumblety presented this duchess with a bouquet of flowers. Quite overwhelmed, she picked up a quill from the table and extemporised a poem on the spot.

---

487 "Ex-chief Byrnes dies of cancer", *New York Times*, May 8, 1910
488 Caleb Carr, *The Alienist* (Sphere, 2011)
489 New York World article quoted in *The Dayton Herald*, February 23, 1889

In memory of the past
To guard the faded flower
When you have gone from me
In memory of the hour
You came to sweet Torquay.[490]

That hardly fits with me being a woman hater, Tumblety exclaimed. He then bombarded the journalist with the usual testimonials from delighted patients overjoyed that he had saved their lives where mainstream physicians had failed. He then breathlessly claimed to have been a member of London's prestigious Carlton Club and Beefsteak Club. Bitterly, he concluded, "It is strange... because I don't remember ever to have done any human being a harm, and I know of a great many whom I have helped".[491]

Tumblety's membership of gentlemen's clubs is something overlooked and worth noting. As the Cleveland Street scandal revealed, these clubs were places where one might find out how to procure the services of male and female prostitutes from other members. A discreet whispered exchange in the library would have informed Tumblety of both where he could find gay prostitutes but also vulnerable women in Whitechapel.

In 1888, the very year that the Ripper was operating, *The Society Herald* described how London's clubs were a secret, self-contained world for rich bachelors, unseen by most of the population. "He breakfasts, lunches, dines, and sups at the club... He lives, moves, and has his being within his club".[492] It formed the backdrop to the lives of both married and single

---

490 New York World article quoted in *The Dayton Herald*, February 23, 1889
491 New York World article quoted in *The Dayton Herald*, February 23, 1889
492 Amy Milne-Smith, "A Flight to Domesticity? Making a Home in the Gentlemen's Clubs of London, 1880-1914", *Journal of British Studies*, Vol. 45, No. 4, October 2006, pp. 796-818

men who "regarded their club as a central part of their lives, functioning as a surrogate home".

These all-male clubs had always attracted upper-class gay men. Members of the Golden Fleece Club adopted camp nicknames on admission like Sir Skinny Fretwell, Sir Gregory Growler, and Sir Nicholas Ninny Sip-all. These were safe spaces for gay men and normally unmolested by the police.

Unless they were less salubrious as was the case with The Vere Street Club raided a few decades earlier. It was a tavern off Lincoln's Inn Fields for a lower class of homosexual and when invaded by the Bow Street "runners", an early form of police, twenty-three men including the landlord were taken into custody for crimes "of a most detestable description". The occupations of those arrested included a hotel waiter, army corporal, and "servant to a gentleman in Portland Place". Two of those arrested, John Hepburn and Thomas White, a sixteen-year-old drummer boy, were subsequently hanged at Newgate Prison.

While in London, Tumblety could very easily have frequented both kinds of establishment: the gentlemen's club and the working-class gay tavern cruising for sex, but also tapping into clandestine networks as he did in America. He boasted about his membership of the Carlton, but it would have been a relatively short walk to the fleshpots of Soho.

Over the years, newspapers observed the slavish relationship between Tumblety and his young male valets, one referring to the "mesmeric force" he exercised over these men and his ability to direct their actions.[493] In the months after Tumblety's return to the United States, rumours circulated that the NYPD, and those English detectives who had tracked the doctor across the Atlantic, were pursuing a new lead. It still involved Tumblety. Though they now believed that one of the doctor's valets

---

493 "Tumblety" *St Louis Globe-Democrat*, January 5, 1889

257

could have been Jack the Ripper - or rather he was directed by Tumblety to carry out the killings.

Police sources spoke of a man "who attracted almost as much attention as the doctor both on account of oddity of characteristics and the shadow-like persistence with which he followed his employer".[494] Journalists were understandably intrigued. One reporter approached a well-known private detective, James Jackson, who was assisting with investigations into Tumblety. Jackson feigned an unwillingness to discuss the case, but the reporter soon got him talking.

Jackson had met Tumblety back in the spring of 1870 in Pittsburgh when the doctor was dabbling in the coal business. He was quite taken by him, describing Tumblety as a dignified and polite man with a military bearing. Tumblety invited the private detective to have a cigar at the Monongahela House. True to form, this was the premier hotel in the city. Abraham Lincoln had stayed there on his multi-city trip to Washington DC in 1861 for his inauguration. Jackson recalled his first meeting with Tumblety.

It was a cold, snowy evening, and smoking our cigars, we walked down to his office. In the meantime he had introduced himself by showing a heavy gold medal which purported to have been presented to him by the citizens of Salt Lake, Utah, for some service.[495]

The doctor was carrying a gold-headed cane, "so heavy that it would tire your hand".[496] Tumblety insisted on giving Jackson a physical examination and "freely gave his advice as to a line of habits which would in a few years make me a perfect specimen

---

494 "Jack the Ripper – Is he Tumblety's Man Friday?", *The Beaver Crossing Bugle*, January 16, 1889

495 Ibid: "Jack the Ripper – Is he Tumblety's Man Friday?"

496 Ibid: "Jack the Ripper – Is he Tumblety's Man Friday?"

of manhood".[497] Jackson was so taken by Tumblety that he visited his work premises frequently and they became great friends. There was a barrel of ale in his office, and they would sit and drink until both men became "somewhat jolly".

The reporter now got to the point of the story:

"Did he at the time have a companion called Jack?"
"What's that?" said the detective.
The question was repeated.
"Well yes," replied the detective in a hesitating, suspicious tone, "I believe he did. But why do you ask?"

Jackson was then told about the rumours that a companion of Tumblety might be Jack the Ripper.

"To tell you the truth," the detective continued, "he did have such a companion, or rather bodyguard. The shadow was with him wherever he went and was known only by the name of Jack. His last name I never heard spoken."[498]

Jackson described Jack in some detail. He was very tall, giant-like even, but his head was always bent over. His deep blue eyes had a "snaky appearance" while his hair was long but his moustache was very small. He was most likely from Texas, where he had been a cowboy of some sort. He didn't speak very much and had a "sneaking movement about him" that made Jackson feel uneasy.

The private detective thought he was "insane and desperate – a man who would do anything". The Texan was sartorially always well presented in a velvet suit. Most likely this was Tumblety's choice of attire for his companion. Five years later

---

497 Ibid: "Jack the Ripper – Is he Tumblety's Man Friday?"
498 Ibid: "Jack the Ripper – Is he Tumblety's Man Friday?"

in 1875, Jackson boarded a train at Aurora, Indiana, and found Tumblety seated in the carriage. Next to him was Jack. It turned out in the subsequent conversation that Jack accompanied Tumblety everywhere including trips overseas.

The reporter posed the key question:

"Is there any possibility that Tumblety's Jack and Jack the Ripper might be some way connected in the recent mysterious murders of London?"[499]

Jackson briefly considered this:

"Well, I have heard suspicions that they might be one and the same," remarked the detective guardedly, "but I don't care to talk about it for certain reasons. I may say, however, that the suspicion is very strong in my mind, and if the inquiries were rightly pushed they might lead to startling developments. I can't say any more to you at present."[500]

This story has been inexplicably overlooked, arising as it did in the last years of Tumblety's life. But it raises the possibility that Tumblety directed his physically stronger valet, a reportedly psychotic Texan, to carry out the Whitechapel killings. Also, note that Mrs Fiddymont, wife of the landlord of the Prince Albert pub in Whitechapel, had seen a man she believed was Jack the Ripper whose clothes were a shabbier version of Tumblety's attire and who was younger than the doctor. Could this have been Texan Jack?

This would have made Texan Jack the second of Tumblety's valets to be involved in acts of murder. Davie Herold had been

---

499 Ibid: "Jack the Ripper – Is he Tumblety's Man Friday?"
500 Ibid: "Jack the Ripper – Is he Tumblety's Man Friday?"

a Lincoln plotter while Texan Jack may have been a perpetrator and the real Jack the Ripper.

What also emerges from the Jackson interview is that Texan Jack had been a feature of Tumblety's life throughout the 1870s and 1880s - a very long time for a valet to last with the doctor. This means that he could have been about forty years old, at the younger end of the age range specified by Mrs Fiddymont regarding the man she saw in her pub downing an ale with spots of blood on his clothes.

The fact that Jack came from Texas opens another can of worms. Three years before the Jack the Ripper case, there was a spate of murders in Texas by a serial killer dubbed the Servant Girl Annihilator. Eight women were slain by this individual also known as the Austin Axe Murderer and the Midnight Assassin. The police investigation was largely ineffective with the husbands of two of the victims being accused of murdering their wives and then acquitted.

Most of the victims were domestic staff and African American, though two white women were also targeted. The level of evisceration in these unsolved cases, clearly the work of the same man, was what struck journalists at the time. And they observed marked similarities between the way in which the body of Eula Phillips, killed in Austin on Christmas night, 1885, was laid out and Jack the Ripper's methodology - especially in the cases of Elizabeth Stride and Catherine Eddowes.[501]

In 1885, Scotland Yard was asked to help track down the Servant Girl Annihilator in the belief that he may have made his way to London. As a result, London detectives questioned several American "cowboys", one of whom was performing in Buffalo Bill's Wild West Show. This was a hugely popular recreation of frontier life with realistic shoot outs. No arrests

---

501 "A Comparison", *The Ottowa Daily Republic*, October 5, 1888

or hot leads resulted from this activity. By 1888, the killer was still at large.

This led one American newspaper, *The Evening World*, to beg readers to go easy on Scotland Yard's deficiencies over the Ripper murders given the lack of any progress on the Austin killings. "Are we not living in a glass house in this respect? Have we a right to throw stones at Whitechapel?"[502] In addition, it noted, there were unsolved murders in Connecticut where the "soil is stained with the blood of victims" and New Jersey which was "rapidly becoming a land of dark mysteries".

If we accept that Tumblety escalated from occasional killing in the line of his medical work to becoming a full-scale serial killer, could he have had a dry run in Texas? And if these grisly murders are connected to Tumblety, did he team up with a local, young psychopath to engage in an orgy of slaying? Jack the Texan was named as a possible Jack the Ripper suspect, so why not the Servant Girl Annihilator? Once the homicidal valet had proven his murderous ability in his home state, did Tumblety then take him across the Atlantic to London's Whitechapel district?

In June 1889, barely seven months after being arrested as a Ripper suspect and then jumping bail, Tumblety found himself in a New York jail cell on a charge of assault. The incident was described in one newspaper as "an echo from Whitechapel in Jefferson Market".[503] Why did the newspaper make this analogy?

Tumblety had been engaged in some nocturnal prowling on the streets of New York when he encountered a younger man, George Davis who lived on Allen Street - now part of Chinatown and the Lower East Side, but then populated by Sephardic and Romanian Jews running basement metal-bashing shops.

The newspapers couldn't agree on the exact details.

---

502 "A Glass House. Don't Throw Any More Stones at Whitechapel", *The Evening World*, November 19, 1888

503 "Tumblety Arrested", *The Evening World*, June 5, 1889

Tumblety and Davis met sometime between 10.30pm and midnight either on Broadway or Fifth Avenue, near what was then Clinton Place. Police reports confirmed that Tumblety was living at number 82 Clinton Place, so not straying too far from his residence. They seem to have conversed and strolled for a while. Tumblety took a fancy to Davis and "tried to walk home with him".

> *Davis told him to go away, but he wouldn't do it. Davis then called him a base name.*[504]

Furious at this insult, Tumblety struck the man across the neck with his cane - or the face in another report. Davis cried out for help. The thrashing continued until the police arrived. Both men then fled, with Davis caught by Captain Brogan of the Mercer Street police station and Tumblety apprehended by police officer McLaughlin.

The next morning, they found themselves before a magistrate in an impressive Gothic building, the Jefferson Market courthouse, known locally as "Old Jeff". In a sign of his vanity, Tumblety declared he was fifty years old but local witnesses who had known him a long time vouched he was nearer sixty. Davis and the police officer told the same story regarding Tumblety's "eccentric behaviour". Tumblety countered that he had refused to give Davis money leading to the fracas. Either Davis was attempting to rob Tumblety or more likely, the doctor resented being asked to pay for sex. The resulting "vile" language fits that explanation more convincingly.

One newspaper reported that Tumblety appeared in court "flashily dressed and sparkling with diamonds"[505]. That would suggest he was the Indian Herb Doctor of yore. But another

---

504 "Eccentricities of Dr. Tumblety", *Pittsburgh Dispatch*, June 6, 1889
505 Ibid: "Eccentricities of Dr. Tumblety"

report contradicted that stating, "he was dressed very shabbily this morning".[506] Admittedly, a night in the cells may not have helped his appearance. Inside his pockets, police found $1,000 in cash which at today's value is roughly $32,000.

In his defence, Tumblety flourished old testimonials singing his praises from the Civil War era journalist and failed presidential candidate Horace Greeley and a renowned physician, Dr Willard Parker. Tumblety produced a book giving an account of his life as a physician, most likely his autobiography, on the cover of which were glowing references from General Sherman and Abraham Lincoln.[507]

It seems astonishing that so soon after being implicated in the Jack the Ripper murders, with all their attendant violence, Tumblety would permit himself to be involved in such an altercation, but now aged around sixty, he still clearly had a compulsive sexual appetite and volcanic temper. So where would Tumblety have gone to find sex in the New York of the Gilded Age?

The LGBT historian Jonathan Ned Katz identifies Broadway and nearby City Hall Park as the main locations where unemployed and working-class men could be found selling their favours. Not only was Tumblety seeking sex, but many New Yorkers with money went to the seedier downtown areas to engage in some poverty tourism, "to witness the depravity of the lower classes and thus to be scandalized or titillated".[508]

Broadway had been a magnet for those seeking same-sex encounters since a German, Charles Ignatius Pfaff, had opened a "bohemian" bar called Pfaff's in the basement of the Coleman House Hotel between 1859 and 1864. A narrow metal staircase

---

506 Ibid: "Tumblety Arrested"

507 Ibid: "Tumblety Arrested"

508 Kathleen Howe, Kathleen LaFrank, "Historic Context Statement for LGTBT History in New York City", *NYC LGBT Historic Sites Project*, 2018

transported visitors into two dimly lit, vaulted rooms, filled with smoke. There were two regulars in the Civil War era: Walt Whitman but also the actor brother of John Wilkes Booth – Edwin, attracted, no doubt, by the bar's "bohemian" crowd and its boast to have "the best of everything".[509]

Tumblety could have chosen a marginally safer option and frequented the emerging homosexual scene around Bleecker Street in Greenwich Village. One venue, The Slide at 157 Bleecker Street, may have been operating already by 1889. It was publicly identified as a gay bar in 1890. A "slide" in the street slang of the time was a place where gay men dressed as women and solicited men. It lasted until 1892 before being closed by police.

On the same street, at number 183, was another venue for same-sex encounters called The Black Rabbit. It enjoyed the distinction in 1900 of being raided in person by Anthony Comstock, the United States Postal Inspector, and head of the New York Society for the Suppression of Vice. Comstock declared he had "never before raided a place so wicked, and that Sodom and Gomorrah would blush for shame at hearing to what depths of vice its habitués had descended".[510]

Reading between the lines of the newspaper report, an ageing Tumblety had gone looking for some casual sex and either inadvertently targeted a heterosexual man, which seems unlikely given his long experience, or been given the cold shoulder by a younger gay man repelled by his advances and demanding money as a pre-condition for sex. An affronted Tumblety then let rip with his fists, feet, and cane.

The case for assault in the third degree was eventually dismissed two months later. It emerged that George Davis was a disreputable character operating under several aliases.

509 Jaap Harskamp, "Charlie Pfaff, Walt Whitman and the King of Bohemia", *New York Almanack*, October 6, 2021

510 "Raid on The Black Rabbit", *New York Times*, October 6, 1900

But critically for the doctor, a character witness of the highest standing came forward to vouch for Tumblety's good name and insist that the case be dismissed.

This was Colonel John R. Fellows (1832-1896) who had fought with the Confederates in the Civil War but became a skilful political operator in New York through the Democrat Party's Tammany Hall machine. The Tammany Hall operation promoted Irish Americans to top political positions and was notoriously corrupt. Between 1888 and 1890, Colonel Fellows, very much championed by Tammany Hall, was the Attorney General of New York, just the kind of friend that Tumblety needed.

And he duly rode to the doctor's rescue:

In recommending the dismissal of the indictment Colonel Fellows said that Dr. Tumblety was a gentleman of the very highest standing and moral character, that the complainant was a confirmed liar, and that to subject the defendant to the risk of a trial would be a gross outrage on justice.[511]

The Brooklyn Daily Eagle, which had led the attack on Tumblety during the immediate aftermath of the Lincoln assassination, ran the headline: "Dr. Tumblety Vindicated".

The question arises why the New York district attorney would stick his neck out for Tumblety? Here was a man who had been accused of being Jack the Ripper in the previous year; implicated in the Lincoln plot twenty-five years before that; and had a long police and court record for vice-related charges?

Tumblety had clearly been wise enough to buy support at Tammany Hall among his fellow Irish Americans through political donations. The doctor was known to have Irish

---

511 "Dr. Tumblety Vindicated", *The Brooklyn Daily Eagle*, August 9, 1889

Republican leanings, like most Irish Catholics in North America, and he retained a sense of kinship and loyalty to his Irish roots. Was this New York's Tammany, Democrat, Irish mafia looking after its own?

Tammany Hall was not immune to sex and gender politics. In 1901, two years before Tumblety's death, it was rocked by a very modern scandal around the gender of one of its leading politicians. Murray Hall was a married man; an energetic local political operative; a regular feature in the saloons of the Fifth Assembly District of the Tammany organisation; and dispenser of charity to the city's poor. However, as a fatal illness struck, this Tammany bigwig was forced to reveal to doctors that he was in fact a woman.

She had been living as a man to realise her political ambitions, but it had all been a lifetime of deception. Shortly after her confession, she passed away. The cause of death was breast cancer. New York politicians were dumbstruck. Irish-born New York Senator Bernard "Barney" Martin (1845–1914) put on a brave face as he received the news calling his old friend "a fine, big woman", even if he could "hardly believe that he was a woman". It had changed his view on the contentious issue of extending votes to female citizens:

Any woman that can act a man's part in every way, even to supporting a wife and family for thirty years, as Murray Hall did, has a right to vote.[512]

Tammany Hall, with its corrupt and lively approach to city politics, seems a natural home for Tumblety. It afforded this son of Ireland some protection and as the Murray Hall case illustrates, there was a large amount of forgiveness on hand for those within its fold of different sexualities and genders.

---

512 "The remarkable career of Murray Hall", *The Farmers Advocate*, January 25, 1901

It stretches credulity to imagine that Tammany politicians were unaware of Tumblety's sexuality, so he got the required shielding.

In recent years, the dreadful reputation of Tammany's machine politics has been reappraised with its positive record on social services and assimilating immigrants.[513] Many of its harshest critics were also rabidly anti-Irish and anti-Catholic. Tumblety's involvement with Tammany ran alongside his support for the Irish National Party in New York, mentioned in an article on the doctor in *The Brooklyn Daily Eagle*. Throughout his life, he remained a keen supporter of Home Rule in Ireland. [514]

But politics was always a secondary consideration for Tumblety who used it primarily as a means for social advancement and building his business. Also, it was another arena for meeting handsome young men with the choicest employed as his valet. However, the intervention of Colonel Fellows in a potentially very damaging legal case for Tumblety shows that keeping his toe in political waters paid dividends when required.

Months after skipping bail and escaping Scotland Yard across the Atlantic to New York, Tumblety was telling journalists variously that he had been acquitted or released. Neither of these claims were true. This was Tumblety out to control the narrative and it revealed a growing confidence that he was untouchable with regards to the Jack the Ripper killings. Basically, he had got away with it.

This merited an updated edition of the autobiography. It included a testimonial from the late President Lincoln alongside glowing commendations from Emperor Napoleon III of France, Charles Dickens, and Samuel Morse, inventor of Morse Code.

Whereas the 1866 first edition of the autobiography

---

513 Terry Golway, Machine Made: Tammany Hall and the Creation of Modern American Politics (Liveright, 2014)

514 "Herbs, Salts and Cider", *The Brooklyn Daily Eagle*, April 27, 1890

reserved its bile for Lincoln's Secretary of War Edwin Stanton, whose warrant had resulted in Tumblety's imprisonment over the presidential assassination, he now took aim at a broader spectrum of perceived enemies. After all, so much had happened since 1866. He even turned on the newspapers that had cultivated his celebrity status, especially those journalists who had dragged his reputation through the mud:

The bitter persecution, venomous assaults and the impudent curiosity, which when balked, becomes malevolent, aimed at the writer from the reptile section of the public press, justify the assumption that the authors of such attacks can only be likened to serpents and similar crawling nuisances.[515]

He was faced with a deluge of slanders all his life but, he declared, this hadn't reduced him to a miserable level but instead heightened his contempt for the liars and critics. He then made an impassioned defence of his record as a doctor. His patients had included the wealthy and distinguished who ignored the sneering from the newspapers and gave Tumblety their full confidence, and money.

Writing this updated biography was nothing to do with vanity or egotism, he continued, but to inform the public that his life had been a "somewhat notable one" that was "distinguished by the intimacy of many eminent personages" and dedicated to medical progress. Sadly, for Tumblety, no institution, society, hospital, or place of learning thought he had advanced the corpus of medical knowledge one inch.

The autobiography throws up a tantalising clue that might explain why he eviscerated women on the streets of London, and possibly elsewhere. Tumblety felt that the medical

---

515 "Tumblety gets mad", *Sunday Truth*, February 10, 1889

establishment did not take him seriously because he was not qualified to cut people open. Real doctors chopped legs off and got blood on their hands delving into a patient's torso. But what was Tumblety? A fraudulent upstart herbalist?

To try and justify himself, Tumblety made a comparision between two London-based early 19th century doctors: Sir Astley Cooper (1768–1841) and John Abernethy (1764–1831). The purpose was to make the point that his patent medicines were as valid as anything going on in hospital operating rooms.

He characterised Cooper, whose statue can still be seen in Saint Paul's Cathedral, as being too eager to cut open a patient, whereas Abernethy was more reluctant, seeking less harmful, non-invasive approaches. Abernethy developed a digestive biscuit named after him to treat dyspepsia. It's still sold in Britain today as a teatime treat. Tumblety, untrained to perform invasive surgery, lauded Abernethy's non-surgical approach.

There is no disputing the fact that the knife is a source of immense mischief to the human family. Every day brings us tidings of some unfortunate man or woman being ushered into eternity through the means of a surgical operation.[516]

His rubbishing of Cooper's readiness to saw off limbs was grounded in Tumbley's underlying inferiority complex over his own lack of authentic medical qualifications. This had been rubbed in his face all his life. Even the repeat fortunes he had made from dubious cures had not lessened the sense of grievance. It was arguably this sense of inferiority that fired those acts of barbaric surgery upon women in the darkened streets of Whitechapel. They were condemned to be the subjects

---

516 Ibid: "Tumblety gets mad"

of his professional wrath. Eviscerating their bodies, he finally got to be a surgeon - a real doctor.

Tumblety distributed his autobiography in person to passers-by as one startled visitor to New York from the town of Olean, in upstate Cattaraugus County, witnessed. On an August morning in 1889, this gentleman boarded a tramcar and grabbed a seat only to notice a "peculiar looking man" getting on. Six feet in height, a square red face, and a gigantic moustache. Tumblety sat next to the startled Oleander.

He immediately recognised Tumblety from pictures in the press and gingerly engaged him in conversation. It began with an observation about the weather and some small talk before the visitor plucked up the courage to ask his name. The doctor extended his hand in greeting.

"Dr. Francis Tumblety, you may have heard it before."[517]

The Oleander said he had, whereupon Tumblety regaled him with the many wrongs he had suffered and pressed a copy of his autobiography into the visitor's hand. This scene shows that even quite late in his life, the doctor was still something of a celebrity. A man from the suburbs, up to the big city for the day, was over the moon to meet a genuinely famous person. And our Oleander was clearly prepared to overlook the disagreeable press Tumblety had received in recent years.

In November 1890, Tumblety was arrested and briefly jailed in Washington DC as a "suspicious character".[518] One of Tumblety's frequent complaints, going back to his arrest over the Lincoln plot, was that the police, or the authorities, robbed him every time he was arrested. Wealth extracted from his pockets or bank account were not returned. One can understand the

517 "Oleanders in New York", *The Olean Democrat*, August 8, 1889
518 "General Intelligence", *Citizen*, November 20, 1890

temptation for arresting officers given the eye watering sums the doctor always carried with him. On this occasion, the police court was informed that Tumblety had $3,000 about his person when arrested. That is just under $98,000 today.

In court, Tumblety testified on his own behalf that he had been waiting for a tramcar at 7th Street and Pennsylvania Avenue when Detective Horne sidled up beside him. The doctor, meanwhile, had been eavesdropping on two young men at the stop who were discussing attractions in New York. Very likely, Tumblety was pondering his next move on them when Horne pounced.

The newspaper report descended into the usual coded language used for homosexual-related vice cases. Reference was made to the gross indecency charges he had been facing in London when initially arrested by Scotland Yard. This clearly irked Tumblety. Under cross-examination the doctor "said that he was never charged with a similar offense in England to that indicated by the officer". Tumblety then denied that he was "mixed up in a scandal implicating certain lords". This was a reference to the Cleveland Street affair of 1889 involving the post office messenger boys and their well-heeled aristocratic clients.[519]

Horne seems to have been on Tumblety's tail for a while observing his "suspicious" behaviour. On this occasion, the doctor had crossed a line and the detective felt able to make his move. Tumblety, however, summoned two character witnesses from his past in Washington DC to rescue him.

A man named as Stable Keeper Keliher swore on oath that during the Battle of Bull Run in the American Civil War, Tumblety "was very active in helping the sick and the wounded".[520] This presents a wholly different picture of the

---

519 "Dr Tumblety free", *Evening Star*, November 18, 1890
520 Ibid: "Dr Tumblety free"

doctor and his time in the Union army to Billy Pinkerton's version of events where he was depicted as a charlatan and pornographer. Could it be possible that the Indian Herb Doctor did something useful during his short term of military service? Also, if Keliher was telling the truth, which of course is open to question, it would lend credence to Colonel Dunham's claim to have first met Tumblety after the Battle of Bull Run.

Another man referred to as Saloon Keeper Harvey remembered Tumblety from the early 1860s and also testified to his "good character". Having heard the evidence, Judge Miller ruled that the account of suspicious behaviour offered by Horne did not come up to the standard of legal proof required to incarcerate Tumblety. The charge was dismissed, though Tumblety would remain under police surveillance.

The Indian Herb Doctor had continued to be a feature of police stations and courtrooms for reasons that dogged him throughout his life. But nothing had arisen of late that bore comparison to the Jack the Ripper killings. However, that was about to change.

On 24 April 1891, the body of a woman was found at a very downbeat lodging house, the East River Hotel. She had been eviscerated in the manner of the Whitechapel murders. The victim, Carrie Brown, was a sixty-year-old woman, possibly Canadian-born, known as Old Shakespeare - apparently because she could quote lines from the Bard's plays after downing a few drinks at the bar.

The old woman, who was known only as Shakespeare among her cronies in the slums of Water Street, was a woman far superior in many ways to those with whom she associated. She was nicknamed Shakespeare because of her knowledge of literature.521

---

521 "Many Arrests", *The Brooklyn Daily Eagle*, April 25 1891

Journalists were initially quite disparaging about this "old hanger on" who frequented the "low resorts of the east side". She was written off as an ageing prostitute who, in summary, would come to a grim end. But New York's Coroner Schulz painted a different picture to *The Brooklyn Daily Eagle*:

> *This woman has occupied a good position in life. She was a domestic recently but was brought down to that level because of her love for drink. She was well connected and well educated.*[522]

Both Coroner Schulz and NYPD Chief Inspector Byrnes were convinced that the killer was London's Jack the Ripper. Captain Richard O'Connor, a right-hand man to Byrnes, told reporters: "it's Jack's work to a dot".[523] Schulz left no room for doubt that the Ripper had crossed the Atlantic and New York had every right to be terrified:

> *He believes the London fiend has visited New York and has begun as series of butcheries here such as those committed by him in London.*[524]

The reporter pressed Schulz on the connection: *Do you think she was killed by 'Jack the Ripper'?* His answer was conclusive:

> *"I believe this case is the same as those of London. In this case, the murderer first strangled his victim and then mutilated her body. There are plain marks of his thumb and finger on her throat. It would appear that she was so*

---

522 Ibid: "Many Arrests"
523 "Killed by the Ripper", *Darlington Democrat,* May 1, 1891
524 Ibid: "Many Arrests"

drunk that she could offer but little resistance."[525]

Jack the Ripper bought enough ale at the bar to sink Carrie into a "drunken stupor", then garrotted the hapless woman with an item of her own clothing. But when that proved insufficient, the Ripper used his own hands. The coroner confirmed that she was dead before he cut her open in the same manner as Annie Chapman removing part of her "viscera".

> *The cut was from the base of the spine up across the abdomen to the breastbone. It was made with the knife found in the room. It was such a cut as must have been made slowly and deliberately. It would appear as though the murderer had pulled the intestines out and spread them on the bed. Then he turned the body over and with the point of his knife scratched a cross on the skin of the left thigh. I do not see any reason to suppose that the crime may not have been committed by the fiend of London.*[526]

In a gruesome twist, Deputy Coroner Jenkins demurred in part from his superior's view on one key point. Having carried out a thorough investigation of Carrie's corpse, he was sure that "the mutilation of the body had begun before life was extinct".[527] In other words, Carrie had been alive during her final torment. Furthermore, Jenkins believed that part of her intestines had been carried off by the murderer.

For Byrnes at the NYPD, this was a golden opportunity to show Scotland Yard that his department could succeed in unmasking the Ripper where the English police had so singularly failed. Remember that Tumblety had mocked the

---

525 Ibid: "Many Arrests"
526 Ibid: "Many Arrests"
527 Ibid: "Many Arrests"

London cops for their incompetence and declared Byrnes would have solved the case by now. Here was the NYPD's opportunity to prove that was true. So, would they come knocking at Tumblety's door?

The day after the murder, Byrnes had every police officer, who could be freed up, on the case. He "put out his drag net in the Fourth ward" and brought every potential suspect down to the 4th precinct police station on Oak Street. The building became a veritable Ripper HQ.

New Yorkers marvelled at the sight of Byrnes running up and down New Chambers Street ordering his officers around. At one point, he bolted into the station yelling at a detective who "did not move as rapidly as the inspector seemed to think he should". Reportedly, Byrnes hadn't slept since being told of Carrie's murder the night before.

Everything that looks like an important clew (sic) receives his personal attention. He is on trial before the world, and he seems to know it. The morning newspapers published dispatches telling of the joy in Scotland yards (sic) because of his inability to catch this man after he had boasted that "Jack the Ripper" could not do in New York what he had done in London.[528]

Byrnes knew every criminal in the squalid neighbourhoods of downtown New York and journalists were soon comparing the area where the murder had taken place to London's East End, where Jack the Ripper had operated.

There is no other part of New York that resembles the Whitechapel district of London as Water street does. The hovels here are filthy, low places whose income is deprived

---

528 Ibid: "Many Arrests"

entirely from drunken sailors. The women who lure sailors into the dive are wretched creatures.[529]

Aside from the drunken sailors, the only other men in the area were petty thieves who worked alongside the prostitutes to rob their inebriated clients. *The Brooklyn Daily Eagle* opined that if Jack the Ripper was looking to stalk the streets of New York, then this was the location he would choose.

Journalists and police were convinced the murderer had studied the area. The crime was planned to precision. Carrie had occupied her usual place in the bar under the hotel, which closed at 1am. But drinks could be bought and taken to the rooms throughout the night.

Jack the Ripper and Carrie had entered the hotel before midnight. But her killer wouldn't have been able to make his escape through the hotel entrance or saloon without asking somebody to unlock a door. So, more than likely, he squeezed through a window, stepping on to a lean-to shed, and dropped down into the street. All of this required advance knowledge.

Those rounded up for questioning included Mary Healey, a friend of Carrie; a witness, William Bekker; Lizzie Carter; Mary Lopez; Alice Sullivan; and Mary Minter the hotel housekeeper. Most of the women interrogated were female acquaintances of Carrie living in similar poverty-stricken conditions.

There were also suspects who police officers thought bore a striking resemblance to the man described as Jack the Ripper. Mounted Patrolman Frank of the 10th precinct took two "tramps" into custody convinced that one of them, John Foley of Newark, New Jersey, was a dead ringer for the Whitechapel murderer.

Meanwhile, Detective Sergeant Carney of the 2nd precinct was on his way to breakfast at 7am when he spotted a very likely

---

529 Ibid: "Many Arrests"

candidate for Jack the Ripper on the corner of Fulton and Hicks streets. Five-feet-eight-inches high; about thirty years old; a prominent moustache "which is the most certain feature of the murderer's description"; and a "battered derby hat".[530] His clothes were dark and soiled.

As Sergeant Carney noted these confirmatory details his heart jumped at the chance that he had got the real 'Jack the Ripper' and his hand was quickly on the lounger's collar.[531]

This arrest provoked a ripple of excitement through the NYPD. Byrnes sent Detective Sergeant McNaughton and a woman named Mary Billiter to take a good look at this suspect. He turned out to be a German-born unemployed butcher, Frederick Strube, aged twenty-six. A hotel clerk at the Glenmore hotel on Chatham Square, five minutes away from the East River hotel, confirmed that a shabbily dressed man with a German accent had tried to check in there at 2am that night with no money and his clothes and face covered in blood.

The night clerk remarked that the man looked as though he had been killing somebody.[532]

Billiter worked at the East River Hotel and had admitted Carrie and her murderer through the entrance that night. The two had filled in the hotel registration book as "Knickloi and wife"[533] even though Billiter knew perfectly well who Carrie was and what she was doing. "The couple were assigned to a room

---

530 Ibid: "Many Arrests"

531 Ibid: "Many Arrests"

532 "Horrible Butchery", *Springville Journal*, May 1, 1891

533 Ibid: "Horrible Butchery"

on the upper floor and went to it at once."[534] Billiter heard no cry for help or any unusual noise that fateful night.

However, as soon as Billiter saw Strube, she was adamant he wasn't the killer. The man seen with Carrie was of slighter build and not so tall. As Strube was ruled out, another officer brought a pair of trousers to the Ripper HQ on which were spots of blood. This led to the arrest of a native of French-controlled Algeria whom the police referred to as "Frenchy". One newspaper adopted a sarcastic and cynical tone:

> *He was immediately placed under arrest. He does not answer the description sent out by the New York police, but because he is called "Frenchy" and says he lives at the Fourth Ward hotel, the name by which the East River hotel is generally known, he is held.*

There ended up being two suspects, cousins, referred to as Frenchy 1 and Frenchy 2. The first Frenchy, an Algerian named Ameer Ben Ali "of the tribe of Ben Asha" was put on trial for the murder. He had been a soldier in the Franco-Prussian war in which Tumblety also claimed at to have served as an army surgeon, hence a glowing testimonial, reprinted by the doctor in many newspapers, from the former French Emperor Napoleon III.

In court, Ben Ali was asked:

Did you kill Carrie Brown?[535]

At which point he burst into tears.

> *I am innocent; I never killed any woman; I implore God to help me!*

---

534 Ibid: "Horrible Butchery"

535 "Ameer Ben Ali as a witness", *The Brooklyn Daily Eagle*, July 2, 1891

Ben Ali would be convicted of second-degree murder and sentenced to life in prison. While incarcerated, he developed symptoms of severe mental illness and was transferred to the State Asylum for the Criminal Insane at Matteawan. In 1901, New York Governor Benjamin Odell (1854–1926) took a personal interest in the case leading to the revelation that the NYPD had forced a confession out of Ali.

Amidst a deluge of criticism against the police, the wrongfully convicted Ali was freed. This of course reopened the question: who murdered Carrie Brown? The English author Philip Sugden (1947–2014) believed it could have been the same man that perpetrated the Whitechapel killings. Only Sugden thought the most likely culprit was George Chapman (1865–1903), a Polish serial killer whose real name was Seweryn Antonowicz Klosowski. In 1893, he adopted the surname Chapman from one of his many girlfriends, a woman coincidentally named Annie Chapman, who was in no way connected to the Annie Chapman murdered by the Ripper in 1888.

There are often overlooked reasons for why he is unlikely to have been either the London-based or New York-based Jack the Ripper. Firstly, Chapman stood trial for the murders of three women in London: Mary Isabella Spink on Christmas Day, 1897; Elizabeth Taylor on 3 February 1901; and Maud Eliza Marsh on 22 October 1902. These confirmed killings were all poisonings.[536]

The Solicitor-General said in his opening address that the body of Maud Marsh was "literally saturated with antimony",[537] a colourless and odourless poison. While he does seem to have had some medical training as a young man in Poland and he worked with sharp blades as a barber, his murderous methodology involved forming relationships, sometimes

536 "Southwark Poisoning Case", *The Daily Telegraph*, January 15, 1903

537 "Southwark Poisoning Case", *The Daily Telegraph*, Mary 17, 1903

bigamous, and killing with poison – not the throttling, stabbing and mutilation that was the hallmark of Jack the Ripper.

Secondly, while he did move between the United Kingdom and United States, there is a high probability he was on the wrong side of the Atlantic when Carrie Brown was murdered. Recently discovered evidence confirms he wasn't in New York at the time.[538] Thirdly, he was too young to be Jack the Ripper, aged twenty-three at the time, if most witness testimonies from Whitechapel are to be trusted.

He would be hanged for the murder of Maud, strenuously denying that his real name was Klosowski or that he was Polish. News reports in the lead up to his execution, with an abortive attempt to get a reprieve from the Home Secretary, were adamant that his movements meant "there is no possibility of his being Jack the Ripper".[539]

Another candidate for Carrie's murderer is James Kelly (1860–1929) who shortly before the Whitechapel killings had escaped from the Broadmoor Psychiatric Hospital where he was being held indefinitely for the murder of his wife. Former NYPD officer and radio host Edward T. Norris (born 1960) has been a leading advocate for the theory that Kelly, an upholsterer by trade, carried out the Ripper killings in London and New York.

However, one suspect is a far more obvious candidate: Francis Tumblety. By now just over sixty, he could have overpowered Carrie, who was an older woman incapacitated by drink. More likely, he used his trusty Texan valet, Jack, to commit the deed. He would certainly fit more closely the description given of the killer.

Carrie was cut open in the same way as the Ripper's victims in London. Could her womanhood have also ended up in one

538 Wolf Vanderlinden, John Hacker, *Ripper Notes: America Looks at Jack the Ripper* (Inklings Press, 2004)

539 "Chapman in his cell", *The Weekly Dispatch*, March 29, 1903

of Tumblety's jars in his cabinet of curiosities? In the days that followed Carrie's death, there were reports of at least three other women being killed in a similar manner. It begs the question whether, after a pause in activity, Jack the Ripper was unable to resist a return to form.

Tumblety had been regarded as a plausible Ripper suspect in London by the police. However, as other Ripper-style murders were committed in London and elsewhere, Tumblety was set aside as a suspect because he was nowhere near the scene of those crimes. But the later killings after 1888 didn't make it into the eventual canonical list, all of whom were killed while Tumblety was in London. Once he left England for New York, murder followed him.

What might have caused Tumblety to continue his ultra-violence, even if conducted through a compliant Texan valet? One answer is syphilis. The clues to his worsening condition can be found in Tumblety's health regimen. The doctor was spending ever more time at the Arkansas spa resort of Hot Springs from the 1880s onwards. He had been visiting before the Ripper murders and continued after his escape to New York.

Tumblety's attendance at this health facility has been overlooked because today its previous reputation as a spa for syphlitics has been largely forgotten.

Tumblety told a reporter at the Toronto Daily Mail in January 1888 that he lived "constantly in dread of sudden death" [540]. The main reason being kidney and heart disease. If he was suffering from cardiovascular problems as well as a general physical deterioration and mental incapacity, then it points very strongly to untreated syphilis. There are accounts of Tumblety rambling to himself in public and appearing uncharacteristically shabby in later years. Prior to the discovery of penicillin, there was no guaranteed defence against the disease. It advanced in

540 "The Travelled Doctor who was suspected of the Whitechapel Murders", *Toronto Daily Mail*, November 22, 1888

well-recognised stages, damaging the central nervous system and other parts of the body.

In the 1890s, when Tumblety was often at Hot Springs, Eugene Carson Hay M.D. – President of the Hot Springs Medical Society – explained to the medical community how the treatments at the Hot Springs of Arkansas were justifiably "a Mecca to all syphilitic subjects".[541] Before 1878, sufferers might have used the free government bathhouse but in the years that followed, palatial hotels were built along Central Avenue to attract a wealthier clientele - people like the Indian Herb Doctor with bulging wallets. The primary mission of the resort was the amelioration of the effects of syphilis as one newspaper reported:

The one great disease which is treated here more successfully than all others is syphilis in its various forms. Undisputed evidence shows that at least 80 percent of all diseases which are treated here are of a syphilitic nature, being either acquired or some form of hereditary syphilis, such as scrofula and many of the blood diseases.[542]

Most people didn't spend longer than three months at the resort on a single visit. While the physicians couldn't offer a complete cure; they were able to provide a temporary respite for two to ten years. So, it was more than likely that any benefit Tumblety received receded over time necessitating further visits. The above report on Hot Springs was disparaging about the treatments offered for other conditions like rheumatism or catarrh but conceded that when it came to syphilis, the resort seemed to deliver on its promise.

---

541 "The Advantages in the Treatment of Syphilis at the Hot Springs of Arkansas", *Journal of the American Medical Association*, 1897, Vol. 28, No. 6, pp. 251-253

542 "Hot Springs, Arkansas", *The Seneca Tribune*, May 15, 1890

Hot Springs became so synonymous with syphilis that advertisements promoted patent medicines for the pox that promised "cures when hot springs fail".[543] One was called S.S.S. and a testimonial from a satisfied customer related how he went to Eureka Springs and Hot Springs, but his condition got worse until he received a bottle of this wondrous ointment. "I feel much better, though my sores are not healed, but they are doing as well as possible, and I am satisfied S.S.S. is going to cure me", wrote happy patient J.W. Reid.[544]

In summary, there is a convincing case that Tumblety was making his repeat visits to Hot Springs to combat a disease whose four stages were well documented. In stage four, the syphilitic experienced damage to the brain, nerves, eyes, heart, blood vessels, liver, bones, and joints. This might take many years to unfold from the initial infection. For those with money, Hot Springs offered the tenuous hope of respite.[545]

Tumblety was attending Hot Springs before the Ripper killings and in the years after he returned to the United States and at the time that Carrie was killed in New York. He brought with him a vast amount of his wealth, which he kept at his hotel. On one occasion, we know that he turned up with about a quarter of a million dollars in cash and jewels at today's value. But it wasn't just his fabulous fortune that attracted attention to the doctor; residents and visitors to Hot Springs were more than aware that Tumblety had been accused of being Jack the Ripper.

In February 1890, Tumblety entered a posh store on Central Avenue, Hot Springs, looking for a male sales assistant he had

---

543 "Cures when Hot Springs fail", *Chattanooga Daily Times*, January 27 1882

544 "More good than Eureka or Hot Springs", *St Louis Globe-Democrat*, November 27, 1881

545 John Parascandola, "In Search of Sexual Health: Diagnosing and Treating Syphilis in Hot Springs, Arkansas, 1890-1940", *Journal of American History*, Vol. 108, Issue 4, March 2022, pp. 853-854

chatted up previously. The only sales staff present on the day were several female employees. At first, he barely registered with them until the doctor introduced himself. Then the penny dropped. Instantly "the fact flashed across their minds that he was the individual supposed to be Jack the Ripper".[546]

...for a few seconds there was a stampede to corners, behind counters, dress forms and other places which offered the least bit of protection.[547]

Fortunately for Tumblety, a leading citizen of Hot Springs appeared at this very moment and reassured the terrified women that Tumblety wasn't about to murder and eviscerate them. Well, not on that occasion anyway. This was unlikely to be an isolated incident and the doctor must have been viewed as a ghoulish monster by many females in the years that followed the global interest in Jack the Ripper.

In April 1891, Tumblety was robbed at Hot Springs. Thieves passed through several rooms in the Plateau Hotel during the night, stealing about $8,000 in cash and diamonds. The most striking thing about this story is that Tumblety was walking around with such a huge fortune on his person. That $8,000 would be about $260,000 today. Tumblety's massive loss was reported widely with one newspaper referring to him as "that well-known mysterious individual".[548] By comparison, Judge A. M. Duffie, staying at the same hotel, suffered the second highest loss of just $2,000.

The detective employed to investigate this burglary and break-ins at neighbouring hotels was none other than Billy

---

546 "A Mysterious Visitor", *Daily Arkansas Gazette*, February 27 1890
547 Ibid: "A Mysterious Visitor"
548 "Couple of burglaries", *Arkansas Gazette*, April 19, 1891

Pinkerton.[549] But his investigation led to no arrests and folded. Tumblety was left out of pocket until 1893. In that year, a certain Cora Sims chanced upon a stash of jewellery from which the settings had been removed, as well as several gold watches, in the basement of a deserted house.[550]

Sims handed over the items to the chief of police who managed to identify most of the owners except, for some reason, the man who had lost by far the most in that robbery: Francis Tumblety. Incredibly, a year later, Sims then sought a court order to seize what were most likely Tumblety's goods back from the police. She took on the services of a lawyer, Jack Page, to "replevin" the valuable objects.

Sensing his client didn't have much money, Page decided not to issue the order but charged Sims thirty dollars for his services up to that point. As she was unable to pay, he took Tumblety's gold watch as collateral, all of which came to the doctor's notice. Now it was Page who found himself at the receiving end of a "replevin" from Tumblety. The outcome of this legal tussle wasn't reported.

Tumblety continued to network furiously, making strategic donations to bank some goodwill for future use. Probably the least expected discovery about Tumblety in writing this book was his support for a strike by New York garment workers in 1890. Four years earlier, six thousand members of the Dress and Cloak Makers Union had come out on strike against the contracting system that made their lives so precarious. They wanted more job security.[551]

The 1886 strike ended up with the bosses claiming victory.

---

549 "Hotel Thieves at work", *Arkansas Gazette*, April 16, 1891

550 "Dr Tumblety's Stolen Watch", *St Louis Globe-Democrat*, December 29, 1894

551 Lawrence Bush, "March 20: The Cloakmakers Strike, 1886", March 20 2013

So, the cloak makers resumed hostilities on May Day 1890.[552] The American Federation of Labor, the United Hebrew Trades, and most unions in New York supported the strike. The overwhelming majority of those taking industrial action were Jewish but there were also Poles, Italians, Germans, Czechs, Hungarians, native Americans, and Irish.

The employers countered with a lockout. The result of this was starvation and eviction. One report detailed "hollow-eyed and miserable men" attempting to survive on the pittance that the union could pay from its strike fund.

Nearly everyone had the same tale of suffering and distress to relate – of a wife and children at home crying for food; of necessary articles of clothing pawned to secure money with which to buy food, and of notices of eviction served on July 1 for non-payment of rent.[553]

Many newspapers characterised the striking workers as socialists or worse - anarchists. There was a widespread fear of anarchism from the 1880s to the 1920s as a wave of anarchist-inspired violence led to the assassinations of the Tsar of Russia, President of France, Empress of Austria, King of Italy, and then in 1901, the third US President to be assassinated: President William McKinley.

On 2 July 1890, the Cloak Makers Union General Secretary Thomas Douglas Garside (1863–1927) issued an impassioned plea for donations. It was clear, he wrote, that "the general public in New York is awake to the great needs of the cloak-makers".[554] Just over sixty dollars had been raised and Garside name checked just one donation as being especially generous.

---

552 Report in *Di Arbeiter Zeitung*, May 1890, translated from Yiddish by Tania Brook Klein

553 "No money left now", *The World*, July 3, 1890

554 Ibid: "No money left now"

Five dollars from "Dr. F Tumblety", which was "gratefully accepted".

This act of philanthropy and concern for the poor echoed the handouts of bags of flour that Tumblety had made so many decades before on the steps of the Merchants' Exchange in Buffalo. A cynical act of PR? Buying support from union bosses that might be required down the road? Or a genuine donation from a man who had grown up in the ghetto?

From the mid-1890s, with a couple of exceptions, Tumblety's name fades for the first time in decades from the newspaper columns. Whether it was paid-for advertising or salacious news stories, scarcely a year had passed without him popping up in the print media. But now as his life reached its end, the light steadily extinguished.

In 1892, some rather curious articles appeared under Tumblety's name in the press with advice on how to lead a long and healthy life.

The body may be looked at as a living machine, delicate and complicated in structure, made to run a hundred years or so, but liable by bad management to be disarranged and brought to untimely destruction.[555]

He condemned "drunkards, debauchees, gluttons and devotees of sensual pleasures" who barely lived out half their days through indulging their baser instincts. One might observe this is rather rich coming from the compulsively cruising, theatre loving, fine wine drinking, cigar chomping Dr. Tumblety. He went on to claim that "physical transgression" could weaken one's offspring.

The main thrust of his argument was that everybody should strive for what we would term today a healthy work-life balance

555 "How to live long", *The Cecil Whig*, June 11, 1892, reprinted from the Chicago Herald

and remain physically healthy to ensure a "green and sunny" old age. Tumblety mentioned the former British Prime Minister William Gladstone, then a very vigorous eighty-three years of age, as being "more than a match for most men at their best".[556] Maybe Tumblety hoped that, like Gladstone, he would live out his final years in good shape - but it was not to be.

On 26 April 1903, a certain Mr Frank Townsend checked into St John's Hospital in St. Louis. He later told an attendant, he had "selected St John's as a convenient place to die". His most likely age was somewhere between seventy and seventy-five, but others later claimed he was well over eighty years old. As death approached in the days that followed, Mr Townsend revealed his real identity as the infamous Indian Herb Doctor, Francis Tumblety.

There was only one other recorded time when Tumblety had used the alias, Frank Townsend. That was when he had fled Scotland Yard for France and from there back to New York in 1888. Previously, the fake names deployed had either been variations of his own surname, such as Twomblety, or the surname Blackburn. His decision to check in to the hospital as Frank Townsend suggests the Jack the Ripper years were foremost on the doctor's mind.

Some accounts claim Tumblety suffered an accident in St. Louis that led him to the hospital. Realising it was unlikely he would leave St. John's Hospital alive, Tumblety summoned an attorney to review his last will and testament as well as a Catholic priest to perform the sacrament of Extreme Unction. From both the lawyer and the cleric he demanded oaths of secrecy.

The lawyer called in to make his last will, T. D Cannon, was stunned by the size of his client's estate. In the 1890s, the impression was sometimes given that Tumblety had been reduced to poverty, living in squalor, and wearing the meanest

---

556 Ibid: "How to live long"

of clothes. While he may have let himself go a bit, Tumblety's wealth was as buoyant as ever.

Though he realised the current illness was terminal, the Indian Herb Doctor insisted on going for lone walks outside the hospital despite his frail condition. Concerned for his wellbeing, the hospital offered an assistant to accompany him on one of these ill-advised strolls, but he refused any help. Returning to the hospital after getting some air, Tumblety sat on the steps of the building.

One account describes Tumblety falling asleep, then rolling forward on to his face and breaking his nose. The shock of this sudden accident proving fatal. He was taken back to his room with little chance of recovery.

On his deathbed the aged physician showed deep religious feeling, and the large amounts he gave to charity indicate the pious disposition of his closing days.[557]

So it came to pass that on 28 May 1903, an "unmarried" man implicated in the Lincoln assassination and the Jack the Ripper murders passed away "without a relative or intimate friend at his bedside".[558] Though in fairness to the deceased, he had insisted that no friends or relatives should be informed of his condition. He wanted to die in peace.

At his death, the obituary writers revealed that Tumblety had continued his after-dark street prowling in several American cities following the Jack the Ripper episode. He also kept moving around, spending the warmer months in the north at various locations then heading south during the winter:

For several years following his arrest in London, Tumblety

---

557 "Fortune won by herbs root of bitter fight", *St Louis Post-Dispatch*, June 28, 1903

558 "Assumed name of Townsend", *The St Louis Republic*, May 29, 1903

resided in Buffalo where he is said to have continued his nightly observations of the seamy side of life. Dr Tumblety was well known in this city several years ago, especially to the night workers, the police and others, for his habit of prowling the streets at night made him a familiar and well known figure.[559]

This Buffalo newspaper referred to Tumblety as a "night hawk" and "masculine street walker" who was "one of the best known habitués of the Tenderloin streets after midnight". In New Orleans, it emerged that he had a very dilapidated room in the French quarter.

The doctor was known in New Orleans as a pronounced woman hater and was often seen in the street in company with small boys, of whom he was very fond. He seemed to delight in street prowling and was often seen on the streets after midnight.[560]

The size of his fortune at death reignited newspaper interest in the Indian Herb Doctor. After years of forgetting his existence, the resulting battle over his inheritance by family and other claimants was good copy. Some were incredulous that he still had so much in the bank while others were less taken aback.

That Dr. Tumblety has left so large a sum of money will not be wondered at by those who knew him well, for though he was eccentric in dress, speech and manner, he was a shrewd money getter.[561]

Tumblety's "love of notoriety", as another newspaper put it,

---

559 "Dr Tumblety's strange life", *The Buffalo Times*, June 27, 1903

560 Ibid: "Fortune won by herbs root of bitter fight"

561 "The adventures of Dr Tumblety", *Democrat and Chronicle*, June 28, 1903

garnered him a fortune at death of $138,000 equivalent to $4.6m today.[562] This was banked with Henry Clews & Co. of New York. His investment acumen was noted, seldom buying stocks except during a period of volatility and then selling at a substantial profit, banking his winnings, then going off on his travels for several months.[563]

His beneficiaries included a niece in Liverpool, England who received $10,000 ($337,000 today) and his former valet Mark A. Blackburn who got half that amount. When this final will and testament was contested, in favour of an earlier one drawn up in the previous year, Blackburn's existence was questioned by other beneficiaries who referred to him as "an imaginary coachman".[564]

Other bequests went to family in Rochester, where he had grown up, while the Catholic church received charitable donations totalling $20,000 ($674,000 today). That still left about $63,000 ($2.1m today) unassigned and fought over.

Tumblety failed to name an administrator for his will and so his family, mainly in Rochester, insisted that the will should be administered in New York state. Other relatives in Liverpool and California took the same view. But the city of St. Louis countered that as Tumblety had been resident there, on and off for forty years, they should administer the monies.

Henry Clews refused to pay out anything until this matter was resolved. For his part the lawyer, Cannon, was convinced that Tumbley wanted to give the outstanding amount entirely to charity. But the late doctor's family saw matters differently.

The city of St. Louis initially triumphed over the family and the city's public administrator Garrard Strode prepared to pay out the inheritance through the Third National Bank of St.

562 "Fight for Tumblety's Cash?", *The Sun*, June 26, 1904

563 "Fortune overlooked in Tumblety will", *The News Tribune*, July 2, 1903

564 "Divides $150,000 estate", *The Baltimore Sun*, June 25, 1904

Louis to which the estate was transferred. However, litigation involving about twenty-five of Tumblety's relatives continued until 1907 when a resolution was finally reached.

One notable donation that emerged out of his various wills was $1,000 to the Home for Fallen Women on North Exeter Street in Baltimore. Eyebrows were justifiably raised at this act of charity given his arrest as a suspect in the Jack the Ripper killings. It's also worth noting that John Wilkes Booth and his family had a house on this very street, bought in 1845 and sold in 1869.

Amidst all the cash, investments, expensive jewellery, and diamonds were two incongruous items: a pair of incredibly cheap imitation rings valued at just three dollars. There are various theories about these items. That they were accidentally or deliberately undervalued by those administering the estate. Or that three dollars wasn't as cheap as we think. That doesn't stack up as the doctor habitually carried gems and gold of far greater value. And finally, that Tumblety unknowingly had some duff jewellery amidst his otherwise glittering and costly items.

But there is another possibility. In 1888, the pathologist examining the heavily mutilated body of Jack the Ripper's second canonical victim remarked coldly in his report that two things were missing from Annie Chapman: her uterus and her rings.

We know already that Tumblety had a bizarre collection of uteruses to which poor Annie's may have been added - which leaves only Annie Chapman's rings unaccounted for. These items in the estate inventory stick out. The two rings, a keeper ring plus a wedding ring, of such little value. They fit uneasily alongside the fortune fought over by Tumblety's family.

Could these rings have been trophies taken by the killer from Annie Chapman - along with her womanhood? The killer being a man responsible for a long string of deaths. A celebrity doctor unable to resist the seedier end of city life. This woman hater and his burning desire to be taken seriously as a man of medicine coupled with a ghoulish collection of women's uteruses. A man taken into custody in 1865 and 1888, accused of two of the greatest crimes of the 19th century.

As he bent over Annie Chapman, drenched in her blood, did he remove her most treasured items from her cold, dead hand? Proving beyond doubt that Francis Tumblety was indeed Jack the Ripper.

Epilogue

The Littlechild Letter
and the Sewer Club

There is one intriguing bit of evidence that reveals the extent to which Scotland Yard believed Tumblety was Jack the Ripper. It's a letter from a retired senior police officer to a high-profile crime journalist. It proves that Scotland Yard was fully aware of the doctor's sexuality and saw this as no barrier to him being Jack the Ripper. Quite the contrary. Applying the new science of psychology, the police thought if anything this proved his guilt. Men of his proclivities were nature's sadists, in their view, evidenced by his misogyny and collection of uteruses. Furthermore, the letter hints that Tumblety was being protected from above by men of his own sexuality.

In 1995, Ripperologist and then-serving police officer Stewart Evans, along with co-author Paul Gainey, brought to light an eighty-year-old letter discovered two years earlier.[565] It dated from September 1913 and was written by a senior retired

---

565 Ibid: *Jack the Ripper: First American Serial Killer*

Scotland Yard officer, Chief Inspector John Littlechild (1848–1923). Back in 1888 during the Jack the Ripper murders he had been chief of what would become the Special Branch.

The letter was addressed to George Robert 'G.R.' Sims (1848–1922), a campaigning journalist and theatre critic. It shared some thoughts on the Ripper investigation and seems to have been part of an ongoing correspondence between the two men. Littlechild confided in Sims the widely held view among London police that Tumblety had indeed been Jack the Ripper. Littlechild leaves no room for doubt in this regard:

> ...among the suspects, and to my mind a very likely one, was a Dr. T... He was an American quack named Tumblety and was at one time a frequent visitor to London and on these occasions constantly brought under the notice of police (sic), there being a large dossier concerning him at Scotland Yard.[566]

Littlechild refers to Tumblety as a *Psychopathia Sexualis*, which was the title of a highly influential book on homosexuality and bisexuality published by the German psychiatrist Richard Freiherr von Krafft-Ebing in 1886, [567] the same year Sigmund Freud opened his private practice in Vienna and just three years after *Sexual Impotence in the Male* was published by Lincoln's former Surgeon-General, Alexander Hammond. *Psychopathia Sexualis* gave us the terms "sadist" and "masochist" so one can see why Littlechild made the association with Tumblety as a homosexual sadist loose on the streets of Whitechapel.

Littlechild points out that Tumblety wasn't openly referred to as a sadist at the time, "which the murder unquestionably

---

566 Ibid: *Jack the Ripper: First American Serial Killer*

567 Richard Von Krafft-Ebing, *Psychopathia Sexualis: The Classic Study of Deviant Sex* (Arcade Publishing reprint edition, 2011, first published 1886)

was", yet "his feelings towards women were remarkable and bitter in the extreme, a fact on record". What Littlechild's letter shows us is that, when confronted with such an unusual and barbaric string of murders sharing certain commonalities, senior police reached for the most cutting edge thinking on mental illness and sexuality.

Then Littlechild details the manner of Tumblety's escape from London:

> *Tumblety was arrested in connection with unnatural offences and charged at Marlborough Street, remanded on bail, jumped his bail, and got away to Boulogne.*[568]

But the retired head of the Special Branch makes a huge and rather careless mistake claiming that Tumblety was "never heard of afterwards" and more than likely committed suicide. It's hard to fathom how such a senior officer at Scotland Yard was unaware that his own detectives had tailed Tumblety to New York and that the Indian Herb Doctor was very much alive in Manhattan. Littlechild states that the Ripper murders came to an end with his departure, which is undoubtedly true if one sticks to the list of canonical murders committed in Whitechapel.

The letter then digresses with some very Victorian bigoted asides on the cruel and degenerate nature of homosexuals. But there is much more to these nasty observations than meets the eye. Because they refer to two huge legal cases at the time and the association between those two cases and Tumblety is very telling. It helps us understand how Scotland Yard and the NYPD really viewed the Indian Herb Doctor.

Firstly, Littlechild references Oscar Wilde. He notes to Sims that "even Wilde used to like to be punched about", proving his view that gay men are inherently predisposed to

---

568 Ibid: *Jack the Ripper: First American Serial Killer*

both sadistic and masochistic behaviour. This was very much in line with the analysis contained in *Psychopathia Sexualis*, where homosexuality was classified as a deviant disorder. And Littlechild was deeply involved in the Wilde trial as he helped build the prosecution case against the disgraced LGBT author in his 1895 trial for gross indecency.

In the same year as Wilde's trial, the Hungarian psychologist Max Nordau (1849-1923) published his key work, *Degeneration*, calling for a concerted attack by the authorities on all forms of immorality which posed an imminent threat to civilisation.[569] His detestation of Wilde echoes much of what was said about Tumblety over the years.

For example, his dress sense. Nordau was disgusted at the sight of Wilde parading down Pall Mall in London "dressed in doublet and breeches, with a picturesque biretta on his head and a sunflower in his hand". He might have imagined, Nordau writes, that this differentiated him from the "Philistine cattle" but it was simply "a sign of anti-social ego mania to irritate the majority unnecessarily, only to gratify vanity" and "a malevolent mania for contradiction".

The men of the Provost Guard in St. Louis were less verbose in their condemnation of Tumblety's dress sense, but the sentiment was mightily similar. This flamboyance in sartorial taste was a sign of moral degeneration to Victorian respectable and academic opinion. It proved incredibly provocative to mainstream heterosexuals who were triggered into feelings of hostility and violence by the sight of Wilde with his sunflower or Tumblety and his plumed helmet.

Littlechild's reference to Wilde, just a few years after his imprisonment and death, would have resonated with the journalist, Sims. It conjured up all the sordid details of Wilde's private life, his male lovers, and poetic defence of the love that

---

569 Max Nordau, *Degeneration* (Appleton and Company, 1895, translated from the German second edition)

dare not speak its name. Tumblety was, as it were, part of the same social and sexual disease.

Then Littlechild digresses again with the case of a well-known homicidal socialite, Harry Kendall Thaw (1871–1947) who was bisexual. Thaw's father was the coal and railroad multi-millionaire William Thaw Senior (1818–1889). Never having to worry about money, Harry sank into a life of heavy partying, narcotics abuse on a monumental scale, and fully indulging his libido.

Littlechild writes about one incident in 1906 where Thaw was a guest at the Carlton Hotel in London, the city's most fashionable hotel in the early 20th century until it was bombed in the Second World War. The story involves the extremely violent abuse of a member of hotel staff:

> *Thaw was staying at the Carlton Hotel, and one day laid out a lot of sovereigns on his dressing table, then rang for a call boy on pretence of sending out a telegram. He made some excuse and went out of the room and left the boy there and watched through the chink of the door.[570]*

The boy couldn't resist temptation and stole one of the sovereigns, at which point Thaw stomped back into the room accusing him of theft. The boy admitted his crime and Thaw asked whether he should call the police or inflict some kind of punishment there and then.

> *The boy scared to death consented to take his punishment from Thaw who then made him undress, strapped him to the foot of the bedstead, and thrashed him with a cane drawing blood. He then made the boy get into a bath in which he placed a quantity of salt.[571]*

---

570 Ibid: *Jack the Ripper: First American Serial Killer*
571 Ibid: *Jack the Ripper: First American Serial Killer*

Why does Littlechild include this story in his letter, which is ostensibly about Tumblety being Jack the Ripper? The answer requires the same level of background knowledge we have about Oscar Wilde. Most people are aware of the criminal charges Wilde faced, the background story, and what happened because of the guilty verdict. But Thaw is a forgotten episode and yet seven years before Littlechild wrote his letter, the sadistic trust-fund kid found himself at the centre of what was dubbed the trial of the century. Yet today it's a historical and legal footnote.

In 1906 – the same year Thaw was leaving sovereigns piled on a hotel table in London – he returned to New York to pump three bullets into the celebrity architect Stanford White (1853–1906). The reason given for this murder, at a busy rooftop restaurant, was that five years before White had drugged and raped Thaw's young wife, Evelyn Nesbit, when she was just sixteen years of age. Nobody then or since has doubted the veracity of this rape claim as White was a well-known predatory seducer of teenage girls, especially if they were from poorer families and therefore more vulnerable.[572]

The murder trial of Thaw was a huge global media event. Both Littlechild and Sims would have known all about it. The author Mark Twain was especially interested having known, but not liked, White and observed that the now-dead architect "ravenously and remorselessly hunting young girls to their destruction".[573] White's great-granddaughter, Suzannah Lessard, has detailed his modus operandi playing the role of paternal benefactor to impressionable girls using his power and money.[574]

572 Nancy Bilyeau, "What The Gilded Age gets right about Infamous Architect Stanford White", Town & Country, February 1, 2022

573 Mark Twain, *Autobiography of Mark Twain, Volume 2* (University of California Press reprint edition, 2013)

574 Suzannah Lessard, *The Architect of Desire: Beauty and Danger in the Stanford White Family* (Random House Publishing Group reprint edition, 1997)

The crucial detail to note in relation to how Tumblety operated for years is that White was part of an underground network of gentlemen in New York determined to gratify every conceivable desire, predominantly sex with underage victims as well as catering for adult heterosexual and homosexual sex. The attitude of these networks, based more on class than sexual orientation, was that the top people in society didn't need to be confined by conventional morality. That was for the great unwashed.

One of these clandestine networks was made up of members of the Union Club and organised "frequent orgies in secret locations scattered about the city". Members of the network included the financier and patron of the arts Henry William Poor (1844–1915) and Thomas Benedict Clarke (1848–1931), headmaster of the Mount Washington Collegiate.[575]

This club within a club called itself, rather appropriately, The Sewer Club. In 1879, White's architect practice McKim, Mead & Bigelow designed the Benedick building at Washington Square Park in New York, named after a committed bachelor in William Shakespeare's play, *Much Ado About Nothing*. From 1888, the Sewer Club, under White's guidance, hosted debauched parties at the Benedick. There were literally no holds barred.

In this sex and drugs fuelled environment, things soured between White and Thaw leading to the former's murder. During the trial of Thaw, the Sewer Club members scattered to Europe, Africa, and Asia to avoid being dragged into court.[576] The trial revealed the existence of these clandestine sexual networks in America's big cities where well-heeled people, old money, and parvenus gathered for the purpose of indulging their vices.

---

575 Simon Baatz, *The Girl on the Velvet Swing: Sex, Murder, and Madness at the Dawn of the Twentieth Century* (Mulholland Books, 2018)

576 "Harry Thaw No Degenerate", *Calgary Herald*, March 11, 1907

Normally, they protected each other from the attention of law enforcement and the newspaper but Thaw had brought the spotlight on to them. However, an expensive legal team managed to generate sympathy in court for Thaw leading to his portrayal in the newspapers as a noble husband avenging the rape of his wife by the now-dead White. In fact, his main grievance seems to have been White blackballing him from various gentlemen's clubs in the city. Thaw escaped the electric chair and was committed to the Matteawan State Hospital for the Criminally Insane. Seven years later he was released but then re-incarcerated after whipping a nineteen-year-old boy.

Ripperologists have often entertained the idea of secret societies being involved in the Jack the Ripper killings but focused on the Freemasons. But in the 19th century, there was a papal ban on joining the Freemasons that would have deterred an Irish Catholic like Tumblety. More plausibly, he gravitated towards clandestine, sleazy networks like the Sewer Club while living in big cities like New York, Washington DC, and London. Elite groupings devoted to illegal sexual activity. In between cruising the streets and theatres, which was always risky, especially as Tumblety was so often under surveillance, he could attend orgies behind closed doors while simultaneously networking the rich and famous.

The Littlechild letter sees a retired senior police officer writing to an experienced journalist. The subject is Tumblety. The references to Wilde and Thaw would have been fully understood by both men given their professional backgrounds. Littlechild had no need to write out all the details of the respective legal cases. Wilde was a story of open and proud homosexuality that society couldn't tolerate. Thaw exposed a network of upper-class people engaging in sexual abuse. Both these were aspects of Tumblety's life. His struggle to be a gay man in the 19th century and the secret networks within which he moved that aided and protected him.

Add to that an ugly, violent streak in his character that every so often bubbled up to the surface achieving its grimmest manifestation on the streets of London's East End in the year 1888. When the letter was written in 1913, the Jack the Ripper murders remained unsolved as they do to this day. But Littlechild was sure the culprit was none other than the Indian Herb Doctor.

There can be little doubt that Francis Tumblety earns the ghoulish distinction of having been at the centre of two of the greatest crimes of the 19th century.

Index of Names

Abernethy, John, 270

Atzerodt, George, 97, 170, 184

Barnum, P.T., 22, 24, 46,109 176

Bennett, Clement R., 196-198

Blackburn, Luke Pryor, 43-44,
188-191

Blackburn Mark (valet of
Tumblety), 9, 43, 168, 192,
292

Blenker, Louis, 122-125

Booth, John Wilkes:
Acting style, 91-94
Assassinates Lincoln, 1, 79,
142-145, 159, 163, 178, 182-
184, 190
Errand boy, 21, 98, 165-167,
171, 186
Early years, 88-90
Knows Tumblety, 4, 20-21,
50, 87-88, 102-103, 154-156,
165, 168-169, 171, 181, 188,
192
Marble Heart incident, 95-96
With Tumblety in Buffalo,
99-103

Syphilis, 77, 79-80

Booth, Asia, 88

Booth, Edwin, 88, 92-93, 100,
151, 178, 265

Booth Jr., Junius Brutus, 88,
151, 187

Booth Sr., Junius Brutus, 91, 151

Bourdet, Édouard, 55

Buchanan, James, 52-54, 63, 74,
81, 104, 157

Bundy, Ted, 30

Brown, Carrie, 273-280

Byrnes, Thomas F., 251, 255,
274-278

Caine, Thomas Henry Hall,
208-215

Cavanaugh, Captain Thomas,
99-103, 165, 167, 179-181,
192

Chamberlin, Thomas, 76

Chapman, Annie:
Death of husband, 225
Discovery of her body, 223-
224
Reports of a boyfriend, 226

Rings stolen by Ripper, 243-244, 293-294

Uterus removed, 227, 275, 293

Wounds described, 228-229

Chapman, George, 280

Colchester, Charles, J., 92

Comstock, Anthony, 14-15, 76, 265

Cooper, Astley, 270

Corcoran, Michael, 131

Coursol, Charles-Joseph, 39-40

Cutter, George Washington, 119-120

Davies, John, 223

Davis, Jefferson, 74, 93, 104, 143-145, 178, 181

Derickson, Captain David V., 56, 58, 74-77, 180

Devlin, Bernard, 39-41

Dickens, Charles, 6, 113, 149, 210, 255, 268

Dirksen, Everett, 55

Donovan, Timothy, 226

Drummond, Lewis, 39-40

Dunham, Col. Charles, A., 30, 140-146, 169, 181, 273

D'Utassy, Frederick George, 125-127

Eddowes, Catherine, 228, 243, 247, 261

Ellis, Abner Y., 56-58

Ellis, Havelock, 98

Ellsworth, Ephraim Elmer, 56-57

Fellows, John R., 266

Fox, Virginia Woodbury, 75

Garfield, James, 218-221

Garrison, William Lloyd, 63-64

Giteau, Charles J., 218-221, 250

Grant, Ulysses S., 182-183, 200

Greene, William "Billy", 56-57, 67

Hammond, William Alexander, 68-74, 130, 240-241, 246, 296

Hart, Fred, 27-28

Hawthorne, Nathaniel, 117-118

Haywood, Edward, 11, 128

Herndon, William, 61-63, 66-67, 77-78, 81-85

Herold, David:
  Attack on Seward, 184
  Company of boys, 170
  Hanged, 4-5, 97, 144
  Meets Booth, 164
  Works for Tumblety, 2, 20-21, 43, 87, 103, 157, 163, 165-169, 171, 179, 181, 186-188, 191-192, 238, 247, 260

Hyams, Godfrey Joseph, 188-190

Irving, Henry, 208, 212

Jack (the Texan), 250, 259-262, 281-282

Jackson, Andrew, 52, 157

Johnson, Andrew, 87, 182, 184, 199

Kauffman, Michael W., 94

Kean, Edmund, 151

Kearns, Elizabeth Ann, 234

Kelly, James, 281

Kelly, Mary Jane, 228-229, 231, 241, 247

Kemble, Charles, 151

King, William Rufus DeVane, 52-53

Kramer, Larry, 98

Leech, Margaret, 75-76

Lincoln, Abraham:
  Assassination, 1-4, 20-21, 43,
    51, 88, 91-94, 100, 142-146,
    154, 163-166, 178, 182-184,
    187-190, 196, 198, 205, 218,
    222
  Captain Derickson, 56, 58,
    74-77
  Crush on Booth, 94-98, 180
  First Chronicles of Reuben,
    60-62
  Joshua Fry Speed, 57, 64-67,
    72-73, 98
  Marriage was hell, 81-83
  Meets Tumblety, 5-7, 32, 49,
    52, 80, 86-87, 94, 106-107,
    115, 121, 131, 135, 157, 159,
    198-199, 208-209, 264, 268
  Rutledge, Ann Mayes, 83-85
  Same sex relations, 54-59, 63,
    72, 74-77, 80-81, 85
  Sense of humour, 59-60, 62
  Syphilis, 77-80, 182, 241
Lincoln, Mary Todd, 62, 74-79,
  81-84, 122, 184
Lincoln, Robert Todd, 56, 79,
  84, 218
Lincoln, Thomas "Tad", 97
Lispenard, Dr W. C., 15-18, 43,
  80, 137
Littlechild, John, 296-300, 302-
  303
Locke, David Ross, 59
Lohman, Ann Trow (Madam
  Restell), 155-156
Mackenzie, Alice, 247
Macready, William Charles, 151
Maguire, James D., 145-146
McCarthy, Joseph, 54

McGee, Thomas D'Arcy, 32-37,
  39, 41
McClellan, George Brinton, 112,
  123-130, 136-139, 179, 216
Melville, Herman, 48-49
Menken, Adah Isaacs, 149
Mordaunt, Frank, 96
Nasby, Petroleum Vesuvius,
  59-60
Nichols, Mary Ann, 228, 247
Nightingale, Florence, 68
Nordau, Max, 298
Pastor, Tony, 154-156
Parkhurst, Charles Henry, 195
Percival, George, 152-154
Pierce, Franklin, 53
Pinkerton, Allan, 117, 135
Pinkerton, Billy:
  Cites Hammond, 72
  Early interest in Tumblety,
    117, 135-136, 245
  Says Tumblety is Jack the
    Ripper, 245-247
  Sees Tumblety in London,
    206-208
  Tumblety as an army medic,
    130, 137-138, 272
  Tumblety leaves Washington,
    160
Powell (Payne), Lewis, 97-98,
  184, 188
Richardson, Amelia, 224
Rogers, Mary, 155
Rosetti, Dante Gabriel, 212
Sandburg, Carl, 54-56, 84
Sappho, 55
Scully, Fenton, 172-174, 193
Seward, William H., 51, 87, 131-
  135, 136, 149, 184

Shaw, George Bernard, 232
Sherman, William Tecumseh, 200, 264
Sims, George, 296
Smith, Emma Elizabeth, 247
Speed, Joshua Fry, 54, 56-58, 62-67, 72-73, 97-98, 180
Stanton, Edwin:
  Arrest of Tumblety, 2, 4, 88, 167, 186
  Attacked by Tumblety, 190, 193, 198-199, 209, 269
  General Blenker, 124-125
  Radical Republican, 60
Stead, William Thomas, 232-234
Stoker, Bram, 208, 212-213
Streeter, Captain W. C., 13, 47-48
Stride, Elizabeth, 243, 247, 261
Sundown, Chief, 19-20
Surratt, Mary Elizabeth Jenkins, 87, 103
Tabram, Martha, 228, 247
Tarbell, Ida, 55-56
Thaw, Harry Kendall, 299-302
Thompson, Jacob, 143-144
Thompson, Lydia, 150-151
Townsend, George Alfred, 96
Tripp, Clarence Arthur, 180
Tumblety, Francis:
  Admits to visiting Whitechapel, 253
  Arrest over Booth's assassination plot, 2, 21, 88, 99, 166, 184, 191
  Arrest in London, 1888, 9, 128, 217, 231, 235
  Arrest by the Provost Guard, 175-177

Arrest in 1890, 271-273
Assault on Fenton Scully, 172-174, 193
Assault on George Davis, 262-266
Attends presidential levée, 121
Burlesque about him, 151-154
Canadian Irish politics, 32-36
Carrie Brown murder, 273-282
Cincinnati, 2-7, 199-202
Claimed marriage, 29-30
Death in St Louis, 290
Display of uteruses, 139
Dog stabbed, 26
Employs David Herold, 163
Garfield assassination, 218-221
Hall Caine, 208-215
Hamilton, Ontario, 26-27
Illegal abortion, 37-40
Introduces Surratt to Booth, 103
Jack the Texan, 250, 259-262, 281
James Portmore manslaughter, 44-46
Jumps bail to avoid Ripper charges, 231, 247-248
Liverpool manslaughter case, 213-214
Lyons legal case, 216-217
Offers medical services to the army, 127-130
Origins, 7-20
Processions on main street, 20-24

Released from Old Capitol
prison, 190
Rides behind President
Lincoln, 105-107
Ridicules Scotland Yard, 254
Robbed in London, 207-208
Robbed in Philadelphia, 161-
162
Robbed at Hot Springs, 285-
286
Syphilis, 77-80
Texas murders, 261-262
Thrown out of Union army,
138
Washington DC, 112-114

Whelpley court case, 109-110
William Seward gift of a
horse, 131
Tyler, John, 117
Van Buren, Martin, 157
Vidal, Gore, 66, 98, 132
Wadsworth, James Samuel, 115
Weik, Jesse W., 77, 84
Whelpley, Charles, 106-111,
162, 192
White, Stanford, 300
Whitman, Walt, 74, 107-108,
122, 178, 212, 231, 265
Wilde, Oscar, 200, 212-213,
297-298, 300, 302